COMPARATIVE POLITICAL ECONOMY

COMPARATIVE POLITICAL ECONOMY

Jan-Erik Lane and Svante Ersson

Pinter Publishers
London and New York

First published in Great Britain in 1990 by
Pinter Publishers Limited
25 Floral Street, London WC2E 9DS and PO Box 197, Irvington, New York, NY 10533

British Library Cataloguing in Publication Data

A CIP catalogue record of this book is available from the British Library

ISBN 0 86187 795 0 (hbk)
0 86187 858 2 (pbk)

Library of Congress Cataloging-in-Publication Data

Lane, Jan-Erik.
Comparative political economy / Jan-Erik Lane and Svante Ersson.
p. cm.
ISBN 0-86187-795-0. — ISBN 0-86187-858-2 (pbk.)
1. Comparative economics. I. Ersson. Svante O. II. Title.
HB90.L35 1990
338.9—dc20 90-7022
CIP

Typeset by Communitype Communications Limited
Printed and bound in Great Britain by SRP Ltd.

Contents

Foreword

Our purpose in writing this volume is to make a contribution to the emerging field of political economy. The emphasis in on the comparative empirical analysis of the interaction between economics and politics, in particular with regard to development in its various connotations. Drawing on theory from a variety of sources including public policy, comparative politics, public choice and economics we analyse the relationship between economic affluence and types of polity as well as the relationship between politics and economic growth. Our study covers rich and poor, capitalist and communist and Third World, European, African, Asian, North American and Latin American countries for which we have managed to gather a small set of data on political and economic variables.

Since it is our hope that the book could be employed for teaching purposes we have deliberately included a large amount of information in many tables which could be used for reanalysis by the reader if he/she so wishes. The level of exposition has been kept elementary so that the volume may be used in undergraduate courses in comparative political economy. The division of labour between the authors is that Jan-Erik Lane has been responsible for the overall layout of the book; he has rewritten the whole book on the basis of drafts put together with Svante Ersson, who has handled the gathering and processing of the data. We have benefited from comments by Duncan O'Leary (LSE) and Arend Lijphart (San Diego). Manfred Holler (Aarhus) and Aaron Wildavsky (Berkeley) took the time to read large parts of the manuscript providing us with much valuable criticism. Francis Castles (Canberra) read Chapters 6, 7, 8 and 9 carefully with several valuable objections.

The initiative to this volume was taken jointly by the International Social Science Council (ISSC) and Unesco under a Unesco contract (no 375.218.6) which resulted in a small manuscript: Development (unpublished). It was recommended to bring the manuscript into a book by the COCTA group — the Committee on Conceptual and Terminological Analysis — which is a standing committee of the ISSC and as such has benefited from the continued interest and support of ISSC.

The volume draws upon articles that we published together in *Political Geography Quarterly*, *International Political Science Review*, *Scandinavian Political Studies*, *International Social Science Journal* in addition to materials in *Statsvetenskaplig tidskrift*.

Jan-Erik Lane, Svante Ersson
Lund, Umeå
February 1990

Introduction: old and new political economy

In traditional usage 'political economy' was used as synonymous with the general word 'economics' (Rothschild, 1989). The study of political economy was the analysis of the economy of a nation-state. Let us quote from *A New Dictionary of Economics (1966):*

> political economy. This term is derived from the Greek polis, meaning a city as a political unit, and oikonomike, denoting the management of a household. The combination of words reflects how inextricably involved are the facts of production, trade and finance with those of government fiscal, monetary and commercial policy. It was not until the nineteenth century that the purely political aspects began to feature less and less in studies of economic phenomena, and economics as it is known today developed. Since the writings of Alfred Marshall (1842-1924), notably his *Principles of Economics*, political economy, as a description of the discipline, has fallen into disuse. (Taylor, 1966: 231)

Although *A Dictionary of Economics and Commerce* (1974) simply states that political economy is the older name for economics (Hansen, 1974: 378), it should be pointed out that books by political economists like Ricardo, Marx and Stuart Mill focused much on the political presuppositions and consequences of the economy. The perspective on economic transactions was that of the political body — the state — and the basic problem concerned the understanding of how economic wealth in a society could be enhanced by the state belonging to that society. Let us quote from Adam Smith's *Wealth of Nations*, Book IV, 'Of Systems of Political Oeconomy':

> Political oeconomy, considered as a branch of the science of a statesman or legislator, proposes two distinct objects; first, to provide a plentiful revenue or subsistence for the people, or more properly to enable them to provide such a revenue or subsistence for themselves; and secondly, to supply the state or

> commonwealth with a revenue sufficient for the public services. It proposes to enrich both the people and the sovereign. (Smith, 1976: 138)

When 'political economy' is now brought back into circulation alongside the general term 'economics', the focus is not the economic phenomena in general but more specifically the interaction between politics and economics (Alt and Chrystal, 1983). Surveying the new literature in the emerging field of political economy, Martin Staniland in his *What Is Political Economy* (1985) states that there is a special set of problems that the new discipline is interested in:

> ...there are several kinds of political economy theory. The criterion for identifying such theory is whether or not it claims to depict a systematic relationship between economic and political processes. Such a relationship may be conceived in different ways — as a causal relationship between one process or another ('deterministic' theory), as a relationship of reciprocity ('interactive' theory), or as a behavioral continuity. Whether or not the theory in question is labeled 'political economy' is secondary: the important issue is its claim to empirical explanation. (Staniland, 1985: 5-6)

In this revised sense of 'political economy' as politico-economic interaction it constitutes a new field of empirical research. One may follow the development of the concept of political economy by comparing the 1899 *Palgrave Dictionary of Political Economy* with the 1987 *New Palgrave Dictionary of Economics*. Let us quote:

> Originally political economy was — as its name suggests — conceived to be the common portion of two arts, 'economy in general' and the art of government. (1899: vol III)

However, the first meaning took precedence over the latter sense at the same time as 'economics' began to drive out the use of 'political economy'. Yet, the latter concept came back in the 20th century:

> ...its first modern usage in the 18th century, its demise from the end of the 19th century, when it was gradually replaced by the word 'economics', and its revival in a variety of forms, largely during the 1960s, which have altered its meaning from more traditional usage. (1987: vol 3)

There is a variety of approaches to the study of politico-economic interaction which are all labelled 'modern political economy' (Frey, 1978): marxist or neo-marxist approaches, systems theory approaches, traditional or institutionalist approaches as well as the public choice approach. Sometimes it is stated that modern political economy involves *one* method — the economic model of preferences, choice and constraint — applied to non-market behaviour (Schneider, 1989). However, such a delimitation to one approach to the exclusion of other approaches is not fortunate. What is common to all kinds of modern political economy is the focus on the reciprocities between politics and economics in a wide sense. Here, we will look at a few but certainly not all major theories about politico-economic interaction. Since the publication in 1953 of Robert A Dahl's and Charles Lindblom's *Politics, Economics and Welfare* there has been a search for an understanding of how political and economic systems interact. This will be our focus which we will pursue on a comparative basis.

Public choice or neo-marxism?

Since the mid-sixties there has been a proliferation of various approaches to the analysis of politico-economic interaction. On the one hand we have the public choice school which is actor oriented and proceeds from a basic assumption about methodological individualism as well as utility maximizing selfish individuals. It has resulted in a number of much debated models: the political business cycle, the political popularity function, the Downsian model of the vote maximizing politician and the Niskanen budget maximizing bureau (Doel, 1979; Frey, 1978; Mueller, 1989; Hibbs and Fassbender, 1981). Although some of these models have been tested in comparative research, there is nothing inherently comparative about them. They may be used to model longitudinal data in one single country. As a matter of fact the public choice models perform differently from one country to another which calls for more of an institutional and less of a comparative approach (Lybeck and Henrekson, 1988).

On the other hand there is a set of marxist or neo-marxist models which are holistic and emphasize macro aspects of political and economic systems: the dependency model, the world systems model and various state models (Frank, 1967; Wallerstein, 1979; Szentes, 1983). These political economy models have a more clear comparative edge than the public choice models as they explicity model country differences in welfare, economic growth and structural dependence. In order to test the idea that there is a world capitalist system that keeps various countries in different relations of autonomy and heteronomy one needs to turn to cross-sectional data about politico-economic performance.

It has been argued that the neo-marxist political economy models refering to world system modelling are weak because of a lack of empirical evidence or even in terms of their capacity to be put to a systematic empirical test (Taylor, 1987). Be that as it may, these neo-marxist models have stimulated the special branch of political economy that we are interested in here, viz. the comparative approach to country differences in political and economic system properties.

The competition between public choice models and marxist political economy has been fierce, but here we will focus on a few models concerning politico-economic interaction that are distinctly comparative. Some distinctive hypotheses deal with system questions about how economics and politics or vice versa are related; the *affluence hypothesis* concerns the relationship between economic affluence and democracy as a type of polity arguing that wealth is a necessary or sufficient condition for the persistence of a democracy; the *'politics matter' theory* claims that politics matter for policy outputs and outcomes rejecting economic determinism which states that public policies are a function of wealth; and the *economic growth hypothesis* argues that economic development is conditioned not only by economic and social factors but also by politics in a wide sense. All these three hypotheses crop up in various approaches or schools like policy analysis, public choice and political economy; and they touch upon problems that are extremely value ingrained and policy relevant. In this book, we analyse and test these three models or three sets of hypotheses, because they are truly complex. No attempt will be made to force the findings into one or the other school in modern political economy.

In *The Rise and Decline of Nations* (1982) Mancur Olson identifies the fortunes of a nation with economic growth. There is no question that material prosperity as measured by the rate of growth of the economy is important, but when one is considering the fate of a nation, equal weight should be given to the political situation in a country. Liberty and equality may be as relevant as economic growth when appraising whether nations rise, decline or develop politically. However, whereas the concept of economic development is a rather clear one, the notion of political development is far more ambiguous.

Albert Hirschman claims in *A Bias for Hope* (1971) that much remains to be done before we reach a basic understanding of how politics and economics relate to each other. What follows below is an attempt to contribute to the creation of some kind of theory of politico-economic interaction by starting from the traditional field of comparative politics and moving towards the emerging field of political economy. What is the impact of socio-economic development on democracy or political development? Or does politics — political institutions or public policy — have an impact on rates of economic expansion? Are there country-distinctive patterns of policy outputs that may be explained by means of political properties?

The distinction between a public choice or rational choice approach and a neo-marxist or radical political economy approach bears on the separation between micro and macro theory, between a focus on microscopic entities and macroscopic units. Rational choice theory intrinsically favour *micro theory*, as it is claimed that actor oriented theories based on *microscopic entities* are superior to structural theory

— often denounced as functionalism. Although the predictive power and formal elegance of public choice approaches must be acknowledged, as must the often severe methodological problems inherent in some systems approaches (Barry, 1970), it is, however, difficult to do without *macro theoretical constructs* when one is interested in wholes or *macroscopic events* (Lijphart, 1977; 1984).

Bypassing the clash between rational choice and structural approaches as well as the gulf between micro and macro theory, we focus on middle range theories about politico-economic interaction (see James L. Paine's *Why Nations Arm* (1989)). Any understanding of how the political system relates to the economic system of a country would have to be founded on an identification of political and economic structures and their properties. The crucial question in a middle range approach is not whether political and economic structures may be ultimately analyzed with a micro theory (reductionism) or requires a macro theory (holism). More important is the problem: if one takes a middle range perspective on the states and economies of post Second World War Two period — OECD-nations, Communist systems and Third World countries — then what concepts are adequate for the anaysis of politico-economic data? We need theoretical constructs, but which ones are the most promising?

Affluence and politics

At times political systems experience large-scale changes. The structural changes in Portugal, Spain and Greece by which authoritarian structures have been dismantled constitute macro changes. The ongoing processes of change within the Communist world introducing democratic institutions and making room for markets and private initiative is another example of structural change in polities. In the Latin American context, we find a circular change process, authoritarianism replacing democratic rule and vice versa. The seminal process of public growth in the rich countries during the post-war period appears to constitute irreversible structural change, as it were.

The political development theme has attracted considerable attention in comparative politics. Yet, confronted with these structural changes, we have to admit that political science lacks a concept of political development comparable to the notion of economic development as measured by rates of growth in overall output or income. The attempts to replace a multi-dimensional conception of political change with some specific notion of political development has not been successful as the concept of political development is surrounded by ambiguity. In fact, it is an essentially contested notion.

The general concept of development — social, economic and political

— has no doubt offered a challenging perspective for the analysis of the Third World countries. The concept of development could be employed not only to approach change in these countries, but also as a way to handle the differences between rich and poor countries. However, has development implied that the Third World should simply become identical with the rich world? In which respects? The concept of development seems to contain a teleological bias, as if there were some goal towards which political change should evolve — the advanced capitalist democracies perhaps? What if change processes moved in a different direction — perhaps this would constitute retro- or under development? Would socio-economic or political development always result in modernization?

The modernization theme contained a hypothesis about linear causality between socio-economic development on the one hand and political development on the other. Political systems would move from a primitive stage towards a developed stage reflecting the seminal trend of social change offset by economic development away from an agricultural economy as if there existed an objective criterion on what is politically developed and not developed. How could one be sure that what was developed in one context, e.g. in the OECD nations, would also constitute development in another context, e.g. the Third World?

There was also the implicit assumption about mono-causation with socio-economic change determining political development which raised crucial questions about the autonomy of political institutions. There was promising work oriented towards the concept of political modernization — see Myrion Weiner's and Samuel P. Huntington's *Understanding Political Development* (1987) — but in the end there was an uncomfortable feeling that severe methodological problems had been left unresolved. No doubt the concept of development was more successful in the field of social studies and development economics.

The study of social and economic change in the Third World resulted in a number of different theories about the sources of economic growth in less advanced economies, from purely economic theories to broad social theories including political institutions — see Peter Hall's *Growth and Development* (1983). There is still no consensus as to the relative weight to be given to various factors that are conducive to economic growth — investments, structure of agriculture, level of urbanization, quantity or quality of human capital or technology, religion, political institutions or public policies of various sorts (Chenery and Srinivasan, 1988). Even if one has come closer to a theory of economic growth, the problem of stating the implications of politics for economic growth remains.

Economic or social determinism cannot be taken for granted. Instead one has to recognize that there could be different paths of socio-economic change within fundamentally different political systems, e.g.

within democratic political systems as against right-wing or left-wing authoritarian systems. The hope for a general theory of political development has to be abandoned. But if the concept of political development cannot be used as a foundation for a comparative analysis of political systems, then which concepts should we employ?

The comparative study of political systems contains plenty of conceptual distinctions between various kinds of systems as well as between various aspects of political systems. Perhaps the most prevalent one is that between democracy and dictatorship. Although the concept of democracy may be delineated in various ways, the distinction appears to have a clear empirical foundation as we may separate between a set of democratic countries and a set of authoritarian countries without too much argument about borderline cases. This distinction may be buttressed by the employment of indicators which allows the specification of when a political system has undergone a regime change, from democracy to dictatorship or from authoritarianism to democracy.

A basic problem in democratic theory raised by Seymour Martin Lipset in a well-known article published in 1959 and discussed at length by Charles Lindblom in *Politics and Markets* (1977) and in Dan Usher's *The Economic Prerequisite to Democracy* (1981) is whether there is any relationship between the democratic organization of the regime and the overall economic structure of society. The comparative study of economic systems builds upon a number of distinctions, but there is one that tends to dominate the others: planned economies and market economies. Whereas it used to be clear which countries predominantly employed planning as the mechanism of allocation and which countries based the allocation of resources on markets, the emergence of so-called mixed economies in the welfare states has made the distinction less clear-cut. The collapse of East European Communism in 1989 may also bring forward new combinations of capitalism and socialism.

However, it still seems possible to classify economic systems as basically market-oriented or as fundamentally planned economies following John M. Montias' work *The Structure of Economic Systems* (1976) or Paul B. Gregory's and Robert C. Stuart's *Comparative Economic Systems* (1989). Combining the distinction between a democratic regime and an authoritarian one with a distinction between capitalist economies and socialist economies, we arrive at the conclusion depicted in Figure I.1:

We will study a large number of countries with the aid of the concepts corresponding to the four cells given in Figure I.1. There is a sort of asymmetry in the framework as we find no real counterpart for the combination of a democratic regime and a planned economy. To what extent is this a pure accidental event or does it reflect some deeper mechanism that interrelates the political regime and the mechanism of resource allocation? This is the old problem of whether democracy and capitalism necessarily hang together.

Figure I.1. Political and economic systems

		ECONOMIC SYSTEM	
		Capitalism	Socialism
POLITICAL SYSTEM	Democracy	I	II
	Dictatorship	III	IV

The fundamental problem of the social and economic sources of democracy involves a number of questions. What is the surface correlation between levels of affluence and democratic regime properties? And how do we account theoretically for the eventuality of a statistical association? According to the well-known study by Irma Adelman and Cynthia T. Morris, *Society, Politics and Economic Development* (1967), there is a strong correlation between various indicators of material affluence and the typical expressions of a democratic regime. Is this still true today and how about the emerging Third World countries? Searching for the socio-economic sources of polities, we have to look at dynamic aspects as well. Does economic growth or the modernization of the social structure promote democracy?

Politics and economics

Turning the focus on politico-economic interaction upside-down, there is the huge problem of how politics affect a country's social and economic conditions. It used to be believed that economic growth could be understood mainly in terms of economic variables like levels or rate of growth in investments — the capital ratio theory of Harrod and Domar or the neo-classical production function approach (Solow, 1988; Chauduri, 1989). As interest began to focus on economic development in poor countries, broader social forces were considered — agriculture by Lewis and religion by Myrdal (Thirlwall, 1986; Chenery and Srinivasan, 1988).

It has also been argued that politics matter, either that political institutions or that public policies have an impact on economic growth. John Zysman (1983) stated that industrial policies matter for initiating and sustaining the so-called Rostow take-off stage. The Olson hypothesis argues that so-called institutional sclerosis in the political fabric of a country reduces average economic growth (Olson, 1982). And the Weede hypothesis claims that democracy as a regime type negatively affects economic development (Weede, 1984b).

From a politico-economic perspective, a few major questions may be identified concerning the relationship between politics in a wide sense and economic affluence. Starting from Figure I.1 again, there is the peculiar type of mixed economy blending private ownership and markets with extensive budget-making: what accounts for the cross-country variation in the size and orientation of mixed economies? In *Budgeting* (1986) Aaron Wildavsky examines the large number of factors that have been suggested as sources of expenditure variations in the public budget. What would an empirical test of these public sector growth hypotheses amount to? Figure I.1 also identies another hybrid — market socialism: what are the country experiences with this type of politico-economic regime? Moreover, we have to analyse at length the difficult question of the sources — economic, social and political — of the country variation in average growth rates in the economy. These three major problems all bear on the distinction between types of polities and types of economic systems. They may be approached in terms of a comparative perspective looking at the empirical variation in politico-economic systems and searching for explanatory factors.

First, there is the seminal process of public sector growth in the set of democratic regimes which rely upon markets to a large extent. What have been the major factors behind this process — the public budget driving out the market mechanism? What accounts for the similarities and dissimilarities between the rich countries with regard to the structure of their public sectors? Harold Wilensky's *The Welfare State and Equality* opened up the debate in 1975 on whether politics really matter for the determination of national policies. Wilensky emphasized the level of economic affluence as the explanation of the country variation in public policies, but should not other factors also be included (Tarschys, 1975; Castles, 1982)?

Second, there was the opposite movement in the Communist world with its frequent attempts to insert market-like mechanisms into a predominantly publicly owned capital structure. How do we explain these attempts and their apparent failure? Is market socialism possible? This has become a highly relevant policy question for the East European countries as they began searching for a new identity both politically and economically in the fall of 1989. Removing the typical Leninist framework of a one-party state in conjunction with a planned economy opens up various system choices (Brus and Laski, 1990).

Third, there is a cluster of questions about how politics condition economic growth in the long run. Does the structure of political institutions matter? Let us look if there exists some significant relationship between economic development and types of polities like democracy or authoritarianism. Is it simply the length of time of institutionalization that has elapsed since the introduction of a modern state that accounts for the variation in economic growth rates? Perhaps public policies promote or reduce economic growth or it could simply be a matter of the less affluent countries catching up with the rich countries (Dowrick and Nguyen, 1987; Castles, 1990, 1991), the level of affluence reducing the amount of change in the economy.

The focus of the volume on politics and affluence reflects a value orientation that guides the selection of the topics or problems considered interesting or relevant. Prosperity or decline of a country involves more than simply growth rates in the economy. Political phenomena like political system institutions or public policies may be evaluated according to the extent to which they contribute to the affluence or material well-being of the population. To promote citizen welfare is by no means a self-evident goal, as the occurrence of state terrorism and genocide testifies (Table I.1).

Genocide presents a basic legal problem because the *UN Convention on the Prevention and Punishment of the Crime of Genocide* of 1946 banishes member states from engaging in such atrocities while at the same time offering no mechanism for the implementation of the prohibition. If the occurrence of genocide is to be prevented, then the only viable alternative must be the purposeful intervention of another state or other states in the internal affairs of the state committing this atrocity, but what would be the legal justification of such an intervention? The *UN Declaration of the Inadmissibility of Intervention* from 1965 makes intervention difficult requiring very special conditions which do not cover the occurrence of genocide.

Many countries in the world are committed to development in the sense of promoting socio-economic objectives, but what are the actual accomplishments with regard to developmental objectives? Moreover, what is development in a political economy perspective? It is vital to discuss how precarious the notion of promoting national well-being may be, particularly in certain countries where Leviathan seems to have ruled for certain periods since the Second World War, and also among countries aiming at a normal rate of economic growth or a certain acceptable level of socio-economic development. It must be underlined that all aspects of development are value-ingrained.

Table I.1. Genocide, 1900-89

Country	Dates	Perpetrators	Victims' identity	Estimated numbers
German Africa	1904	German army	Herero	65 000
Ottoman Empire	1915	Young Turks/ Kurds	Armenians	800 000- 1.8 million
Soviet Union	1929	Russians	Kulacks	1 million
China	1931	Japan	Manchuria	?
Germany	1941-45	Germans	Jews	5-6 million
			Gypsies	48 000+
Sudan	1955-72	Sudanese army	Southern Sudanese	500 000
Indonesia	1965-67	Vigilantes backed by the army	Communist supporters	200 000- 500 000
Nigeria	1967-70	Nigerians	Ibos	2-3 million
Bangladesh	1971	West Pakistan	Bengalis	1 247 000- 3 million
Burundi	1972	Tutsis	Hutus	100 000- 200 000
Paraguay	1974	Paraguayans	Guayaki Ache Indians	?
East Timor	1975	Indonesian army	Timorese	60 000- 100 000
Kampuchea	1975-79	Khmer Rouge	Kampucheans	740 000- 3 million
Uganda	1976-78	Ugandan army	Ugandans	500 000

How is it that states behave differently with regard to the objective of citizen affluence? The emerging new interest in state theory requires that we understand what various objectives mean to state interests (Dunleavy and O'Leary, 1988). What are the degrees of freedom for the state with regard to the welfare of its population? If political regime is not a strict function of economic development and politics may matter for the rate of economic growth, then how can we explain the dismal failure of some countries to raise material well-being or the tragic occurrence of genocide and state terrorism? Whereas raising the level of material well-being of citizens is a major if not the major objective for some nation states, the governments of Argentina, Chile, Uruguay, Uganda and

Kampuchea have at times pursued very different objectives in relation to their people (Harff,1984).

Data, countries and indicators

We attempt an empirical analysis of politico-economic interaction in the rich world, the Communist world as it existed up to 1990 and Third World countries evaluating a few theories of how political institutions and public policy interact with socio-economic development in a reciprocal fashion. More specifically, we focus on some questions about development — economic as well as political — and the socio-economic determinants of polities, the pattern of public policies in various political systems and their explanation as well as the impact of political institutions and public policy on economic growth.

An attempt will be made to classify countries in various parts of the world according to a set of politico-economic concepts. A number of indices will be employed in order to render a quantitative statement possible. The study comprises various sets of countries in the different chapters selected for the main problems dealt with in each chapter, but included are the OECD-nations, several Communist countries and at least some forty Third World countries or sometimes more. And the social and economic correlates of polities will be searched for in order to find out how political structure is conditioned by the social and economic structure on the macro level. The indicators employed and the data sources used are stated in appendices to each chapter. It hardly needs to be pointed out that the problems in finding reliable information about several countries are great. How they are to be resolved is an open question. Thus, the statistics on economic growth within Communist countries are probably not strictly reliable. And often no data at all are available on Third World countries, particularly so for the 1950s and 1960s. In what ever way these difficulties are met, the solutions to the problems of data validity and reliability are bound to have an impact on the substantive findings.

Contents of the volume

The first chapter in this book contains an introduction to some basic concepts in political economy in terms of a discussion of the two basic modes of allocating resources, the budget or markets, in relation to income distribution and ownership structures. In the second we deal with the general social science notion of development. Chapter 3 is devoted to the analysis of a specific kind of development, namely socio-economic development, where the main question is how much countries — rich market systems, Communist systems and Third World countries — vary on various indicators of social or economic well-being. The more troublesome concept of political development is examined in Chapter 4 in an effort to unpack the different notions covered by the ambiguous qualification of development as political development. We search for the social and economic determinants of polities in Chapter 5 and inquire into the interpretation of the well-known empirical association between affluence and democracy.

Then, we move towards the analysis of public sector growth, looking for factors that account for the variation in welfare state expenditures, firstly among the West European countries in Chapter 6 and then, secondly, more generally among different politico-economic systems in Chapter 7. Chapters 8 and 9 deal with the effects of politics on economic growth, first concentrating on the differences in growth rates among the rich market systems or, more precisely, the OECD countries, and then moving to a more general analysis of the variation in economic growth among rich, Communist and Third World countries. Chapter 10 explores how politico-economic regimes may be evaluated on the basis of explicit economic and political criteria of performance. The conclusion weighs up our findings concerning how economic development impinges on politics with our analysis of the ways in which politics influences economic growth.

1 Allocation, distribution and ownership

Introduction

Political economy is the study of how politics and economics are interrelated. The distinction between the public and the private sectors and its implications for the polity and the economy is the principal focus. It deals with how the state is involved in the economy of a society and the economic consequences of the size and structure of the public sector (Palgrave, 1899: vol III; Palgrave 1987, vol 3). We need conceptual tools for interpreting the various ways in which the state may be related to the economy in a society and vice versa.

In this chapter we will introduce some basic concepts in political economy which will be elaborated upon in the following empirical chapters. There is a set of political economy concepts in terms of which politico-economic theories are formulated and which may be employed to identify types of politico-economic regimes. They refer in one way or another to mechanisms for the allocation of resources, the size and orientation of the public redistribution of income and wealth, and structures of ownership of the means of production (Margolis and Guitton, 1969; Stiglitz, 1988).

In any society resources or different factors of production have to be allocated among various usages and income as well as wealth be distributed to the households (Musgrave and Musgrave, 1980). Overlooking such phenomena as gift exchange and heritage there are in principle only two mechanisms for deciding about allocative and distributive matters: markets and politics in a wide sense (Arrow, 1963; Akerloff, 1970). The use of politics as the mechanism of allocation implies budget-making and planning as well as the resort to hierarchies to implement the budget document or plan. When markets are trusted with allocating resources the basic mechanism of choice is individual agreement or voluntary exchange (Buchanan, 1967; 1986). Distributive questions may be handled by markets, but the results of or the preconditions for voluntary exchange may be the target of public policy-making, the state attempting redistribution of income and wealth by means of the budget (Hochman and Peerson, 1974; Binder et al, 1974).

It is not always easy to distinguish between allocative and redistributive programmes in the public sector, as redistribution does not have to be in money but may involve goods and services — redistribution in kind. The welfare state with its high public budget mixes allocative and redistributive programmes to such an extent that it is difficult to tell which programme is which (Musgrave and Musgrave, 1980; Atkinson and Stiglitz, 1980). A very salient problem in political economy is to identify criteria for the determination of the size of the allocative and redistributive budget. Such criteria may be either normative, looking for an optimal size of budget allocation and budget redistribution (Margolis and Guitton, 1969; Haveman and Margolis, 1983). Or they may empirical, i.e. the actual factors that explain the variation in the size of the public sector and the welfare state commitments, among the nations, in the world (Wilensky, 1975; Castles, 1982; Wildavsky, 1986).

Although modern political economy has focused considerably on the variation in allocative and redistributive programmes in search for positive explanatory factors, the classical questions about ownership of the means of production: capitalism or socialism retain their relevance. The ownership problem remains central in the political economy approach, but this simple distinction no longer captures the complexity of the separation between budget allocation and market allocation. Although ownership of the means of production may be predominantly either private or public, the size of the welfare state or the tax state refers to another politico-economic dimension.

The political economies of the nations of the world differ along these three dimensions: mechanism of allocation, extent of redistribution and ownership structure. A basic problem in political economy is whether and how the variation in types of polities and economic development is related to how the basic politico-economic system is built up around the allocative, distributive and ownership structures (Pryor, 1968; Eckstein, 1971; Kornai, 1986). Actually, we have here a whole set of problems for comparative research into how political and economic variables are interrelated, some of which we will look at in the ensuing empirical chapters.

Allocation and ownership

One basic problem in any society is how to allocate the resources in an efficient manner. A second fundamental problem is the ownership question or how the means of production are to be owned. The efficiency question is how to devise a system whereby the resources are allocated to various uses in such a way that it would not be possible to achieve a better result had the resources been allocated differently. The ownership problem relates to basic questions about equity and power in society. Although the two problems are different their solutions are related to each other. How is an efficient system to be devised given the restriction that the means of production are predominantly owned publicly or privately?

One fundamental type of resource allocation system employs competitive prices as the tool for allocating resources to producers and consumers. It presupposes the existence of markets where scarcity prices are determined by the interaction between demand and supply. Could such a market system exist in a society where ownership is predominantly public?

The other fundamental type of resource allocation system employs planning and central coordination. A ministry of production and consumption — a central planning board — decides how resources are to be allocated among alternative employments — budget allocation. Such an allocation system is typically employed in an economic system where the resources are owned by the state. But could such an allocation system really be efficient? It is one of the basic results of microeconomic theory that both market and plan lead to identical allocation if the plan and the market satisfy the marginal conditions for efficiency, to be outlined below. The difficult problem is, however, the extent to which *actually existing institutions* in market allocation or budget allocation come close to the ideal type starting point.

Figure 1.1. Allocation and Ownership

		ALLOCATION MECHANISM	
OWNERSHIP		Predominantly market	Predominantly budget-making
	Predominantly public	Market socialism	Command economy
	Predominantly private	Capitalism	Mixed economy

Resources could be owned predominantly by the public or the private sector. And resources could be allocated by means of the budget or the market mechanism. Combining these distinctions we arrive at the basic alternatives shown in Figure 1.1, remembering that all existing politico-economic systems combines these properties in some mixture (Dahl and Lindblom, 1953; Lindblom, 1988).

The contradiction between capitalism and traditional socialism meaning a command economy arises in about two of the possibilities in Figure 1.1. However, there are two other ideal types identified in the figure which are relevant for the comparative analysis of politico-economic systems. In the Western World the developments in their politico-economic systems since the Second World War have meant that more budget allocation has been inserted into an economic system that used to be very much based on private ownership (Galbraith, 1975; Johansen, 1977-78). Finally, there is the somewhat imaginary, ideal type of market socialism. It is difficult to find actually existing counterexamples of this brand.

Two different reasons lie behind the seminal process of public sector growth among the rich market economies: public policy in relation to so-called market failures and policy-making with regard to income redistribution (Head, 1974; Lane, 1985; Wildavsky, 1986; Wolf, 1988). Budget allocation and market allocation have been combined in more equal doses than envisaged in the pure model of decentralized capitalism — the so-called mixed economy of the welfare states (Brown and Jackson, 1978; Lybeck, 1986; Lybeck and Henrekson, 1988). At the same time the seminal development in the OECD countries of a process of public sector growth has meant that public ownership of resources has increased. The mixed economies of the OECD countries differ, however, in terms of both size and orientation — why?

How can we account for the strong variation in welfare state commitments among rich and Third World countries in terms of an empirical analysis? The convergence hypothesis was suggested in the 1960s as a prediction to the effect that welfare state expenditures between market countries and Communist systems would become more and more similar (Tinbergen, 1967; Galbraith, 1975). Is it really true that public policies tend to grow more similar between countries as the level of affluence increases? Perhaps politics matter for public policy outputs or outcomes as discussed in the literature on policy determinants (Danziger, 1978; Sharpe and Newton, 1984)?

A number of important questions for research may be identified in relation to Figure 1.1. Is public sector growth related somehow to the state of the economy or to the structure of the polity (Wilensky, 1975)? How far is it possible to expand budget allocation within the confines of extensive private ownership of the means of production? How does public sector expansion affect economic growth? The major development in the socialist world has been the opposite one, to try to insert more of market allocation into a system of public ownership of the means of production (Lindblom, 1977). Is it possible to achieve an introduction of markets into an economic system based on public ownership of the means of production?

The four combinations of types of ownership and types of allocation mechanism in Figure 1.1 may be regarded as ideal types. Their relevance to countries in the Third World cannot be doubted. The basic problem of development administration is to make crucial choices about allocation mechanism and ownership structure in order to promote development goals (Hirschman, 1958; Verma and Sharma, 1984). The Indian debate, for example, about the place of planning in an economy with extensive private ownership is highly relevant in this context (Mareshwari, 1984; Baradhan, 1984).

The concept of planning is often employed in discussions about politico-economic systems. How does it relate to the concepts discussed so far? Actually, it is far from clear what is meant by 'planning' (Wildavsky, 1972). Several distinctions may be made between different kinds of planning (Johansen, 1978; Cave and Hare, 1983):

- Macroeconomic planning or the regulation by the state of fiscal, monetary and trade parameters in order to influence macro-economic targets.
- Microeconomic planning or the control of the state of basic decision parameters.
- Comprehensive planning or the attempt to control the whole economy in more or less detail.
- Indicative planning or the effort to influence the economy by means of selective measures that work out their own consequences.

In a market economy some kinds of macroeconomic planning by means of indicative planning mechanisms had been considered relevant after the great depression in the 1930s. Yet, macroeconomic planning began to be questioned in the 1970s, as there was a reaction in several OECD nations against a too optimistic and perhaps naive adherence to Keynesian macroeconomic principles (Sawyer, 1989). Microeconomic planning is not in agreement with a market economy which may accommodate indicative planning on the other hand. Comprehensive planning is typical of command economies.

Whereas planning may be employed both in systems based on market allocation as well as in command economies although differently, the distinction between competition and budget allocation as the medium of allocation is a sharp one. Budget allocation occurs in both command and market economies although in quite different amounts. Whereas budget allocation in socialist systems covers all types of goods, in market economies it used to be confined to the provision of public goods. In a system where the state or the public owns most of the means of production is it necessary to resort to a command economy?

Is it possible to employ efficiently market-type decision mechanisms and achieve planning although different from the comprehensive planning of a command economy (Tinbergen, 1952; 1967)? In any economic structure the role of prices is crucial, but we must distinguish between competitive prices and administrative prices. To what extent may various ownership structures be combined with different allocation mechanisms?

Market economy and efficiency

The concept of efficiency in resource allocation has a precise and specific meaning (Layard and Walters, 1978; Bohm, 1986). Three conditions are sufficient and necessary for an allocation system to be efficient:

1. Efficiency in consumption: on the demand side of the economy consumers trade with each other in order to maximize their individual utilities. An allocation is efficient if it is not possible after a trade to retrade and arrive at a position where the utility of at least one consumer can be increased and the utility of no other consumer be decreased.
2. Efficiency in production: on the supply side of the economy producers deliver goods and services. An allocation is efficient if it is not possible to increase the supply of at least one good while the supply of other goods remains constant.

Efficiency in production means that it is not possible to increase output by changing the composition of the factors of production employed. Overall efficiency also requires that efficiency in consumption matches efficiency in production, i.e. we have:

3. Product-mix efficiency: the value to the consumers of a good equals its marginal cost.

It is possible to show that a market economy may under certain conditions fulfil these efficiency requirements by the employment of the price mechanism as the allocation instrument (Arrow and Scitovsky, 1972; Mishan, 1981). Given a set of competitive prices concerning goods and factors of production, the market mechanism will arrive at a situation where there is efficiency in consumption and in production as well as in the overall economic sense (Debreu, 1959; Lachman, 1986).

These efficiency conditions apply under certain conditions which render the market appropriate for certain types of goods and not others. The market is suitable for the allocation of private consumer goods, i.e.

divisible goods that have few externalities and are characterized by rivalry or no jointness (Bator, 1958; Head, 1974; Musgrave and Musgrave, 1980). The market economy faces severe problems when it comes to indivisible goods or public goods and externalities. Moreover, the market is not able to handle overall macroeconomic decisions like consumption versus investments. Finally, the problem of determining the distribution of incomes is not solved. We may apply an independent criterion of justice to the outcomes of the operation of the market forces (Nath, 1969; Rawls, 1971).

The basic problem in a market economy is not its internal functioning. On the contrary, if the conditions for market allocation are satisfied there is no cause for hesitation as the efficiency requirement is met. Problematic in relation to market allocation is its applicability as the conditions for a perfectly functioning market economy are narrow (Buchanan, 1985). Wolf identifies four sources of so-called market failure or situations where the typical conditions for the successful operation of markets do not apply: (1) externalities and public goods; (2) increasing returns to scale or jointness; (3) market imperfections in terms of actor misinformation or factor inflexibility, often called internalities; (4) distributional equity (Wolf, 1988: 20-29). The situation with regard to a command economy is the very opposite one, as it is the internal mechanics of such a resource allocation system that are problematic.

Theoretically, it is possible to prove that the employment of competitive prices in markets with perfect competition and adequate production technology results in allocative outcomes that satisfy the necessary and sufficient conditions for efficiency. But this is all just theory. The practical institutions of market regimes — capitalism — involve much more than simply perfectly competitive markets. In his *The Economic Institutions of Capitalism* (1985) Oliver E. Williamson states:

> Firms, markets, and relational contracting are important economic institutions. They are also the evolutionary product of a fascinating series of organizational innovations. The study of the economic institutions of capitalism has not, however, occupied a position of importance on the social science research agenda. (Williamson, 1985: 15)

The practical feasibility of market allocation is bound together with the occurrence of market failure. The new transaction approach within economics emphasize that basic contractual problems of asymmetrical information, moral hazard and adverse selection limit the applicability of market exchange and that they may be handled in terms of a variety of institutional responses (Williamson, 1986; Mueller, 1986; Ricketts, 1987).

How wide-spread market failure is depends on both the evaluation of externalities and inequities in market outcomes as well as the occurrence of internalities and inefficiencies in market operations, but also the probability that government action and bureaucratic implementation constitutes a real alternative to market failure. The Coase theorem implies that market failure may not be a condition for state intervention, if the likelihood of government failure is even larger (Buchanan, 1986). Thus the practicality of a market oriented society is tied into the fundamental problem of a demarcation line between the private and the public sectors in societies with extensive private property institutions. Budget allocation of resources or budget redistribution of income ameliorate market failure, but there are limits to the size of the public sector when economic efficiency is considered.

In a comparative perspective it seems important to separate between various kinds of capitalist regimes and attempt to evaluate how they perform on political economy criteria. Thus the so-called rich market economies perform very differently in terms of such a crucial criterion of evaluation as average economic growth. How can we explain performance differences among different existing capitalist systems?

We need to proceed from the pure theoretical argument about the superiority of competitive market allocation in combination with capitalist institutions to empirical research into the similarities and differences between various politico-economic systems. One tentative distinction is that between decentralized capitalist, capitalist-state and mixed-capitalist systems on the one hand and socialist regimes on the other hand (Chapter 10). A step forward may be taken by an empirical analysis of the performance variation both *between* these categories and *within* each category itself. Such a research programme involves an analysis of other performance dimensions besides the differential rates of economic development of politico-economic systems.

Command economy and inefficiency

The allocation mechanism in a command economy is the command or directive stemming from the authority of the state. The ministry of production in a command economy faces the same requirements for efficiency in consumption and production which the market handles by the invisible hand. How is it possible for a command economy to meet the efficiency requirement in consumption and production? It is necessary to distinguish between two problems in relation to a command economy. The first problem is one of *theoretical possibility:* could a command economy satisfy the general conditions for efficiency in resource allocation? The second problem concerns *practical feasibility:* is it possible in a real world sense to devise a system of resource allocation that satisfies the efficiency conditions although it allocates resources by command?

It has been argued that the ministry of production could create such an information system as well as such a command system that it would be able to allocate goods and factors of production to consumers and producers in such a way that the efficiency criteria are met (Barone, 1935). However, although this may be theoretically possible, the basic problems concern its practical feasibility (Hayek, 1935; Bergson, 1982). When looking at the existing examples of command economies it seems as if the practical problems are enormous (Ward, 1967; Roberts, 1971; Bornstein, 1973). Before we begin the empirical evaluation of the model of a command economy, we will look at some of the difficulties from a theoretical point of view.

The practical problem for the central planning board in a command economy is to build up an information system so vast as to include each and every consumer, producer and good. Attempts have been made to formulate a model of a command economy with regard to the production side (Kornai and Liptak, 1962; Heal, 1973). Its key components include:

> The centre, instead of quoting prices, proposes at each step an allocation of all the goods and services in the economy amongst various uses. Then, having proposed an allocation, it receives information that enables it to assess the marginal contribution to social welfare that a good or service makes in each of its uses. Knowing these marginal contributions, it calculates a new plan in which, by comparison with the first, inputs have been moves from uses where their marginal values are low, to those where they are high. (Heal, 1973:156)

Leaving the consumption aside for the moment grave doubts must be raised as to the practical feasibility of this planning model. How could any central authority store or master knowledge about the marginal productivities in a total economy? This is not possible in a changing world (von Mises, 1936; Caiden and Wildavsky, 1974). Even if the *information problem* could be solved in a small economy the *incentive problem* would still remain. Since it would be rational for each producer to disguise their information about technologies a strategic game would result. Participants would try to promote their interests by biased information. If the ministry of production attempts to force the directives on producers, then there is no incentive to search for a rational technology.

A command economy may use prices instead of explicit commands like in a war economy, but these prices would not constitute market prices. Prices may be employed for several purposes (Johansen, 1978). They may reflect the interaction between demand and supply, but they may also express central authority directives. In a command economy prices have the function of conveying to the participants in the economy the conditions for their activity as the central authority considers the situation. The prices of goods and services as well as of the factors of production are strictly controlled, meaning that they express the intentions of the central planning board, not the demand and supply of consumers and producers — administrative prices. It has been suggested that this could be resolved by a sort of Groves-Ledyard mechanism (Varian, 1984), but whether it is practical remains to be seen.

The advantages of a command economy is that it may make certain types of planning easy. The state could decide the overall direction of the economy. Macroeconomic planning that made distinctions between consumption and investment as well as between collective goods and consumer goods would become much easier as the amount of central control is so much larger. The central planning model emphasizes knowledge of technological factors for the governance of the economy in accordance with the preferences of the central planning board (Dobb, 1940).

The disadvantages of the command economy derive from the fact that it tends to be badly inefficient with regard to the allocation of consumer goods or capital. Although it is true that the ministry of finance or the budgetary authority could, in principle, employ efficient shadow prices or exchange ratios between different kinds of resources or production factors, the practical feasibility of such a mechanism is open to doubt. Controlling prices and employing them as tools for commanding the economic decisions of consumers and producers means most probably that neither efficiency in consumption nor efficiency in production will be met. In practical situations we find the curious expressions of a command economy: severe shortages for some goods, enormous overproduction of other goods, mismanagement of capital resources and a peculiar allocation of the labour force (Zaleski, 1980; Kornai, 1986).

These difficulties are well-known from studies of the East European systems (Grossman, 1960; Ellman, 1979; Nove, 1986; Åslund, 1989). A huge planning bureau uses prices to allocate resources, but these prices do not reflect changes in demand and supply. They are cost-plus prices, meaning that they are based on the average unit production cost in enterprises producing a good (Eidem and Viotti, 1978). The planning bureaux base their administrative decisions on available technology in terms of how much of the input resources are needed to produce an output unit given the existing knowledge about production functions. Moreover, the planning bureau may also adjust these prices in accordance with national priorities concerning the goods that should be produced, replacing consumer sovereignty with collective preferences interpreted by a group of planners (Spulber, 1969; Dyker, 1983; Bergson and Levine, 1983; Amann and Cooper, 1986).

In an ideal command economy there would be no need for prices. The state would know the relative value of each good in terms of preferences. No existing economy could, however, be governed in this way. Although, for example, the Soviet economy is basically run by means of a large planning framework — allocating resources to various regions, factories and consumers — it employs some sort of prices: administrative prices (McAuley, 1979; Nove, 1986, 1987; Kornai, 1990; Dyker, 1976, 1985). The single units in the Soviet economy are given a budget within which to make economic decisions about resources. This does not mean that these decisions guide resource allocation, but simply that there is a limit as to how far planning can proceed. The economic decisions of consumers and producers are still largely determined by the plan (Nove, 1986).

Major economic changes, then, also have to come from the plan. The administrators of the economy must employ various devices in order to gather information about how to increase efficiency. The state has to remain alert to various signals from producers and consumers that the allocation of resources must be changed — queues, overproduction, misallocation, wastage. On the one hand, the state must be able to coordinate and process a vast amount of knowledge. The problems with a planning system are that the state may not get the right information from producers and consumers and that the state may not be able to process such a vast amount of information. There are limits to the capacity of any group of actors to control social systems, in particular economic ones. On the other hand, there is the serious incentive problem: what is the reward for the various participants in a planned economy — consumers, producers and administrators — when they search for and transmit the best available knowledge?

Change in production and management becomes particularly difficult in a command economy as there is little scope for innovation and few rewards for individual initiatives. To devise a number of performance indicators does not help as they may be strategically manipulated in a system based on hierarchical control (Leeman, 1963). The sudden and almost dramatic collapse of the East European command economies in the late 1980s appears to have been a mature reaction to long-term system problems of the kind outlined above.

The structural problems inherent in a pure model of a command economy are not only theoretical but may also be found and loom large in the existing command economies when socialist systems are analysed — see *From Marx to the Market: Socialism in Search for an Economic System* (1990) by W. Brus and K. Laski — or compared with existing capitalist regimes (Davis and Scase, 1985). The East European countries have given up trying to cope with them when they started in 1989-90 to dismantle their command economies without a clearcut replacement model.

This is not the place to discuss the probable future developments in

Eastern Europe, as we move on to the attempts to formulate an alternative theoretical model of a socialist politico-economic regime. The serious problem of efficiency in a command economy resulted in a search for another resource allocation model that is based less on planning and recognizes the fundamental importance of prices — scarcity prices. The socialist models of Lange, Taylor and Lerner are based on an attempt to combine public ownership with market prices (Lange, 1936-7; Lippincott, 1938; Lange and Taylor, 1964; Lerner, 1944; Mandel, 1986).

The competitive socialist model

The so-called Lange-Taylor model is interesting as it explicitly tries to accommodate a socialist system of resource allocation within the standard efficiency criteria. It is not based on the notion of a command economy with a huge planning office directing the economy by means of state authority.

The Lange-Taylor model attempts to combine the trial and error procedure of a competitive price mechanism with public ownership of production. The assumptions of the model include:

1. The allocation of capital is to be based on administrative criteria.
2. The allocation of labour and consumption goods is to be determined by the interaction between demand and supply in free markets.
3. The producers of goods are to be instructed to obey the following rules: (a) to choose the combination of factors which minimize the average cost of production; (b) the scale of output is to be determined where marginal cost is equal to the price of the product (Lange, 1964).

Given these initial conditions, the state authorities are to start the trial and error process by arbitrarily setting the prices for goods and labour. The interaction between consumers and producers on various markets will then in successive stages lead to a state where the prices are adjusted by the price board until the efficiency conditions are met. Thus, a socialist economy could be using real prices and achieve an efficient allocation of resources with a Walrasian auctioneer.

Two detailed models of resource allocation in a socialist economy employing scarcity prices have been developed. The so-called Lange-Arrow-Hurwicz model is an attempt to copy the competitive mechanism of a market economy in a socialist system (Arrow and Hurwicz, 1960). The LAH planning procedure may be outlined as follows:

> At a given distribution of resources amongst consumers, the central planning

> board (CPB) quotes a vector of prices. Producers then calculate the production programmes that would maximize profits at these prices, and inform the centre of the supplies, demands and profits that would result. The profits are distributed as the centre may see fit amongst consumers, who then, facing given profit shares and wage rates, choose their most preferred consumption bundles, and inform the CPB of these. The centre now acts as an auctioneer, raising prices of goods in excess demand, and vice versa: and so the process continues. (Heal, 1973:79)

An alternative to the LAH model is the so-called Malinvaud process where the centre employs a competitive price mechanism in order to arrive at knowledge about the production possibilities of the firms which may be used to determine an efficiency locus. The Malinvaud model places a much stronger role with the Central Planning Board (Malinvaud, 1967).

It has been argued that the trial and error method suggested in the LAH model of a socialist system of resource allocation will face severe practical information problems. Will the successive reconsideration of prices by a state board really work? Would there not be too slow a process of price adaptation to information about the relationship between demand and supply? How is the remuneration to labour to be decided? Is it really possible to have an equal distribution of income at the same time as the wages are to be determined in the market? According to Hayek, the iterative revision of prices to be fed into market operations would require a board of supermen, with perfect knowledge about all production technologies and the behaviour of managers (Hayek, 1940). It has also been argued that the so-called competitive solution would not handle macroeconomic disturbances well (Dobb, 1940; Wright, 1947). The Malinvaud process has been criticized as requiring too much coordination between producers.

Another basic problem in the competitive solution remains to be pointed out: the incentive problem. Why would managers in the various production units follow the assumptions of the model meaning that they would be socially rational without any remuneration? Why would it not be possible that the managers of production might try to influence the price board to set the prices in such a way that any losses will be recovered? Why would managers attempt to minimize costs if they are not allowed to capitalize on the profits? If the profits are to be returned to the price board, why would managers care about production costs?

The socialist bias in the LAH model is apparent in the restrictions on capital. Capital would be owned and controlled by the state and profits, interests and rents earned in government enterprises would be distributed as a sort of social dividend unrelated to labour income. But how could there be efficiency in capital allocation given these restrictions?

What is the exact meaning of competition in the LAH model? Could there really be competition on either side of the economy if severe socialist restrictions concerning wages and ownership were upheld? It may be argued that from a static point of view the competitive solution might achieve efficiency, but how about a dynamic perspective? Why would managers care about the introduction of new technology if the profits are not to be capitalized in one way or another? According to the Austrian school, there will be no stationary solution as the economy is always in a process of change and adaptation. If risk and uncertainty is inherent in management, then the incentive problem will be most severe as there would be no reward for the embarkment on a process of innovation (Schumpeter, 1944). What is really the difference between the central planning solution and the competitive solution?

The competitive solution suggested by Lange, Taylor and Lehner is an attempt to solve the efficiency equations by means of the market mechanism instead of the administrative solution in the central planning model. The administrative solution is deficient because there is no such vast and reliable information system available as required. The competitive solution aims at replacing the administrative mechanism with a trial and error mechanism in combination with some severe socialist restrictions. What is the difference in reality?

It would seem as if the competitive solution reduces the tasks of the ministry of production from a giant comprehensive planning body to a small price board making adjustments here and there. This is not so, however. The price board in the competitive solution would need extensive knowledge — pure information undisturbed by tactical considerations — in order to control the behaviour of managers. Is average cost really minimized? Is price really equal to marginal cost? Why could not various managers co-operate and try to influence the price or hide information about the cost function? Who could judge whether there really is free entry to the market in a socialist state where the state controls access to capital? Is it not conceivable that it will be difficult to operate markets where the availability of capital is not free?

Some goods may display economies of scale, meaning that there will be losses for the managers when price is set equal to marginal costs. If the price board is asked to change the price so that losses are eliminated, then why could not the board be equally willing to change the prices for other goods? Would it not require the same amount of extensive information as in the command economy to be able to judge the cost function of various enterprises? It seems as if the competitive solution also requires a central planning board.

The information requirements are no less formidable in the competitive solution than in the central planning solution. And both face the same incentive problem: how could the participants in this type of resource allocation be trusted with an ambition to act according to the rules? Just as there would be an advantage for managers in a command economy to misrepresent costs in order to maximize their own advantage, so there would be no incentive for managers in the competitive solution to minimize costs, if they could not count on some of the profits being made available to them.

The difference between a central planning board and a price board would in effect be marginal. No central planning board would ever be able to allocate all resources without the use of some price mechanism. And no price board would ever reach an efficient allocative state if it did not have access to comprehensive knowledge about production possibilities as well as make the correct decisions about the release of the socially owned capital resources.

These theoretical generalizations about the prospects for a market-type reform of the command economies may be checked against oberservations on the developmental trends in existing economies in the communist world (Brus and Laski, 1990). The zest for a fundamental but still socialist reform of the command economies in eastern Europe and in mainland China has cropped up now and then as a reaction towards the rigidities, shortages and inefficiencies of the command economies (Ellman, 1979; Kornai, 1979; Åslund, 1989). However, these reform movements in the command economies accomplished less than hoped for and this is the reason why the East European countries decided in 1989 to look for alternative economic systems outside the various socialist models. What is the basic difficulty in the theoretical argument for a new kind of socialist politico-economic regime — market socialism (Nove, 1983; Miller, 1989; Le Grand and Estrin, 1989)?

Market socialism?

The idea of market socialism was launched as a result of the inefficiency problems of a centrally planned economy. The informational requirements on a Central Planning Board would simply be too great to handle by any social organization. However, the proposals for or models of a combination of markets and a socialist economy are ambiguous with regard to two basic problems, the position of a coordinating body and the range of the use of markets to allocate resources. From a theoretical point of view we may predict serious difficulties in implementing market socialism in an existing politico-economic system. Let us pinpoint these problems before we look at the attempts at other socialist models.

All models of market socialism assume some coordinating board, but the scope of its operations and its power differs. Given the fact that the Coordinating Board has the responsibility for allocative efficiency it seems difficult indeed to restrict its operations. Even if it employs competitive prices it would still face the requirement that it itself operates rationally. What mechanism in market socialism would guarantee that the coordinators make the correct decisions? It seems as if the theories of market socialism simply assume that the Coordinating Board will consist of highly competent people that are unambiguously devoted to the efficiency goal. But why would this be the case? *Sed quis custodiet ipsos Custodes*?

The incentive problem recurs at the management level (Bergson, 1982). There is no mechanism that will reward the managers to act in a way that is socially productive as long as profits cannot be capitalized by the managers. The same problem appears again with regard to labour. If wages are to be set on the basis of an equality requirement, then it is difficult to see why labour would behave in way that is conducive to collective rationality.

On the consumption side market socialism was meant to strengthen the principle of consumer sovereignty in socialist economies. The use of administrative prices in command economies means that effective demand may show up in ways other than via the price mechanism. There is a constant danger in a command economy of replacing consumer preferences with the preferences of the coordinators. Not even market socialism could accept the principle of consumer sovereignty as the coordinators would make crucial choices about the division between consumption and investment as well as the long-range orientation of the overall economy. What would be the incentives for coordinators to make the correct decisions?

The incentive problem is the most difficult problem that market socialism faces. How is it to be solved given the tension between the use of market prices on the one hand and the restrictions of a socialist economy on the other? The literature on capitalism versus socialism tends to focus on the information problem that arises as markets are replaced by planning, but the incentive problem is more severe. It accounts for the widespread feeling of apathy in several socialist countries where reforms aiming at market socialism have been tried but where the incentive problem has not reached a satisfactory solution. It also explains the development of a sharp tension between the official economy and the unofficial or black economy in socialist systems.

Could a socialist production system be efficient? What amount of market-type operations and mechanisms could be inserted into a socialist economy in order to raise productivity and affluence? These questions have been much debated by economists over the last fifty years. The debate is clearly relevant to the recent attempts in the communist world to promote efficiency in their economies. The practical lessons are that a command economy is possible but not efficient. In order to promote efficiency the price mechanism has to be resorted to in the sense that prices reflect scarcity of values. This in turn requires that the reward function of the price system is recognized in the *incentive system* of the society, meaning that it will pay for the participants to communicate truthfully and behave rationally in relation to economic parameters.

Only if a socialist state allows private incentives is it possible to employ the price system to allocate resources in an efficient way. The socialist restrictions of the Lange-Taylor model mean that the competitive solution will be a variant of the command economy model. How could there be efficiency in production if managers are not allowed access to a capital market as well as being permitted to capitalize profits without the intervention of the state?

How far is it possible to accommodate private incentives without breaking the socialist assumptions of the economic system? The debate about the possibility and efficiency of a socialist economy has focused far too much on abstract equilibrium conditions and bypassed crucial institutional problems. The basic difficulty in a socialist economy is not to derive a set of solutions to the standard efficiency conditions but to devise and maintain institutions that implement these solutions in the short run as well as in the long run. It seems as if the two models of a socialist economy — the competitive model as well as the central planning model — make far too strong or simplistic institutional assumptions about the practicability of managing a large economy along socialist lines.

It is impossible to discuss the possibility of change in allocation mechanism without taking the institutional structure for ownership into account. If market mechanisms are to be employed instead of planning or administration, then private ownership must be allowed. If one favours efficiency in resource allocation, then one has to accept the institutional requirements and consequences of the working of the market. The fact that a country has an ownership structure that is fundamentally public implies that there are definite limits to the scope for the operation of the market mechanism.

The introduction of market socialism in communist systems has always been of limited significance and restricted to a few types of divisible goods. Often it is accompanied by a process in which attempts to broaden the relevance of the market mechanism is curtailed by a fear for the consequences for the structure of ownership and property rights. Public ownership limits the use of the market mechanism to such an extent as to make the whole idea of market socialism superficial.

Looking at the various attempts at some type of market socialism in the communist world — in the Soviet Union, Hungary, Yugoslavia, China — we may predict on theoretical reasons that these reforms will pass through an ambiguous process of implementation characterized by opposite forces. Either the reforms will be curtailed after a while or restricted to a narrow sector of the economy. Or there will be a severe incentive problem as apathy will be the response to a situation where private initiatives are allowed but not rewarded. Or, finally, the communist state has to recognize private initiative to an extent that must have system power implications which call for a very delicate balance between the established order and the new initiatives.

The relevance of market socialism to developing countries is limited due to the fundamental contradictions between the need to maintain control and the pressure to extend market operations. It is symptomatic that the economies characterized by rapid and steady growth have not attempted to adopt the model of market socialism. On the contrary, the economies of the pacific area have successfully tried a model of market capitalism introduced and supervised by government (Zysman, 1983). If the institutional analysis is widened to include trade unions and political factors, then the practicability of market socialism would have to be even more confined.

It is often stated that Yugoslavia and Hungary are the only countries where market socialism were tried on a significant scale (Brus and Laski, 1990). We need to look at these cases of socialist reform for various reasons. First, there was a mix of regime reforms in Yugoslavia, all of which can hardly be subsumed under the label of market socialism (Singleton and Carter, 1982; Estrin, 1983; Lydall, 1986). The participatory schemes for workers have attracted international attention as a way to reform the rigid bureaucratic nature of the command economy (Dahl, 1985), but it is an open question as to what extent these participatory reforms really imply market socialism. Second, the reform of the Hungarian economy away from the command model towards the market socialism model never managed to introduce real market mechanisms as the enterprises remained dependent on the state. Third, it is vital to evaluate empirically the extent of success in these two system experiments, because the Yugoslavian one failed as the 1980s were hardly a period of economic progress whereas the Hungarian one will most probably be replaced by more capitalist inspired reform attempts.

Budget allocation, voice and exit

Extensive budget allocation instead of market allocation in a system with considerable private ownership of the means of production and consumption has become typical in the OECD countries. The relevance of budget allocation has been on the increase in capitalist systems for several decades transforming these private societies to mixed economies, although the seminal process of public sector expansion has now come to a halt (Webber and Wildavsky, 1986; Wildavsky, 1986). It would appear there is a limit to the process of public sector growth. The distinction between a mixed economy and a command economy is a qualitative one and the transformation of a society with strong private ownership and existing market mechanisms into a system oriented towards the planning mechanism would require structural changes that are far more encompassing than yearly increments in a slow process of public sector growth.

Budget allocation takes place in the yearly budgetary process where requests seek appropriations and appropriations result from the consideration of competing requests (Wildavsky, 1984, 1988; White and Wildavsky, 1988). The principal tool for deciding which requests will be which appropriations is the authority of government, not the voluntary agreement between producers and consumers. Budget allocation is characterized by considerable stability in that there is a short-term plan about how resources are to be employed and for what purposes which is of a determinate form.

The mechanism of allocation in the budgetary process is not based on competition and exchange but rests on the authority of government to decide on the basis of cost calculations from one supplier, the bureau. Budget allocation is a strategic game between two actors, the government demanding a service and the bureau supplying the service on the condition that total costs will be covered. Thus, we have the typical feature of the budgetary process that programme quantity will not be set where marginal value equals marginal cost (Niskanen, 1971).

Budget allocation is based on monopoly and hierarchy. Goods and services are produced by one supplier and consumed by the citizens without any choice of an alternative. Quantity is determined by the authorities on the basis on various considerations including citizen preferences as revealed in some political process or collective preferences as defined by some authority. The programme is uniformly provided by the authority to be consumed in equal ways by its clients. Quantity is determined in the budgetary process as a result of the game interaction between government demanding a programme and the bureau supplying the programme. There is large scope for negotiation and strategic behaviour in the budgetary process as described by Aaron Wildavsky in a series of studies of the budgetary process (Wildavsky, 1964, 1984, 1988; Heclo and Wildavsky, 1974; Wildavsky, 1976, 1986; White and Wildavsky, 1988).

Price and cost in budget allocation serve administrative functions. On the one hand, the appropriation informs the bureaux about the amount of resources they are entitled to use. On the other hand, the authority mobilizes resources either in the form of taxes or charges. Producer costs are the appropriations which reflect the bargaining power of the two principal actors in the budgetary process. Consumer prices may be fixed on a variety of grounds from allocative purposes to redistributional criteria. The remunerations to labour and capital are affected by political deliberations. Labour costs are a function of the bargaining power of the public employees in relation to government, whereas capital costs are handled by means of various administrative criteria.

The basic principles of public administration structure budget allocation. The means and ends of programmes are determined in a plan document which singles out the supplier and identifies the production functions. There is a predetermined structure of monopoly suppliers, the bureaucracy. There is no competition between the bureaux as they have been assigned long-term tasks which are unique for each bureau. Clear standards for the operation of the bureau are laid down and the output of the bureau is regulated by means of technical and legal criteria. Complaint is to be expressed by means of voice, not exit.

As Albert Hirschman argued in *Exit, Voice and Loyalty* (1970), the difference between budget and market allocation appears most clearly in the handling of allocation failures and the expression of dissatisfaction. Whereas the consumer may exit from the market when faced with a product or service he/she dislikes, the citizen in a voting context has no such powerful tool at his/her disposal. Instead the dissatisfied citizen has to go through the tiresome and lengthy process of complaining to those responsible for the provision of the good or the service, which is a lot less expedient than simply turning to a competitor in the market.

Long-term planning in a mixed economy is of a different nature. It is also based on a plan document but it lacks the determinate form. It is more of a projection and a guess than a real commitment as to the path to be travelled. Short-term budget allocation and long-term planning have certain advantages which may make them attractive alternatives to market allocation. However, there are certain disadvantages which have become more apparent in the era of big government.

The budget in a mixed economy

The government budget is a promise about who can expect what money. It is a real commitment that there is a high probability that resources will be forthcoming, particularly in rich countries. In his comparative model of the budgetary process, Wildavsky employs two conceptual pairs in order to derive four ideal types. On the one hand, we have the predictability of the budgetary process as to whether its appropriations will lead to safe expenditure in accordance with what was planned, or the state budget is characterized by instability in that budgets are remade continuously. On the other hand, there is the environment of budget-making — how rich or poor the economy is that supports the public sector. Typical of the *incremental* budgetary fashion that has been prevalent in the mixed economies is the combination of stability and affluence, whereas *repetitive* budgeting typical of Third World countries takes place in a poor environment where the budgetary process tends towards instability (Wildavsky, 1976).

The variation among the so-called rich market economies may be further explained by looking more closely at the budgetary contexts in the leading OECD countries. Wildavsky explains the variation in budget size by the interaction between the containment of conflict and the support on spending where the first factor reduces whereas the second factor enhances budget-making (Wildavsky, 1986). The question of variation in the public finances is one of the core problems of political economy. We will deal with this problem of the size and orientation of the public budget in empirical analyses of both the variation within the OECD set of countries and the variation between rich market economies, communist systems and Third World countries.

Budgetary stability has a one-year periodicity. Typical of short-term budget allocation is, however, that the one-year periodicity tends to extend to a long-term stability as stated in the theory about incrementalism. Once appropriations are fixed they are non-negotiable. People can predict what services and goods are forthcoming and employees may trust that their salaries will be paid (Rose, 1989). The budget document is transformed into expenditure decisions which may be called upon in due time. Uncertainty is minimized, predictability maximized.

Stability when considered advantageous tends to characterize the development of the budget meaning that yearly changes will only be marginal. The theory of incrementalism used to be the established explanation of the short-term budgetary process. It was considered valid until budget-making became more erratic and shifting as a reaction to a more volatile environment. Yearly changes became non-marginal and programmes were really extinguished. It remains to be seen whether non-marginal budget-making amounts to a real change or if it is simply the exception that confirms the rule. The relevance of incrementalism hinges on the interpretation of the concept of marginal changes as well as the occurrence of changes in appropriations. It could be the case that incrementalism overemphasized the extent of stability that used to take place before the turmoil of the early 1980s or that the 1980s really meant a decisive break with the past.

A society that trusts budget allocation for a large number of services and goods values control and predictability highly. Government lays down what to expect for one year for a wide variety of utilities. This enhances security of employment and makes it possible to control outputs in accordance with regulations. Short-term cost efficiency is traded for long-term stability and predictability. Budget allocation is the attempt to make the future controllable and predictable in terms of predetermined criteria. The information contained in the budget is a one-way communication that states what will take place and how.

Budget allocation is the authoritative allocation of values for a society. And authority if benevolent may accomplish beneficial outcomes.

Budget allocation enhances similarity. The emphasis on similarity follows from two sources: technical rationality and a preference for equality. Budget allocation is a method to inform about how resources are to be used to accomplish a number of goals. And such information has its own requirements. In a system of big government it becomes impossible to take each and every factor into account and to treat each appropriation differently — hence the need for standardization and similarity. To allocate by means of a budget is to employ rules and rules are expedient if they are universal with as few exceptions as possible.

The drive for similarity is further strengthened by the preference for similarity in societies with big government. Big government is both an effect and a cause of the trend towards similarity. In relation to the set of public goods there can be no choice between budget and market allocation, because there is so called market failure. However, in relation to other kinds of goods and services there is a real choice between politics or markets. Often budget allocation is preferred to market allocation because it makes possible the control of outputs which in turn makes standardization possible at the same time as it further enhances similarity for its own reasons.

Budget allocation initiates a need for yet more budget allocation. Budget allocation creates clients who tend to hang on to their appropriations and if possible extend them further. And people are always looking for new appropriations to become clients of budgetary programmes. Budget allocation has its adherents among those who favour stability and value predictability. Once an item of expenditure is accepted on the budget it has a strong probability of remaining there for long periods of time. A variety of arguments have been put forward to account for the expansion of budget allocation (Tarschys, 1975; Larkey, Stolp and Winer, 1981; Rose, 1984; Wildavsky, 1985).

The growth of the state is essentially a political process through which the budget has driven out the market as the mechanism of allocation. The process is a universal one in systems with a structure of predominantly privately owned means of production. It is considered that a number of problems and deficiencies may be better attacked by the use of the budget instrument — public policy solutions to market failure. Essentially, it is a preference for stability and predictability as well as similarity. The mixed economy or the bargaining society (Johansen, 1979) means that allocative processes comprise a limited number of choice participants as well as that allocation decisions may be influenced if not controlled by government and its bureaux.

Whereas there is a search in communist systems for more market allocation and its derivatives — rapid adjustment, flexibility and mutual adaption — the opposite tendency has characterized the development of the political economies of the OECD countries. One has resorted to government in order to allocate the welfare state goods and services, although neither could these goods and services be classified as pure public goods nor is budget allocation often based on the occurrence of externalities or economies of scale. The budget instrument has been considered superior to market allocation in relation to a number of basically private goods and services where the elements of jointness and non-excludability have not been conspicuous. In relation to health, social services and education predictability and similarity have been deemed more important than flexibility or efficiency.

Hierarchy has replaced markets in the economies with extensive private ownership. The budget instrument appears to handle the transaction costs in a complex society characterized by bounded rationality and opportunism with a small number of powerful actors better than the market. Internal organization will drive out market exchange systems when these conditions obtain (Williamson, 1975) whether in the private sector or in society in general. Combining the transaction argument with the stability and similarity argument, there is a strong case for budget allocation in relation to semi-public goods.

However, there are institutional limits to the expansion of the budget. The structure of privately owned means of production implies some amount of individual choice which works against the expansion of budget allocation. Budget expansion may be conducive to individual freedom but it basically means that resources are allocated by one actor in accordance with standardized rules. Regulation is typical of budget allocation, but there is a limit to the regulative capacity of government in systems with private ownership. When take-home pay goes down the period of budget expansion is bound to come to an end in systems with private ownership (Rose, 1985). The larger the budget the more serious the efficiency problems. A simple diagram may be employed to display two basic problems with an extensive public sector (Figure 1.2). We have two allocative situations, in principle.

On the one hand, governments may regulate the private sector in a way that restricts competition (Buchanan *et al*, 1980; Spulber, 1989). Economic regulation would involve a movement away from the optimum Q_{opt} towards the monopoly point Q_{mon} where there is a welfare loss to society. The consumer surplus — the triangle ABE in the competitive case — is much less in the monopoly situation — P_2BC — meaning that there has been a redistribution to the advantage of the producer.

On the other hand, budget allocation of resources may involve a budget maximizing bureaucrat (Niskanen, 1971) choosing instead of the competitive solution — Q_{opt} — a situation where the entire consumer surplus goes to the bureau producing the good or service — the triangle EFG equating the triangle ABE, or Q_{nis}. A large public sector may involve both extensive regulation and high public resource allocation by means

Figure 1.2. *Efficiency Losses in Public Regulation and Budget Allocation*

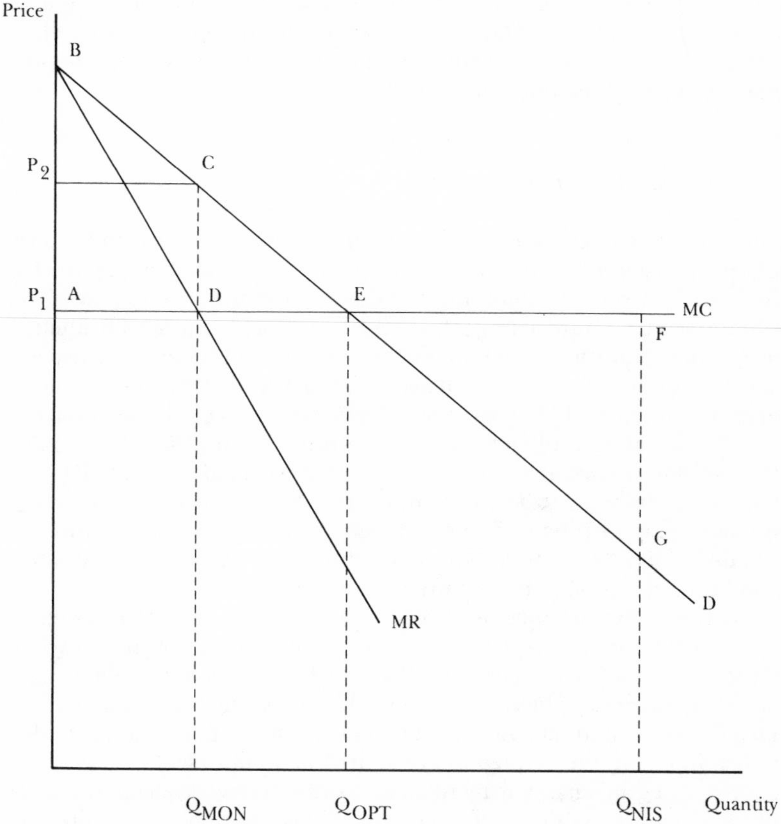

of bureaux. There is, then, a high probability that various public programmes will result in situations that are either more close to Q_{mon} or to Q_{nis} than to the optimal situation, Q_{opt}.

Budget allocation presupposes a set of bureaux or structures of public administration. And the problem of efficiency and productivity in budget allocation is very much tied up with the problem of bureaucracy (Lane, 1987). The distrust of the 1980s in bureaux as producers of goods and services applies not only to the rich market economies or the so-called mixed economies but equally to the Third World countries where there has been a reassessment of planning and bureaux as the tool for managing development objectives.

Planning and development

Planning is typically resorted to for a different reason than to keep the public household going, namely to plan the overall development of resources in society. Planning for the long-term development of the economy is a mixture of projection and decision. Planning both attempts to predict the future development of markets and their outcomes and also to influence the working of markets in a manner that is conducive to macro-economic objectives. Short-term planning of the economy or budget allocation is often based on long-run planning though the link is far less tight as was once expected. Planning is considered advantageous because it could contribute to stability and predictability. And planning procedures are strong in societies where stability and predictability are highly valued. There is, however, a limit to how much planning can be combined with a structure of private ownership.

Planning may be increased to a certain extent within a system of privately owned resources. In a process of public sector growth where more and more resources are allocated by government, planning is bound to increase. There is a need for planning the development of the public household above and beyond what is possible in budget allocation and the strong increase in the public sector calls for a coordinating mechanism in relation to the market system. However, there comes a point when planning takes over the basic decision functions of the market. Markets and planning may coexist to some degree only. The continued existence of privately owned means of production presents a challenge to planning systems as private incentive mechanisms reject the drive for control and predictability. The tension between planning and markets implies that either there will be even more planning or planning will not work efficiently due to the unpredictable and uncontrollable interaction with markets.

Planning became as popular in rich as in poor countries after the

Second World War, identifying almost all kinds of budget-making and administration with planning (Wildavsky, 1972). In the Third World outside the communist systems there was a strong belief in combining planning with market allocation as a way to bypass the conflict between capitalism and communism (Caiden and Wildavsky, 1974). Developmental planning was the technique to steer the economy towards the goals of five-year plans stating collective objectives. It motivated the expansion of the role of the state in society calling for a number of political and administrative measures. Not only would the economy grow but developmental planning would assure the right kind of economic growth. The strength of these planning techniques varied from country to country. India is perhaps the most well-known example of developmental planning with a strong socialist dose, though maintaining a structure of private ownership (Little, 1982; Marathe, 1989; Cendit, 1989).

The many failures of developmental planning have resulted in a reconsideration of the place of market forces in processes of development as well as a strategic instrument to bring about economic growth (Toye, 1987; Balassa, 1989). There is less trust in politics and bureaucracy as the mechanism for resource allocation mainly because of the difficulties to come to grips with bureaux as producers of goods and services. Budget allocation builds upon a structure of bureaux and the larger the stake of the state in the economy of a country, the more the prospects for goal achievement are tied up with how the bureaucracy works. But there are many different ways to structure systems of public administration: which model is the one to be recommended?

The development administration approach to socio-economic change in Third World countries not only faces the typical problems inherent in public sector expansion (see Figure 1.2). It also has to recognize that the fundamental properties of bureaucracies vary considerably from one country to another — see Heady's *Comparative Administration* (1979). The comparative study of public administration has shown that bureaux in the public sector may be structured very differently. This finding is of relevance for the question of promoting efficiency in resource allocation in Third World countries by choosing proper institutions. Which are the lessons from the study of public administration?

At first public administration had a narrow, parochial and formalistic approach which came under severe criticism at about the same time that there was a search for new models in the comparative study of social institutions (Cantori and Ziegler, 1988). Robert Dahl pointed out that the study of public administration was not scientific because it lacked a comparative focus. Much of the work done in this field was country specific and practical in tone. Dahl stated:

> Conceivably there might be a science of American public administration and

> a science of British public administration and a science of French public administration; but can there be a 'science of public administration' in the sense of a body of generalized principles independent of their peculiar national setting? (Dahl, 1947: 8)

The development administration trend was a response to the atheoretical predicament of the study of public administration. The so-called developmental administration perspective was a quest for a theory of the place of public administration in Third World countries aiming at modernization. The merits of the development administration approach has been a matter of serious contestation, but it rendered necessary a reorientation of the traditional perspective on public administration.

A variety of models of the structure, role and function of public administration in developing countries were suggested which stemmed from a comparative perspective on the similarities and differences between administrative systems in different countries, rich or poor, democratic or non-democratic. Development administration combined theoretical ambitions at understanding country specific patterns of public administration and policy implementation with relevant practical concerns about recommending the proper course of actions in relation to the achievement of economic growth and human betterment. Public administration was regarded as of strategic importance for the accomplishment of developmental objectives, economic as well as social ones.

Although the development administration trend was a response to the atheoretical predicament of the study of public administration, the main criticism against this trend was that it was too theoretical and lacked an empirical evidentiary base as well as concrete practical applications (Dunsire, 1973). The criticism of this comparative theory of public administration claims a number of shortcomings of the development administration approach: no paradigmatic consensus, cosmic or grand theory perspectives instead of middle-range approaches, serious data problem limiting comparability between various countries and confining several inquiries to case-studies, too little of administrative and organizational theory and too much of general political theory.

It is now believed that Max Weber's concept of bureaucracy affords a more suitable basis for comparative public administration. The concept of bureaucracy may be looked upon in terms of a Weberian perspective (Weber, 1964). The various interpretations of Weber's conception in the literature (Albrow, 1970; Siffin, 1971) consider the following properties typical of bureaucracies: (1) hierarchy, (2) differentiation or specialization and (3) qualification or competence. The first aspect refers to the structure of authority, the second aspect to the division of work in bureaux whereas the third one stands for the criteria of recruitment and professionalism. And these three aspects may vary in a manner that makes comparative bureaucracy analysis feasible. Each and every public administration system has to devise some kind of practical solution to the following three problems: (i) dominant internal operating characteristics of the bureaucracy for its composition, hierarchy, and specialization; (ii) the multi-functionality of bureaucracy; (iii) external control over the bureaucracy (Page, 1985).

The major systems of public administration — the French and German systems, the Great Britain and United States systems as well as that of the Soviet Union and the Japanese system of modernizing administration — display how differently the three basic problems may be solved when structuring the public sector in terms of a system of bureaux. There was no single best model for the Third World countries to adopt, were they to try the development administration approach.

Conclusion

Competitive prices in markets have several advantages over administrative prices in a planned economy. They are conducive to efficiency in resource allocation. They enhance flexibility and rapid adjustment. They reveal the value of goods and services momentarily and serve as an optimum medium of communicating preferences. Their weakness is lack of stability and predictability (Stigler, 1966).

Competitive prices presuppose the operation of markets with numerous suppliers and demanders. Producer and consumer differences are to be reflected in the market by means of price and quantity. This model may operate well in a society with capitalist institutions including private ownership and a variety of incentive mechanisms where individuals may express preferences in the form of possessions as long as the problems in relation to externalities, economies of scale and distributional equity have been resolved somehow. If, however, the emphasis is on control and predictability then market allocation may be questioned as the appropriate medium of communication.

Theoretically speaking, in any society resources have to be allocated between alternative uses. There are, basically, two *institutional* mechanisms for the allocation of resources: markets and budgets (Borcherding, 1977). They complement each other only to a limited extent, as stated in the theory of public goods (Baumol, 1965; Samuelson, 1983; Arrow, 1980). Resources may be owned in two basic ways, publicly or privately. The structure of ownership sets limits on the employment of the two mechanisms of allocation. It may be derived from political economy theory that there is a definite limit on the tendency of publicly dominated ownership structures to move towards the use of markets. Similarly, the continued existence of private ownership means that there is a boundary for the growth of government or the expansion of the scope of budget allocation. The so-called mixed economy is an impure hybrid of market and budget allocation.

It has been argued that the welfare state could be dismantled in favour of market allocation with regard to welfare state goods and services (Buchanan, 1986). This presupposes considerable transfer payments in order to maintain a minimum level of income equality. Such a society would constitute a market society that would maximize individual choice and preferences if transactions costs would not become staggering. It would be a volatile society in contradistinction to an economy with a large public sector. Planning, if it at all works, operates differently, as it is conducive to stability and predictability as well as to control and similarity, at least in theory.

We now turn to data about existing politico-economic regimes in order to determine whether some or all of these theoretical notes hold up in the face of empirical evidence. We shall begin by pinning down the elusive concept of development to specific empirical procedures which allow us to begin to look at the real world in terms of a comparative perspective. What, then, is the variation in economic affluence which, it is belived, is such a powerful predictor of social well-being as well as of political regimes or public policy patterns? Moreover, is there something that may be called 'political' development?

2 The concept of development

Introduction

Development is a key word when comparing nations. Some countries are said to be highly developed, some rapidly developing, whereas other countries are labelled underdeveloped. Even if these words are not used similar distinctions are singled out by means of other more diplomatically phrased terms. In the official statistics we find the following categories: low-income economies, middle-income economies and high-income economies, industrial market economies and non-market economies (World Bank). Or developed market economies are distinguished from developing countries and centrally planned economies (World Economic Survey).

At the same time the notion of development is an essentially contested conception (Sen, 1988). It has been argued that the concept of development is a value-loaded notion, expressing Western preconceptions about basic values in social life. It presupposes or requires that the non-Western world adheres to a similar culture to that of the advanced economies giving priority to economic growth and its derivatives. Moreover, it has also been claimed that there could be no general concept of development as the country specific patterns of evolution are simply too diverse (Meier, 1984).

Problems in the development concept

The concept of development is a multi-dimensional concept. It stands for a set of properties that refer to economic, political or social aspects of life. Theories about development may focus on various aspects of development (Lewis, 1988; Bardhan, 1988). *An Asian Drama* (1968) — a treatise on development by Gunnar Myrdal — focuses on the social and economic aspects of the phenomenon:

> What is actually meant in characterizing a country as 'underdeveloped' is that there is in that country a constellation of numerous undesirable conditions for work and life: outputs, incomes and levels of living are low; many modes of production, attitudes, and behavioral patterns are disadvantageous; and there are unfavorable institutions, ranging from those at the state level to those governing social and economic relations in the family and the neighborhood (Myrdal, 1968:1840).

One of the most debated problems in development theory is the extent to which social and economic indicators on the level of development of a country tend to covary. Thus it has been argued that a simple economic indicator on development like GDP per capita does not tap the social aspects of development (Adelman and Morris, 1973; Morris, 1979). The level of social development involves more than just an average income measure like the extent of inequality in the distribution of income and wealth or the real life access to basic necessities like food, physicians and shelter. We will look at the hypothesis that social and economic aspects of development are related somehow in Chapter 3. Mydal argues that there exists a:

> general causal relationship among all these conditions, so that they form a social system. It is the task of the study of underdevelopment and development to determine this relationship within the social system (Myrdal, 1968: 1840).

Myrdal emphasizes the orientation of development towards economy in particular and social well-being in general, but we may ask if there is not also a political aspect of development — political development? Thus, within the field of comparative politics in political science there has been a search for a counterpart to the notion of socio-economic development, namely political development. With the aid of such a concept one would understand the transition from a so-called primitive political system to what is called a 'modern' one. We will deal with the concept of socio-economic development in Chapter 3 and the idea(s) of political development in Chapter 4. A much debated issue in comparative research concerns the possibility of a causal relationship between socio-economic development and political development (Rustow, 1970; Huntington, 1984; Laband, 1984) — a theme to be discussed in Chapter 5. Or perhaps political development conditions economic development (Goldsmith, 1987; Pourgermani, 1988)?

Another much debated problem in development theory concerns the value-loaded character of the concept. Myrdal raises this issue in the following way when talking about the constellation of development attributes:

> They are evaluated undesirable — or low or disadvantageous or unfavorable — from the standpoint of the desirability of 'development' — a characterization afflicted with vagueness but definite enough to permit its use (Myrdal, 1968: 1840).

When the implicit positive values hidden in the development notion are made explicit, it is often claimed that there are alternative routes to development. Whereas there is at least some agreement about what socio-economic development amounts to, it is an ideological task to define the ends and means of political development.

The concept of development presents two difficulties. On the one hand, it seems feasible to make a distinction between development in general and political development in particular. On the other hand, there is every reason to suspect that the notion of development or political development is a so-called value-loaded concept (Myrdal, 1961). Both problems — how to separate a neutral concept of political change from a normative notion of political development as well as how to distinguish between general social development and political development in particular — reflect the genesis of theories of change or development in the grand sociological theories of the coming of a Western society (Higgott, 1983).

The emergence of the occidental type of society and polity is described with pairs of polar concepts: community versus society (Tönnies), mechanical versus organic solidarity (Durkheim), modernism versus traditionalism (Weber), primary versus secondary social attachment (Cooley), status versus contract (Maine), folk versus urban culture (Redfield) and sacred versus secular social orders (Becker).

The first difficulty means that one faces a severe problem as to how to model the relationship between development in general and political development in particular. One may distinguish between economic, social and cultural development (Portes, 1976). Are we to believe that political development is some function of social development? Or is a modern polity an aspect of the phenomenon of social development? If one allows for the possibility that the relation between social development and political development is an empirical one — a so-called synthetical problem and not an analytical one — then we may approach either phenomenon as the dependent variable recognizing that political development may not only reflect but also trigger social development. In any case, we need to sort out theories of political development from general theories of social and economic transformation. Here we focus primarily upon what theories of development amount to with regard to politics and economics, government, the state or the economy, whichever concept one may prefer.

The second difficulty concerns the direction of change involved in the notion of national development or political development. Sometimes it is admitted that we may talk about both positive and negative development, but the overall impression is that political development is something inherently valuable, i.e. the opposite of political development is political decline or decay. If this is correct, then a theory of political change would have to be far more encompassing than a theory about political development. It has been argued that the value component in theories of development reflects a Western bias (Wiarda, 1983; Leftwich, 1990).

The word 'development' is both an ordinary term in everyday language and a technical term in several scientific theories. It may be interesting to map some of its usages in these two contexts before we deal with the phenomenon of development in its socio-economic appearance as well as in an assumed political form(s).

Semantics of 'development'

In ordinary language there is the basic meaning of 'develop' as unfold that lies behind the various different connotations that we are interested in when talking about country development. Let us quote from some standard dictionaries.The *Oxford English Dictionary* (1961) contains the following entries, among others, on 'development'.

> 1. A gradual unfolding, a bringing into fuller view. 2. Evolution or bringing out from a latent or elementary condition. 3. The growth and unfolding of what is in the germ; Evolution 4. Gradual advancement through progressive stages, growth from within. 5. A developed or well-grown condition; a state in which anything is in vigorous life or action. 6. The developed result or product; a developed form of some earlier and more rudimentary organism, structure, or system.

Testifying to the complexity of the notion of development, Webster's *Third New International Dictionary* (1965) has a heavy set of entries on 'develop' , some of which we quote to convey how difficult the concept is to handle. Thus we have:

> De-vel-op also de-vel-ope. 1a: unfold, unfurl b: to change the form of (a surface) by applying point by point of a specified surface; c: to lay out or evolve into a clear, full, and explicit presentation. 4: to open up: cause to become more completely unfolded so as to reveal hidden or unexpected qualities or potentialities. 5a: to make (something latent) active: cause to increase or improve: promote the growth of b: to make actually available or

> usable; 6a: to cause to unfold gradually: conduct through a succession of states of changes each of which is preparatory for the next, b: to expand by a process of growth. 7: 1 a: to go through a process of natural growth, differentiation, or evolution by successive changes from a less perfect to a more perfect or more highly organized state.

Evidently, development relates to a process in time of some kind. In scientific usage development is often qualified by 'economic', 'social' or 'political'. We may then expect more substantive definitions.

Scientific usage

Fred W. Riggs points out that the concept of development occurs in several disciplines. Thus one talks about individual, attitudinal, cultural, group, organizational, social, community, urban, global and model development. It must by no means to be taken for granted that 'development' in these contexts has the same meaning (Riggs, 1984: 132-3). Sometimes the word is employed in relation to improvements (land, capital), sometimes to activities (plans, projects), sometimes to agents (persons, organizations) or parameters (resources), sometimes to Third World countries (developing countries) or industrialized areas (developed areas), or sometimes in relation to studies (development studies) (Riggs, 131-2). Moreover, the word 'development' may denote a process or a state of affairs — a condition. It is important to keep this distinction in mind when one proceeds to the phenomenon of development in a context that interest us, e.g. the seminal trends in Third World countries. Riggs presents a neat model for this distinction between process and condition which is reproduced below in Figure 2.1.

In social science contexts a number of treatises on development may be found. What are the major connotations of this word when used by economists, sociologists and political scientists? We now present some quotations from leading scholars in the fields of development studies and the analysis of development processes.

Economics

'Economic development' used to be synonymous with 'economic growth' or even 'economic progress' in general (Sen, 1988). It was measured by the rate of expansion in gross domestic product (GDP) per capita. The difficulty was not the meaning of the term nor how it was to measured in aggregate national statistics, but how to account for economic development, i.e. to identify the forces that were conducive to a rapid expansion of income per capita. There was sharp disagreement between alternative theories or approaches to economic development —

Figure 2.1 A model for the concept of development

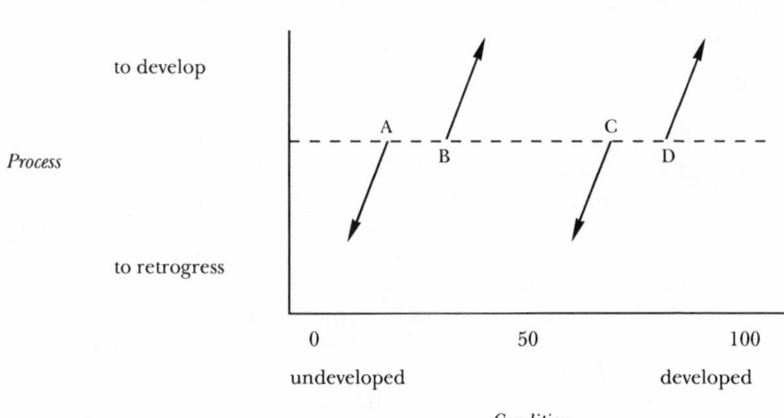

Source: Riggs, 1984 : 134.

neo-classical, Keynesian, institutionalist, dualist, dependence, neo-liberal schools (Thirlwall, 1986; Todaro, 1985; Bardhan, 1988).

During recent years this solid foundation for the concept of economic development has been eroded, as the development notion has come to be more and more an essentially contested one *per se* — see *Handbook of Development Economics* (1988, 1989). It has been argued against a simple notion of economic development that 'economic development' refers to more than simply growth in national income per capita. One has to consider broad welfare indicators — the so-called *social indicator approach*. Moreover, the handy equation, economic development = economic growth, bypasses the distributional problem of how national income is divided among social groups or in general how the resources are allocated to various collective or individual purposes. Finally, it is argued that the implicit value bias in economic development as economic growth should be brought out explicitly as one cannot take for granted that economic growth is under all circumstances something positive. It may even be the case that what is labelled economic development is conducive to underdevelopment of a country within the confines of a world capitalist system (Streeten, 1972; Toye, 1987; Lewis, 1989; Sen, 1988; Syrquin, 1988)

It is no doubt easy to find references to economic development where it is regarded as the key to human progress. Look at the following:

1. Most would agree that development implies more than just a rise in real national income; that it must be a sustained, secular rise in real income accompanied by changes in social attitudes and customs which have in the past impeded economic advance. But at this point agreement on what constitutes development would probably end. (Thirlwall, 1983: 22)
2. Development must, therefore, be conceived as a multidimensional process involving major changes in social structures, popular attitudes, and national institutions, as well as the acceleration of economic growth, the reduction of inequality, and the eradication of absolute poverty. (Todaro, 1985: 85)

What can be done here is to make some distinctions without any claim as to the true meaning of 'economic development'. It seems important to separate between the following: (i) level or rate of growth in GDP total or per capita; (ii) level or rate of change in a set of social indicators measuring individual well-being on an average; (iii) the distribution of income or wealth and measures of skewness in relation to these.

We may then approach the problematic nature of economic development as two hypotheses as to whether higher levels of national income per capita also means greater welfare or a more equal distribution of incomes. The traditional approach to economic development bypasses the simple fact that a larger GDP may be spent on purposes other than the reduction of poverty — defence, national symbols or conspicuous consumption. In Chapter 3 we will approach economic development in such an open-ended fashion. In *The Odyssey of Rationality* (1989) Albert Lauterbach summarizes the debate on the concept of development in the field of economics stating:

> instead of the manifold and fluctuating meanings of 'development' in general, perhaps the following concept could be agreed upon for the basic aim concerned: 'Striving for the better in the condition of the general population groups concerned in line with their own felt needs and without sudden disruption of their established value systems and ways of life'. (Lauterbach, 1989: 221)

Such an approach to the development concept implies a broadening of the perspective from economic indicators to social indices. However, it seems to be a good strategy to associate the analysis of economic development with the test of established growth theory. As A.P. Thirlwall underlines in his *Growth and Development* (1986), it is possible to conceive of economic growth without economic development taking place at the same time, but it is hardly conceivable that there may be a process of economic development without a basis in sustained economic growth.

Sociology

Sociologists tend to take a broader view on development than economists, generally speaking, though a general concept of social development may come close to the notion of social change. The term 'development' appears, more specifically, to denote a major process of social transition or transformation from some earlier stage called 'primitive society' or 'traditional society' to some later stage referred to as 'modern society' or simply 'modernity'. What kinds of social change are involved here? Let us look at some quotations:

1. Development takes two forms, industrialization, which is dynamic and innovative as a consequence of the allocation of new information to technology, and modernization, which is derivative. (Apter, 1971: 6)
2. The process of social change whereby less developed societies acquire characteristics common to more developed societies. (Lerner, 1968: 386)
3. Economic diversification within an advanced industrial technology; heightened social mobility and the movement toward impersonal and rationalized social relationships; a concentration of the population in cities and in more comprehensive social units generally; and the mobilization of persons en masse through popular education, organization, and communication. (Scalapino, 1964: 65)
4. Advanced, non-traditional practices in culture, technology and economic life are introduced and accepted on a considerable scale (Deutsch, 1961: 493).

The model of a kind of broad social transformation often called 'modernization', which recurs in the quotations above, may be illuminating when one speaks generally about problems in Third World countries, but it may be highly misleading if one looks in particular at a specific country and its social transformation.

Countries differ in terms of social change. We must therefore be aware of the possibility that some countries may display some but not all of the properties typical of modernization while other countries display other properties. In fact, the idea of a model of social transformation implies a number of empirical hypotheses about the relationships between various aspects of social systems. Perhaps the notion of modernity replacing tradition (Eisenstadt, 1973) was less deficient because of its western value biases than weak in terms of actual empirical research conducted on the ways in which social change takes place in Third World countries.

Political science

Basically, there are two different approaches to development among political scientists. Firstly, there is the derivative approach focusing on the political consequences of socio-economic transformation on the political system. Secondly, there is the non-derivative approach trying to identify a path of political change that would be more or less self-sufficient.

The derivative approach focuses on political development as an aspect or effect of socio-economic development. It is thus committed to the belief that there exists such a general phenomenon and that political factors are truly determined by socio-economic ones. Let us offer quotations of this theory of political development as the adaptation to profound social and economic change — the coming of modernity.

1. The expansion of roles, increased functional specificity, and the concomitant construction and/or reconstruction of social, economic, and political institutions to reflect, cope with, and channel this expansion. (Benjamin, 1972: 24)
2. The overall processes of social, economic, intellectual, political and cultural change that are associated with the movement of societies from relatively poor, rural, agrarian conditions to relatively affluent, urban, industrialized conditions. (Huntington, 1976: 17)
3. The elaboration of new and more complex forms of politics and government as societies restructure themselves so as to absorb progressively the stock and flow of modern technology which is, essentially, uniform. (Rostow, 1971: 3)
4. ...a disposition to accept new ideas and try new methods; a readiness to express opinions; a time sense that makes men more interested in the present and future than in the past; a better sense of punctuality; a greater concern for planning, organization and efficiency; a tendency to see the world as calculable; a faith in science and technology; and, finally, a belief in distributive justice. (Weiner, 1965: 3-4)

Although it must be important to look at the political implications or consequences of social or economic change, particularly so when it is a matter of the broad movement from the agrarian society to the industrial society, there is the basic problem that these political effects may be very different from one country to another. Is there really a general phenomenon of socio-economic development which causes the same kind of major political changes?

It is far from certain that we will be able to identify these consequences for the political system under one single concept — the notion of political development. It is obvious from the above quotations that the concept of political development tends to be a highly general one with little specific content. Actually, this conception of political development as the adaptation to socio-economic transformation on a large scale is essentially a set of hypotheses that need elaboration and testing (Leftwich, 1990).

The non-derivative conception of political development claims that there is a single path of political change that implies development of the polity but that it cannot be modelled as uniformly caused by socio-economic factors. How is political change conceived? A few quotations suggest what constitutes a process of political development:

5. Any two political systems (may be compared with respect to) capabilities, performance of process functions, and performance of socialization and recruitment. (Almond and Powell, 1966: 309)
6. The new requirements which are demanded of institutions if they are to maintain stability and cope responsibly with social conflict. (Binder, 1972: 472)
7. The level of ... adaptability, complexity, autonomy, and coherence of (any political system's) organization and procedures. (Huntington, 1965: 394)
8. The rationalization of authority, the differentiation of structures, and the expansion of political participation. (Huntington, 1968: 93)
9. Increasing governmental efficiency in utilizing the human and material resources of the nation for national goals. (Organski, 1965: 9)
10. Four dimensions: stability, legitimacy, participation, and capacity; within a certain unspecified range development along any one of these dimensions can vary independently of the other three. (Sigelman, 1971: 12)
11. A process whose goal is a political system which can provide for the functional requirements of long-term persistence... the capacity to direct the course and rate of social and economic change. (Von Vorys, 1973: 63).

The common core of these definitions of 'political development' is that political system change is a process with *a logic of its own* and not just the automatic impact of socio-economic transformation. What the more specific content of this type of political change that implies political development may be is very much up in the air considering the above quotations. A variety of phenomena are mentioned as the content of political development: structural differentiation, functional performance, institutionalization, adaptation, increased governmental capacity, stability and legitimacy as well as democratization. The abstract nature of these definitions of 'political development' calls for a more concrete approach that searches for empirical variables that somehow measure these dimensions.

It may be the case that a certain kind of macro political change process is caused by social structure change, but that is an empirical question to be answered by investigating the various sources of such a political development. However, what unites these various definitions is much less than what divides them as it is far from obvious that 'political development' stands for one and the same process in these quotations. The semantic ambiguity surrounding the concept of political development makes it imperative that we take a closer look at the various properties or dimensions identified with political development in Chapter 4.

Conclusion

The semantic inquiry above leads one to the conclusion that there is so much uncertainty and ambiguity surrounding the notion of development that one better make a preliminary distinction between economic, social and political development. Although there are ties between these aspects of development, they should be handled as hypotheses about relationships that need corroboration from empirical research using a variety of indicators on each of these aspects. Further distinctions are preferably made within each of these three separate aspects of development between different manifestations of economic, social and political development, respectively, as the empirical analysis of various manifestations of development proceeds.

The various modes of economic and social development are treated in Chapter 3 whereas Chapter 4 takes up the concept of political development. The purpose is to create some ground for the empirical analysis of the interaction between these phenomena in the chapters that follow. It is necessary to move away from the abstract modelling of development and its various modes towards a concrete look at variables that indicate the various dimensions of development as well as permit a test of empirical hypotheses about their interaction.

All the time it is recognized that the word 'development' is highly ingrained with value notions as it pictures a macro process of change that is also to be something desirable. Amartya Sen argues that:

> What is or is not regarded as a case of 'development' depends inescapably on the notion of what things are valuable to promote. (Sen, 1988: 20)

He separates between two types of value dependence: value heterogeneity and value endogenity. It is not only the case that economic change may be valued differently by various people; economic change may also bring about alterations in the values of those involved in economic development. How is such a value ingrained concept to be handled in neutral and objective social science research?

By attempting to separate the factual component from the value-loaded element in the concept of development we wish to make an empirical inquiry into the variety of phenomena denoted by the term 'development' without any commitment as to whether any such phenomenon is intrinsically good or just. Let us begin with the concept of economic or socio-economic development.

3 Socio-economic development

Introduction

A fundamental issue in political economy is the problem of priority as regards economic factors and politics with regard to causality. Precedence is often given economic variables which according to several well-known hypotheses are claimed to explain political phenomena. At the same time economic determinism in whatever shape it may come has been challenged by the opposite hypotheses which attribute economic phenomena to political factors. We will evaluate these contrary claims in the chapters to come. Here we wish to present an overview of the socio-economic differences between major countries in the world by taking up one well-known development theory (Lal, 1983; Jones and Kenen, 1984; Chenery and Srinivasan, 1988, 1989).

The so-called the gap theory figures prominently in the interpretation of development data (Thirlwall, 1986). The hypothesis states that the income differences between a set of rich countries and a set of poor countries are tremendous and tend to increase over time. The hypothesis is pessimistic about development as it predicts that the between-country differences in affluence will increase. We will question whether the gap theory is confirmed when a large number of countries, rich as well as poor, are included in the analysis of development data.

It is often stated that the income gap between rich and poor countries is increasing and that there is a north-south divide hidden behind these sets of countries (Brandt Report, 1980). This trend, if true, is certainly a cause of concern since it would counteract the ambitions behind the development ideology as interpreted by the United Nations. The quest for development has no doubt dominated much of the planning in several Third World countries and it has inspired the UN to initiate its programs for developmental decades and its call for a new international economic order.

We will look into how valid these statements are to the effect that the so-called developing countries are not only not catching up but also lagging behind even more than before. The set of developing countries is not a homogeneous one, which implies that we need to look at the variation in levels and rates of development not only between rich and poor countries but also within different sets of so-called less developed countries or LDCs (Syrquin, 1988). There may also exist a variation within the set of rich countries that needs to be pinpointed as this set covers not only the rich market economies but also the communist systems in the northern hemisphere, i.e. excluding mainland China. The use of the concept of newly industrializing countries — the NICs — seems to imply that the identification of rich and poor countries may change over time. In order to pinpoint the issue it is necessary to consider how the concept of development is to be measured.

Indicators and data

There is no single unanimously accepted definition of development in the literature (Todaro, 1985; Thirlwall, 1986; Sen, 1988). When some national income statistic is mentioned in relation to development it is clearly understood that it is only one among several possible indicators. Myrdal approached the concept of development as multidimensional referring to: production output and incomes, conditions of production, levels of living, attitudes towards life and work, institutions and policies (Myrdal, 1968:1860). Although Myrdal treated these aspects of development as separate from each other, he also claimed that they co-vary, each reinforcing the others in a process of circular causation (ibid.: 1859-66). No doubt income measures are given priority in the development literature, in particular GDP per capita (Gersovitz et al., 1982). GDP measures the total final output of goods and services produced by an economy by residents and nonresidents regardless of the allocation to domestic and foreign claims. It is calculated without making deductions for depreciation. Let us start from this rather simple but helpful indicator turning to more complex measures of well-being later on.

This statistic — GDP per capita — may be employed to measure the level of economic affluence. It is an open question whether other indicators on social welfare co-vary considerably with the GDP per capita indicator. The GDP per capita indicator displays problems concerning both validity and reliability. In terms of indicator validity GDP per capita measures are sensitive to the size of the money economy, the price level and the currency exchange rate. With regard to reliability the national income accounts of various countries have been estimated with different procedures, which affects the comparability of the information (Kuznets, 1965, 1966, 1968; Streeten, 1972; Little, 1982).

The raw data about gross domestic product rendered by various countries have to be examined and recalculated in order to remove a number of errors and make the data series comparable between nations. If a GDP per capita index is constructed from such a cautious procedure, then the GDP per capita indicator may be used to arrive at a crude but informative picture of economic differences between various countries. We have employed a standardized series — real GDP per capita in 1980 international prices relative to the US dollar — compiled by Summers and Heston (1988). The data series give annually, in addition to population and exchange rates, real product and price level estimates for four different national income concepts estimated for some 130 countries from 1950 to 1985.

From the Summers and Heston data set, where several of the problems of indicator validity and reliability have been taken into account, we have selected some 120 countries divided into subsets corresponding to the OECD countries (24), Latin American countries (23), African countries (36), Asian countries (21) and communist countries (13) (see Appendix 3.1). The classification has been chosen in an attempt to evaluate the gap theory looking at both the between- and the within-set differences and how they have developed during the post war period. Average growth rates may also be calculated with regard to these countries or sets of countries for various time periods.

The rich set of countries would consist of the set of OECD nations and the set of communist systems with the exception of China. Mainland China may be properly classified in the set of Asian countries as it is an LDC and does not enter the Comecon bloc. Since the analysis goes up to 1985 the set of communist countries comprise basically East European communism disregarding the major system changes that started in 1989. We have not included a few rich countries in the evaluation of the gap theory, because they are marginal from the standpoint of this exercise (Israel, South Africa, Hong Kong). Nor are the super-rich oil-exporting countries covered (Saudi Arabia, Oman, Kuwait, United Arab Emirates). We will report on the level of real GDP/capita for 1950, 1960, 1970, 1980 and 1985 in standardized prices and the rates of growth in real GDP per capita between 1970 and 1985. Reliable information for all the 110 countries is not available for 1950 and 1960 which means that we have had to reduce the number of countries covered.

A more fundamental objection to the use of the standard GDP or GDP per capita indicator on economic affluence is that it says nothing about the distribution of affluence in a country. This is a real limitation of this indicator as a growth in total output or overall national income over and above the population increase does not necessarily imply that poverty has been reduced for all social groups. Economic growth in poor countries implies that there are more resources to be distributed among various social strata, but which groups benefit is an open question.

The GDP per capita indicator needs to be complemented with an index that measures the extent of inequality of the income distribution. The literature contains a few indices measuring the variation in income between households or regions: the Gini-index, some kind of Lorenz curve and a coefficient of variation measure tapping the regional distribution in income or output. It should be pointed out that there is a reliability problem when handling income distribution data for a large set of countries. In some countries the statistical information is not quite accurate and the definitions of income or economic affluence vary from one country to another, which reduces the comparability of such data. In this chapter we will employ the Gini-index on the basis of data referring to the 1970s.

The gap theory

First, the gap theory implies that there was a sharp gulf in economic affluence between a set of rich countries and another set of poor countries at the end of the Second World War. Second, the gap theory suggests that this gap has increased during the entire post-war period, not only during the 1950s and the 1960s but also during the 1970s and the 1980s. Third, the gap theory claims that this unbridgeable gulf coincides roughly with a major geographical separation between the northern and southern parts of the hemisphere. Fourth, the gap theory predicts that the income differences within the sets of rich countries and the sets of poor countries are less than the differences between these sets.

The Summers and Heston data series allow us to evaluate these implications of the gap theory by taking a close look at the variation in levels of overall economic well-being between and within sets of countries from 1950 to 1985. An analysis of the growth differentials in real GDP per capita complements the study of levels of average GDP per capita. The differences between the five sets of countries are as important as the variation in real GDP per capita income within these sets of countries. The coefficient of variation (CV) may be employed to indicate the within-group differences where a CV score of more than roughly 0.25 may be said to indicate substantial variation.

Levels of affluence

Allowing for all the objections to the use of a GDP per capita indicator on the average economic affluence in a country, we may establish that this measure really indicates profound between- and within-country set differences. Let us start with the year 1950 and look at national averages between the different sets of countries as well as the variation within these sets themselves (Table 3.1).

Table 3.1. GDP/capita for five sets of countries, 1950*

	Mean	Max	Min	CV
OECD countries (N=24)	3 235	6 401	822	0.48
Communist countries (N=8)	1 883	3 124	1 069	0.37
Latin American countries (N=17)	1 461	3 800	720	0.58
African countries (N=7)	374	524	223	0.31
Asian countries (N=8)	580	1 262	212	0.52

* International US dollar at 1980 prices.

Source: Summers and Heston (1988)

The average income per capita in the set of OECD countries amounts to $3 235 whereas the average income in the communist systems reaches some $1 883 which indicates that after the devastating effects of second World War the average economic affluence would be roughly twice as high in the former countries compared with the latter countries. However, we must note the substantial variation within the market-oriented systems and the planned economies. In the United States which fought in the war mainly outside its borders, the average income was about six times ($6 401) higher than in Turkey ($822) and Japan ($1 129). There was also considerable variation among the planned economies, e.g. between Czechoslovakia with a high $3 124, which is comparable to the mean average income in the OECD set, and a low $1 101 in Yugoslavia.

Around 1950 the level of affluence in these types of countries, market-based economies versus planning-oriented systems, is not typically far higher than in the Third World. It is true that the average income scores for African countries ($374) and Asian countries ($580) are far lower than both the OECD average score ($3 235) and the mean country values for the communist systems ($1 883), except for China. But the set of Latin American countries that also did not have to fight a war within their borders constitute an exception.

Not only is the Latin American mean real GDP per capita of $1 461 almost on a par with that of the planned economies, but the maximum score in Venezuela ($3 800) surpasses the mean country score for the OECD countries. Had one looked only at the data for 1950, it is far from obvious that the gap interpretation had been proposed at all. Although we lack information about the GDP per capita income in Brazil and

Argentina, it remains a fact that Latin America does not fit the simple classification: rich versus poor or North versus South.

The average income of the OECD countries is about five times higher than that of African and Asian countries but only roughly twice as high as that of Latin American countries as well as that of the communist systems. In order to indicate somewhat more extensively the country differences at the beginning of a long period of overall economic growth and of staggering expansion in world trade, we will look at the variation within these three sets of countries. Let us consider Table 3.2.

Table 3.2. GDP/capita in OECD and communist countries, 1950*

OECD		*Communist countries*	
USA	6 401		
Canada	5 337	GDR	2 119
UK	3 993	Poland	2 179
Ireland	2 047	Hungary	2 208
Netherlands	3 404	Czechoslovakia	3 124
Belgium	3 462	Yugoslavia	1 101
Luxembourg	5 286	Bulgaria	1 306
France	3 125	Romania	1 069
Switzerland	4 886	Soviet Union	1 966
Spain	1 640		
Portugal	937		
FRG	2 713		
Austria	2 318	Mean	1 883
Italy	1 929		
Greece	986		
Finland	2 758		
Sweden	3 980		
Norway	3 802		
Denmark	4 241		
Iceland	3 592		
Turkey	822		
Japan	1 129		
Australia	4 331		
New Zealand	4 531		
Mean	3 235		

* International US dollar at 1980 prices.

The gap theory is based on a hypothesis about a north-south divide in the separation between rich and poor countries. Yet we see from Table 3.2 that geographical situation does not coincide with the division into rich and poor countries. Australia and New Zealand were among the most well-off countries in 1950, second only to the United States, Canada and

Switzerland. In addition, there was a rather sharp north-south division within rich western Europe, as Turkey, Greece, Portugal and even Spain scored lower than Venezuela, Uruguay and Trinidad. In fact, both Spain and Ireland were more close to the average values for the Communist world than for the OECD set.

As we turn to country data for the developing nations a lot of variation is to be expected since we know that the countries in the Third World have walked along different paths of economic development since 1850 (Reynolds, 1985). Table 3.1 indicates that the country variation within the three subsets of developing nations was larger than within the two subsets of rich countries. What does this mean when we take a closer look at single countries (see Table 3.3)?

Table 3.3. GDP/capita in Asia, Latin America and Africa, 1950*

Asia		*Latin America*		*Africa*	
Iran	—	Dominican Rep	744	Senegal	—
Iraq	—	Mexico	1 652	Liberia	—
Cyprus	1 262	El Salvador	897	Ghana	—
Jordan	—	Costa Rica	1 175	Cameroon	—
Korea Rep	—	Panama	1 059	Nigeria	478
India	416	Colombia	1 188	Zaïre	223
Pakistan	510	Venezuela	3 800	Kenya	401
Sri Lanka	787	Ecuador	916	Tanzania	—
Thailand	638	Peru	1 235	Ethiopia	261
Malaysia	—	Brazil	—	Zambia	—
Singapore	—	Bolivia	1 004	Malawi	—
Philippines	591	Paraguay	1 060	Madagascar	—
Indonesia	416	Chile	—	Morocco	524
China	429	Argentina	—	Algeria	—
		Uruguay	2 864	Tunisia	—
		Haiti	—	Egypt	427
Mean	580	Jamaica	—	Uganda	299
		Trinidad	2 717		
		Barbados	—	Mean	373
		Guatemala	1 165		
		Honduras	720		
		Nicaragua	1 143		
		Guayana	1 501		
		Mean	1 461		

* International US dollar at 1980 prices.

Although not very many countries in Asia, Africa and Latin America can be compared at this time due to problems with reliable data, what is most striking is not the general poverty in the Thirld World but the substantial variation. First, there was a clear gulf between Latin America and the other parts of the Third World, which hardly fits in with the gap theory. If data had been available for Argentina and Brazil the overall picture might have been somewhat but hardly much different. Clearly, it would be misleading to designate Mexico ($1 652), India ($416) and Ethiopia ($261) all as underdeveloped countries, as if they were of one kind.

The country differences between the set of African and Asian countries were not pronounced in 1950. China ($429) and Indonesia ($416) had a low GDP per capita as had Nigeria ($478) and Egypt ($427). There were also a few extremely poor countries in Africa: Zaire ($223) and Uganda ($299). Had information about more countries been available this gloomy picture of Africa may well have been more pronounced. In order to find out whether these country differences are stable or change as the gap theory predicts, we compare the 1950 data with similar information for 1960 (Table 3.4).

Table 3.4. GDP/capita for five sets of countries, 1960*

	Mean	Max	Min	CV
OECD countries (N=24)	4 322	7 380	1 255	0.39
Communist countries (N=8)	2 949	4 516	1 705	0.35
Latin American countries (N=22)	1 868	5 308	605	0.69
Asian countries (N=19)	994	2 527	306	0.57
African countries (N=35)	531	1 302	208	0.43

* International US dollar at 1980 prices

Source: Summers and Heston (1988)

The overall developments of the 1950s corroborate the gap theory as the distance between the two sets of rich countries and the three sets of Third World countries increased. This is particularly true of how average per capita income developed in the OECD on the one hand and in Latin America and Africa on the other hand. As the world economy entered a long period of staggering growth in output and trade, the mean average income in African countries actually did not increase much between 1950 and 1960 whereas that of the set of Latin American countries increased slowly. The differences between the 1950 and 1960 data may reflect the simple fact that we cover more countries in 1960. Although we find in the data for 1960 signs that indicate the gap theory, not all the facts confirm the gap theory. Let us take a closer look at the variation within our subsets (Tables 3.5 and 3.6).

Table 3.5. GDP/capita in OECD and communist countries, 1960*

OECD		*Communist countries*	
USA	7 380	GDR	4 258
Canada	6 069	Poland	2 826
UK	4 970	Hungary	3 218
Ireland	2 545	Czechoslovakia	4 516
Netherlands	4 690	Yugoslavia	1 778
Belgium	4 379	Bulgaria	2 339
Luxembourg	6 112	Romania	1 705
France	4 473	Soviet Union	2 951
Switzerland	6 834		
Spain	2 425		
Portugal	1 429	Mean	2 949
FRG	5 217		
Austria	3 908		
Italy	3 233		
Greece	1 474		
Finland	4 073		
Sweden	5 149		
Norway	5 001		
Denmark	5 490		
Iceland	4 664		
Turkey	1 255		
Japan	2 239		
Australia	5 182		
New Zealand	5 571		
Mean	4 322		

* International US dollar in 1980 prices

During the 1950s all the so-called rich countries benefited from high levels of economic activity with the possible exception of Australia and New Zealand where average GDP per capita grew modestly. The increase in GDP per capita in Japan was a high 100 per cent in this decade, but other rich countries also expanded their national income rapidly: the FRG, Spain, Portugal, Italy and the DDR.

Several countries in Asia hardly increased their average income per capita at all during the 1950s, mainly as a result of sharp increases in population. Some Asian countries faced a severe poverty problem around 1960 although it is somewhat arbitrary to identify a poverty line: Burma with $306, Indonesia with $480 and Pakistan with $558 per capita — all nations with tremendous populations. However, in the set of Asian countries there were also some examples of an average GDP per capita higher than the min value in the OECD set: Iran with \$1 839, Singapore with \$1 528, Syria with \$1 234 and Malaysia with \$1 103 per capita.

Table 3.6. GDP/capita in Asia, Latin America and Africa, 1960*

Asia		*Latin America*		*Africa*	
Iran	1 839	Dominican Rep	956	Senegal	756
Iraq	2 527	Mexico	2 157	Liberia	449
Cyprus	1 692	El Salvador	1 062	Ghana	534
Jordan	1 124	Costa Rica	1 663	Cameroon	507
India	533	Panama	1 255	Nigeria	552
Pakistan	558	Colombia	1 344	Zaïre	314
Sri Lanka	974	Venezuela	5 308	Kenya	470
Thailand	688	Ecuador	1 143	Tanzania	208
Malaysia	1 103	Peru	1 721	Ethiopia	285
Singapore	1 528	Brazil	991	Zambia	740
Korea Rep	690	Bolivia	882	Malawi	237
Philippines	874	Paraguay	991	Madagascar	629
Indonesia	480	Chile	2 932	Morocoo	542
Syria	1 234	Argentina	3 091	Algeria	1 302
Afghanistan	671	Uruguay	3 271	Tunisia	852
China	716	Haiti	605	Egypt	496
Taiwan	866	Jamaica	1 472	Uganda	322
Burma	306	Trinidad	4 904	Mali	396
		Barbados	1 747	Benin	595
		Guatemala	1 268	Mauretania	414
Mean	994	Honduras	748	Ivory Coast	743
		Nicaragua	1 588	Guinea	411
		Guyana	—	Togo	415
				Gabon	804
				Central Afr.	485
		Mean	1 868	Chad	515
				Congo	563
				Burundi	412
				Rwanda	244
				Somalia	483
				Angola	880
				Mozambique	798
				Niger	284
				Sierra Leone	281
				Sudan	667
				Mean	531

* International US dollar at 1980 prices

Already in 1960 Africa was different from Asia and Latin America as poverty was much more prevalent. The set of African countries really constituted a special Third World set of countries where the average income tended to be always below that of the mean income in the other two sets of Third World countries. The standard predicament in Africa was one of extreme poverty: Malawi with $237, Rwanda with $244, Sierra Leone with $281, Zaire with $314 and Kenya with $470 per capita. Only in the Northern countries and in the Portuguese colonies was there a more decent level of income: Algeria with $1 302 and Tunisia with $852 per capita versus Angola with $880 and Mozambique with $798 per capita.

In relation to the 1950 and 1960 data the gap theory fails to recognize the large difference between Africa and Latin America. Some countries in Latin America did fairly well around 1960 even when compared not only with Communist systems but also with some OECD nations. High average income scores were to found in Venezuela with an astonishing $5 308 per capita and in Uruguay with $3 271, Argentina with $3 091 and Chile with $2 932 per capita.

The 1960s was again a decade with strong expansion in the world economy and several countries achieved high yearly growth rates in their economies. Yearly growth rates of about 3-4 per cent were not uncommon and some countries accomplished even more. What was the impact of a decade of high levels of economic activity on the global income distribution between countries? Does the gap theory prediction of larger differentials between the rich countries and the Third World hold true? We can see from examining Table 3.7.

Table 3.7. GDP/capita for five sets of countries in 1970*

	Mean	*Max*	*Min*	*CV*
OECD countries (24)	6 235	9 459	1 702	0.32
Communist countries (N=8)	4 207	5 836	2 563	0.28
Latin American countries (N=23)	2 469	6 957	550	0.66
Asian countries (N=19)	1 418	3 317	398	0.65
African countries (N=36)	659	2 082	268	0.58

* International US dollar in 1980 prices.

Source: Summers and Heston (1988).

Partly the gap theory prediction of a widening gap between the rich and the poor countries fits the data from around 1970. The decade of strong economic growth around the world benefited some countries more than others. The OECD nations and the communist systems except China increased the income gap to Latin America as well as Africa. The already dismal development of African Third World countries continued with the exception of northern Africa.

Partly, however, the gap theory is not validated due to the

developments in a few Asian countries, the so-called baby tigers of Singapore, Hong Kong, South Korea, Taiwan and Malaysia. These countries entered what Rostow referred to as the take-off stage in the 1950s which resulted in growth rates that bridged the gap to the affluent world (Rostow, 1960). Perhaps also Japan should be included among these aggressive new industrializing countries as the average income per capita in Japan grew from $2 239 in 1960 to a staggering $5 496 in 1970. How does the mixed picture of 1970 compare with data for 1980 which indicate how the gap theory fared when the world economy went into a sustained period of recession?

Table 3.8 has the information about mean average country values for the five sets of countries around 1980.

Table 3.8. GDP/capita for five sets of countries, 1980*

	Mean	Max	Min	CV
OECD countries (N=24)	8 191	11 404	2 319	0.29
Communist countries (N=8)	5 577	7 891	3 946	0.23
Latin American countries (N=23)	2 882	7 161	696	0.53
Asian countries (N=19)	2 164	5 817	483	0.70
African countries (N=36)	722	2 973	224	0.76

* International US dollar in 1980 prices.

Source: Summers and Heston (1988).

The recession in the world economy in connection with the oil crises did not break the pattern that emerges when data about levels of average income per capita are compared since 1950. The increase in the mean value for the OECD and the communist systems continued during the 1970s. We may note a secular trend towards more homogeneity in the two sets of rich countries. The CV scores drop continuously from 1950 to 1980, meaning that the between-country differences within these two sets have become less extreme.

At the same time the CV scores for the three sets of Third World countries have increased since 1950 which means that there is cause for being cautious when comparing levels of affluence in various parts of the Third World with that of the advanced economies. Again, the development pace among the Asian countries was far higher than that of the Latin American countries and that of African countries. The gulf between the rich world and the world of LDCs and NICs increased with regard to Africa and Latin America but not in relation to Asia. More recent data are presented in Table 3.9.

The trends of the early 1980s implied a break with the seminal tendencies from 1950 to 1980. Several countries suffered real setbacks in their average GDP per capita income, in particular Latin America and Africa. And the variation within all the five sets of countries increased, suggesting that the setback in the world economy hit countries differently.

Table 3.9. GDP/capita for five sets of countries, 1985*

	Mean	*Max*	*Min*	*CV*
OECD countries (N=24)	8 779	12 623	2 533	0.30
Communist countries (N=8)	5 945	8 740	4 273	0.25
Latin American countries (N=23)	2 616	6 889	631	0.56
Asian countries (N=19)	2 581	9 834	526	0.85
African countries (N=36)	709	3 103	210	0.86

* International US dollar at 1980 prices.

Source: Summers and Heston (1988).

Table 3.10. GDP/capita in OECD and communist countries, 1985*

OECD		*Communist countries*	
USA	12 532	GDR	8 740
Canada	12 196	Poland	4 913
UK	8 665	Hungary	5 765
Ireland	5 205	Czechoslovakia	7 424
Netherlands	9 092	Yugoslavia	5 063
Belgium	9 717	Bulgaria	5 113
Luxembourg	10 540	Romania	4 273
France	9 918	Soviet Union	6 266
Switzerland	10 640		
Spain	6 437		
Portugal	3 729		
FRG	10 708	Mean	5 945
Austria	8 929		
Italy	7 425		
Greece	4 464		
Finland	9 232		
Sweden	9 904		
Norway	12 623		
Denmark	10 884		
Iceland	9 037		
Turkey	2 533		
Japan	9 447		
Australia	8 850		
New Zealand	8 000		
Mean	8 779		

* International US dollar at 1980 prices.

Looking at the data for 1985 we can make a more definitive evaluation of the gap theory. The basic implication is a widening gulf between the rich sets of countries or the North and the sets of Third World countries or the South. This holds only with regard to the comparison between the OECD countries and communist systems on the one hand and countries in Africa and Latin America on the other. It is not generally true in relation to all parts of the Third World. Let us examine the individual country information more closely (Tables 3.10 and 3.11).

Up until 1980 the planned economies were not outdistanced by the OECD countries. Had there been later data available, then there would have been an even larger distance than that in the 1985 data. The decline of Poland from $5 006 per capita in 1980 to $4 913 in 1985 was not a single phenomenon among the East European economies during the 1980s although the setbacks had not shown up in a striking manner by 1985.

Among the OECD countries there is a sort of north-south division as the northern parts had a higher level of economic affluence than the southern parts with the exception of United Kingdom and Ireland. Japan ($9 447) had by 1985 passed Australia ($8 850) and New Zealand ($8 000) in spite of the fact that in 1950 the gap was quite large as Australia ($4 331) and New Zealand ($4 531) had a per capita income three times higher than that of Japan ($1 129). Had Japan been classified as a Third World country, then there would have been one major exception to the gap theory. In 1985 the average income in the OECD set of countries was three times that of the average income of the set of Latin American countries and eleven times that of the African set of countries.

The economic development among African countries has been negative since 1970. The average income among the African countries included in this analysis actually declined from $722 per capita in 1980 to $709 per capita in 1985. The northern parts of Africa developed differently, as Algeria with $1 998 in 1980, Tunisia with $1 845 in 1980 and Egypt with $995 in 1980 show. The trend was similarly negative among the Latin American countries where an average income per capita of $2 882 declined to a level of $2 616 in 1985. The shift to a lower level of economic activity in the world economy in the 1980s hit some parts of the Third World more harshly than others.

What invalidates the gap theory is the continued strong increase in real GDP per capita in several Asian countries. Even when the world economy went into slump the average income per capita among the set of Asian countries grew, from $1 418 in 1970 to $2 164 in 1980 and $2 581 in 1985. Whereas in 1950 the average income per capita was six times larger in the set of OECD countries than among the set of Asian countries, the same gap had narrowed down to a 3:1 ratio in 1985. The sharp advance of this part of the Third World was not, however, evenly distributed within that set as the between-country variation did increase from 1970 to 1985.

Table 3.11. GDP/capita in Asia, Latin America and Africa, 1985*

Asia		*Latin America*		*Africa*	
Iran	3 922	Domincan Rep	1 753	Egypt	1 188
Iraq	2 813	Mexico	3 985	Sudan	540
Cyprus	5 310	El Salvador	1 198	Senegal	754
Jordan	2 113	Costa Rica	2 650	Liberia	491
Syria	2 900	Panama	2 912	Ghana	349
India	750	Columbia	2 599	Cameroon	1 095
Pakistan	1 153	Venezuela	3 548	Nigeria	581
Sri Lanka	1 539	Ecuador	2 387	Zaïre	210
Thailand	1 900	Peru	2 114	Kenya	598
Malaysia	3 415	Brazil	3 287	Tanzania	355
Singapore	9 834	Bolivia	1 089	Ethiopia	310
Korea Rep	3 156	Paraguay	1 996	Zambia	584
Philippines	1 361	Chile	3 486	Malawi	387
Indonesia	1 255	Argentina	3 486	Morocco	1 221
Afghanistan	609	Uruguay	3 462	Algeria	2 142
China	2 444	Haiti	631	Tunisia	2 050
Taiwan	3 581	Jamaica	1 725	Mali	355
Burma	557	Trinidad	6 889	Benin	525
Nepal	526	Barbados	5 212	Mauretania	550
		Guatemala	1 608	Niger	429
Mean	2 581	Honduras	911	Ivory Coast	920
		Nicaragua	1 989	Sierra Leone	443
		Guyana	1 259	Gabon	3 103
				Central Africa	434
				Chad	254
				Madagascar	497
		Mean	2616	Guinea	452
				Burkina Faso	377
				Togo	489
				Congo	1 335
				Uganda	347
				Burundi	345
				Rwanda	341
				Somalia	348
				Angola	609
				Mozambique	528
				Mean	709

* International US dollar at 1980 prices.

In the set of Asian countries we note the so-called baby tigers: Singapore,

Taiwan, Malaysia and South Korea. How precarious it is to generalize about a development pattern in the Third World appears evident from a comparison with these aggressive growth nations and the more populous countries. Thirty-five years of development in India and Pakistan and Bangladesh has enabled these countries to increase their living standards only marginally in excess of the income implication of the strong population growth. The gap theory fails to take into account the tremendous income differences within the Asian part of the Third World: Singapore with $9 834 and Taiwan with $3 581 versus India with $750 and Burma with $557. Note the $3 922 of Iran.

The same objection to the gap theory may be made with regard to the set of Latin American countries and the set of African countries. It is true that there was little progress between 1960 and 1985 in countries like Zaire ($314-210), Zambia ($740-584) and Nigeria ($552-581) as well as in Argentina ($3 091-3 486), Venezuela ($5 308-3 548) and Uruguay ($3 271-3 462). But on the other hand there are countries with exceptional economic progress in the same sets of countries: Tunisia ($852-2 050), Algeria ($1 302-2 142) and Egypt ($496-1 188) as well as Brazil ($991-3 282) and Ecuador ($1 143-2 387). The country differences in development pace are most substantial in the Third World; as a matter of fact, they are so large that the general notion of a set of rich countries becoming richer than a set of poor countries is more confusing than clarifying, at least as long as it has the connotation of the north versus the south or the OECD and communist countries versus the Third World generally.

Average economic growth rates

An analysis of average growth rates in the economy may complement the focus above on country differences in levels of affluence. The pace of economic development may be measured by various indicators. We will employ the real GDP per capita measures collected by Summers and Heston as well as GNP data by the World Bank and calculate average growth rates for the sets of countries specified above. It should be pointed out that using GDP per capita data for measuring economic growth means that we take the population change directly into account. A country may have a strong increase in total production, yet show little economic growth due to strong population increase.

The gap theory implies a definitive country pattern with regard to average growth rates. The yearly growth rates of the economy of a country may hover due to short-term factors. However, here we focus on seminal growth trends over long time periods. If it were true that the overall income differences between the sets of rich countries on the one hand and the sets of Third World countries on the other were increasing over time, then there would be higher average growth rates in the economies of the rich countries than in the economies of the Third World countries. Is this true? Let us look at Table 3.12 with GNP/capita data. GNP measures the total domestic and foreign output claimed by residents. It comprises GDP plus net factor income from abroad.

Table 3.12. Average growth rates in GNP/capita, 1965-85

	Mean	Max	Min
OECD countries (N=22)	2.6	4.7	1.4
Communist countries (N=8)	5.0	5.8	4.1
Latin American countries (N=21)	1.3	4.3	−2.1
Asian countries (N=14)	3.9	7.6	1.0
African countries (N=32)	0.5	4.0	−2.6

Source: World Development Report (1987).

Economic growth from one year to another reflects a number of temporary factors which increase or decrease the pace of economic development. Of interest here is the average growth rates over longer periods of time, i.e. the speed of economic expansion when the yearly economic fluctuations have been taken into account. Countries differ considerably in terms of average growth rates, but is the variation in accordance with the prediction of the gap theory?

The mean average growth rates between 1965 and 1985 differ among the five sets of countries. It is true that the mean average growth rates in the sets of OECD countries and communist countries are higher than that of the set of Latin American countries or that of the African countries — as the gap theory implies. However, the mean average growth rate among the Asian countries is larger than that of the OECD countries, which is exactly where the gap theory falters.

Developing countries are not of one kind as if there were one single average growth rate for all Third World countries. On the contrary, there are considerable differences in economic growth over time within all five sets of countries. Let us look at the country variation within the so-called set of poor countries with regard to 1970 and 1985 when the world economy in general did not develop as it did in the 1960s (Table 3.13).

The average mean country growth rate among the OECD countries was 2.7 per cent between 1970 and 1985. The finding is again that there are several Third World countries that have been successful in bridging the gulf between themselves and the rich countries. There are also several countries that have fallen behind even more, but that does not change the fact that the gap theory implication is not confirmed. Besides the gap theory we need a theory about the so-called NICs that develop in a manner different from the pattern of the gap theory. Note the high yearly growth rates in Indonesia and Thailand in South-East Asia.

Table 3.13. Percentage increase in GDP/capita, 1970-85

Rapid increase		*Slow increase*	
Singapore	15.2	Mozambique	−3.1
Korea Rep	9.8	Angola	−2.9
China	8.8	Venezuela	−2.9
Taiwan	8.5	Chad	−2.8
Indonesia	7.8	Zaïre	−2.6
Malaysia	7.8	Ghana	−2.4
Tunisia	5.7	Liberia	−1.9
Brazil	5.3	Jamaica	−1.8
Syria	5.2	Madagascar	−1.6
Thailand	4.9	Sudan	−1.3
Egypt	4.8	Argentina	−0.8
Cyprus	4.7	Bolivia	−0.8
Ecuador	4.4	Ethiopia	−0.6
Paraguay	4.2	Nigeria	−0.5
Barbados	4.1	Peru	−0.5
Cameroon	3.5	Chile	−0.3
Colombia	3.2	Uruguay	0.2
Sri Lanka	3.2	Kenya	0.5
Gabon	3.1		
Jordan	3.0		
Morocco	2.5		
Algeria	2.4		

Source: Summers and Heston (1988).

Quality of life

Economic or socio-economic development typically relates to a positive change — a real increase — in total output or in the well-being or material welfare of the citizens of a country. The value component of the concept of development is here quite explicit and straightforward: a developing nation is a country that is becoming better off and a developed country is one that is well off. But here the agreement between scholars also ends. What is contested is how to measure the extent of welfare of a nation as well as how to explain which factors are conducive to development as increased well-being. We will deal with the two counter-arguments one at a time.

Often a simple economic indicator such as level or rate of growth in GDP is considered a tool for analysing welfare in a society. There are basically two counter-arguments: on the one hand, it has been claimed that an indicator like GDP per capita does not adequately map individual welfare which includes other things like health, employment, housing and so forth, meaning that we have to pay attention to broad social indicators; on the other hand, we have the argument that what matters is not the overall size or growth rate in GDP but its distribution among various social groups. Attempts have been made to construct more complex indices measuring more generally social welfare like e.g. the Physical Quality of Life Index and the Disparity Reduction Rate which taps the change in physical quality of life over time (Morris, 1979; Pourgerami, 1989). A rising national income may be used for many purposes except raising the level of affluence among the poor. Thus we have to look at the extent of inequality as measured by, for example, the Gini-index.

It is not necessary, however, to commit oneself to any of these positions as one may approach socio-economic development in an open fashion. To what extent do various measures — economic or social — co-vary in a data set covering some seventy-five nations in various parts of the world? What is the main relationship between affluence on the aggregate level and the distribution of income? The indicators employed and the set of countries covered are presented in Appendix 3.1.

The problem when comparing countries in relation to the general notion of affluence or rate of change in affluence are well known (Kuznets, 1966). First, there are the difficulties in getting access to data; for some countries this has been difficult except for the last ten years. Generally, longitudinal data series are more problematic than cross-sectional data. Second, there are severe problems of interpretation and comparability (Meier, 1984; Thirlwall, 1986). How can we know that the indicators measure the same phenomenon? Problems of indicator validity and reliability are confounded by culture barriers: indicators that tap one dimension in one context cannot be transferred to another context with a similar interpretation. These data problems impose limits on what can be achieved in terms of country comparison, but they do not exclude an analysis of levels or rates of development.

It may be worthwhile to penetrate the extent to which the above picture about differences in affluence is generally true when alternative indicators of affluence are resorted to. Are we to conclude that the per capita differences in income as measured by GDP co-vary with similar country differences in standards of living? Material well-being or social welfare is a difficult notion to pin down in measurement indices. A number of social indicators are relevant for consideration in the measurement of welfare. We include the following indicators: infant mortality, number of doctors, energy consumption, life expectancy, literacy, school enrolments, telephone, radio, TV, real GDP/capita 1980, and calories per capita.

The claim that underdevelopment is a general predicament that distinguishes between countries implies that these social indicators co-vary to a high extent. Moreover, development theory also implies that the per capita income indicator co-varies strongly with each of the social indicators. Table 3.14 comprises a factor analysis with findings that are relevant for these beliefs.

Table 3.14. Factor analysis of welfare indicators

Indicators	*Factor 1*	*Factor 2*
Life expectancy	0.884	0.357
Literacy	0.875	0.338
School enrolment ratio	0.860	0.308
Infant mortality	−0.850	−0.359
Number of physicians	0.775	0.450
Calories per capita	0.728	0.521
Real GDP/capita 1980	0.610	0.740
Television	0.542	0.817
Energy consumption	0.396	0.802
Telephones	0.387	0.817
Radio	0.208	0.841
Explained variance:	75.8%	9.4%
N = 75		

Source: World Handbook of Political and Social Indicators (3rd edn, 1983).

The findings of the factor analysis offer substantial evidence to the fact that there is a general predicament of underdevelopment because there is strong co-variation between the indicators. Countries that have a low level of affluence as measured by the GDP per capita indicator tend consistently to score low on the most basic indicators of material well-being, but there is also a more luxurious aspect to welfare that these basic indicators do not co-vary with, radio, TV and telephones. The fact that underdevelopment is a general social predicament does not imply, however, that there are two homogeneous sets of countries, developed and underdeveloped.

The Kuznets curve

A higher average GDP per capita does not imply a higher standard of living for the entire population. The standard indicator on levels of economic affluence says nothing about the distribution of economic affluence. The Kuznets theory proposed in 1955 suggested that a rise in economic affluence had a somewhat contradictory impact on the pattern of distribution (Kuznets, 1955). At first, the income differences would increase but later on these differentials would decrease. Thus, there would be something like an inverted U-shaped curve linking levels of affluence with some measure on the extent of inequality in the distributions of incomes. A similar hypothesis was suggested by Myrdal (1957) and Hirschman (1958; Taylor and Arida, 1988).

There has been a lot of research on the Kuznets theory but so far there has been no conclusive answer (McCormick, 1988). Part of the difficulties in testing theories about income distribution arise from the lack of reliable data for a large number of countries. Various indicators may be employed, but there are not enough cross-sectional or longitudinal data for more refined tests. Part of the confusion also stems from the interaction between the two entities. A low or high level of economic affluence may have one kind of impact on the income distribution whereas the income distribution may have another kind of impact on levels of economic affluence. Moreover, other factors like public policy may change the impact of the two variables on each other. It is also an open question as whether the Kuznets theory should be tested by means of cross-sectional or longitudinal data (Bigsten, 1987).

The data set employed here does not allow any strict treating of the Kuznets curve but it may be employed to illuminate some aspects of the relationship between income distribution and levels of economic affluence; relating the two entities to each other in a statistical analysis does not permit us to draw any conclusion about the direction of the causal interaction between the variables. Income inequality is measured by means of the Gini-index with regard to data from the 1970s, whereas the GDP information is supplied by the Summers and Heston data (1984). The higher the score of the Gini-index, the larger the amount of inequality in the distribution of income between the households.

Looking at the relationship between average real GDP per capita in a country around 1980 and the degree of inequality in its income distribution between households, we have a negative relationship between level of affluence and income inequality ($r = -0.66$), although a nonlinear test would be more appropriate (Ahluwalia, 1976; Weede, 1980). Whether the finding that income inequality is reduced the larger the national income per capita of a country is in accordance with the Kuznets U-curve may be discussed (Adelman and Robinson, 1989).

Even if it is true that income inequality may vary considerably between Third World countries like Brazil and Pakistan, it is still the case that income inequality decreases the larger the average GDP per capita in a country. It is true that income inequality rises somewhat as we move from very poor countries to countries with a higher level of affluence, but in general, the richer a country the larger the probability that its income distribution is more equal. The Kuznets curve suggested in the 1950s may be partly traced in the data from the 1970s (Figure 3.1).

Figure 3.1. GDP per capita 1980 and income distribution 1970-80

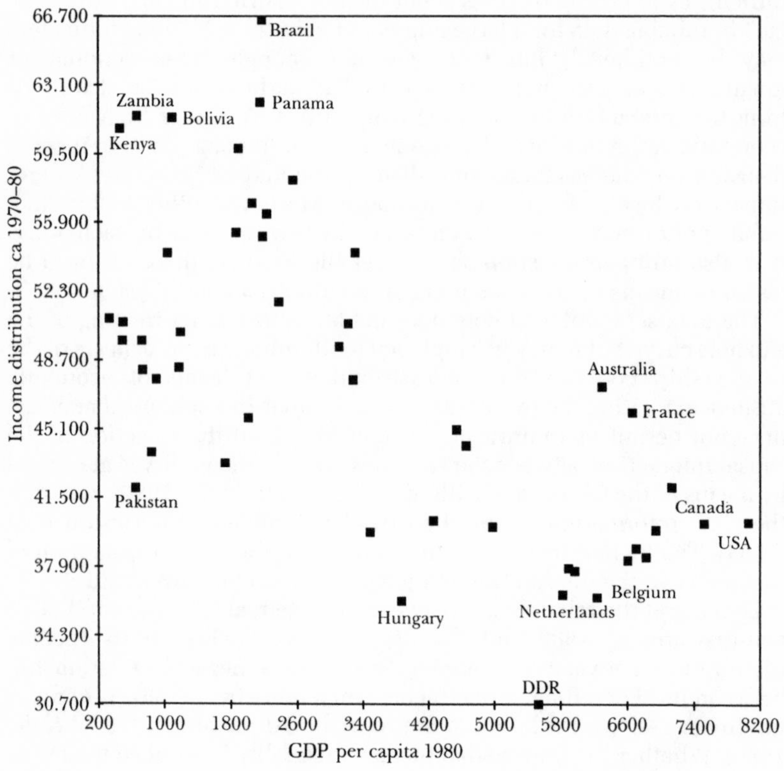

Figure 3.2. Economic growth 1960-80 and income distribution 1970-80

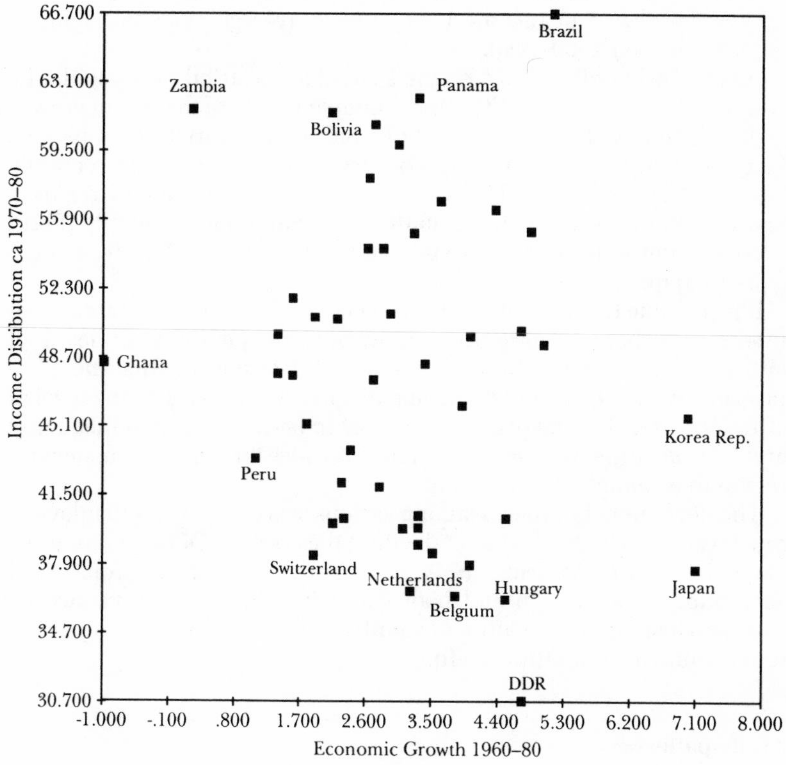

The cross-sectional test of the Kuznets hypothesis may be complemented by a longitudinal test. It is often argued that the extent of income inequalities in a country like India and Brazil has increased over time (Mathur, 1983; de Carvalho and Wood, 1980). Since there has also been some economic development during the same time period, it may be argued that the Kuznets curve fits longitudinal data about an association between economic growth and income inequality. Figure 3.2 relates the degree of income inequality to average rates of economic growth between 1960-1980.

Again, the hypothesis of a Kuznets curve is not strictly validated. The amount of income inequality varies independently of the rate of growth in the economy. It is not possible to predict the variation in income inequality knowing the average country growth rates in the economy between 1960 and 1980. There are cases of all conceivable extremes: a low growth rate and much inequality (Zambia) or more equality (Peru) versus a high rate of growth and much inequalities (Brazil) or more equality (Japan).

It is possible to trace out a reminiscence of a Kuznets curve around an inverted U-shaped curve linking income inequality with level of affluence. An interpretation of more recent data suggests that there is a probability that the extent of income inequality increases, as the level of affluence rises, but the overall relationship between income inequality and level of affluence is negative. There is cause for more optimism with regard to economic development.

The development process among various sets of countries displays so much variation both between and within these sets — OECD, communist countries, Latin America, Asia and Africa — that the traditional separation between rich and poor countries, the northern versus the southern hemisphere, or affluent countries and Third World countries is more confusing than illuminating.

Trade patterns

A seminal hypothesis in development theory argues that foreign trade is characteristic of advanced or developing countries. The theory of international trade implies that the more a country engages in trade with other countries, the more likely is it that it will benefit from the consequences of an open economy in a way which improves the prospects for rapid socio-economic expansion at home. The basic Richardian theory of comparative advantages claims high gains for all the interacting countries from productive specialization and trade (Yarbrough and Yarbrough, 1988). Although the debate on the potential benefits and costs of extensive international trade between countries has developed far beyond the simple Ricardian model (Lal, 1983; World Bank, 1987), there is still the fundamental notion that trade or openness of the economy is typical of countries with a high level of affluence or with a high level of average economic growth (Bhagwati and Ruggie, 1984; Caves and Jones, 1985; Choksi and Papageorgiou, 1986; Chacholiades, 1985; Pack, 1988; Bliss, 1989; Evans, 1989).

Table 3.15. The impex indicator on economic openness of OECD and communist countries.

	1960	1970	1980	1985
USA	9.4	11.1	20.8	17.0
Canada	36.8	44.7	58.6	56.0
UK	43.6	45.8	54.0	57.3
Ireland	67.4	80.5	122.5	137.5
Netherlands	93.3	91.1	105.2	122.5
Belgium	65.9	84.7	123.8	149.8
France	27.7	32.0	46.2	47.6
Switzerland	57.5	64.9	74.1	73.4
Spain	17.9	28.1	33.8	45.0
Portugal	38.6	49.4	71.7	82.7
FRG	35.5	40.0	54.3	61.3
Austria	50.4	64.2	80.4	81.4
Italy	28.2	34.9	53.0	46.7
Greece	25.4	27.9	44.6	54.4
Finland	46.2	54.1	70.6	58.5
Sweden	46.4	49.2	62.4	70.1
Norway	85.2	85.6	92.1	87.3
Denmark	65.5	58.9	69.5	76.2
Turkey	8.4	14.3	21.7	45.6
Japan	21.2	20.4	28.9	25.8
Australia	33.0	30.4	36.4	35.9
New Zealand	47.1	47.5	60.5	67.5
GDR	—	—	—	—
Poland	—	—	61.8	35.6
Hungary	—	62.6	79.8	85.4
Czechoslovakia	—	—	—	—
Yugoslavia	31.4	42.2	45.0	59.7
Romania	—	—	—	—
Soviet Union	—	—	—	—

Source: World Bank, World Tables 1984 and 1987.

Is it true that extensive international trade characterizes rich countries and that a heavy concentration on the home market is typical of poor countries? Let us test this simple idea in relation to an indicator on the scope of trade in an economy: the *impex index* or the sum of exports

Table 3.16. The impex indicator on economic openness of Third World countries.

	1960	1970	1980	1985
Iran	35.9	46.2	—	—
Iraq	82.8	60.4	—	—
Jordan	—	64.8	133.3	146.2
India	13.6	9.0	17.8	16.1
Pakistan	23.5	22.4	34.1	33.5
Thailand	36.4	38.1	55.4	54.8
Singapore	334.1	244.3	452.0	—
Korea Rep	16.0	38.2	82.5	74.5
Philippines	21.3	39.1	46.5	39.6
Indonesia	50.0	29.1	55.0	45.8
China	—	—	15.4	24.3
Mexico	23.0	17.6	46.7	28.3
Haiti	42.1	31.8	48.9	40.2
Jamaica	73.2	73.8	111.5	150.7
Trinidad	81.3	84.3	90.1	61.0
Guatemala	27.5	37.2	47.0	41.8
El Salvador	45.6	50.1	68.2	55.1
Costa Rica	48.0	64.1	66.5	70.6
Colombia	31.5	31.2	32.9	32.0
Venezuela	54.8	45.0	58.3	51.2
Ecuador	34.5	33.2	53.5	51.3
Peru	39.4	32.2	28.2	39.8
Brazil	12.1	13.5	19.9	20.1
Bolivia	32.6	37.9	34.3	28.5
Paraguay	35.6	31.6	28.5	67.2
Chile	31.0	30.2	51.5	62.9
Argentina	20.8	18.4	16.2	26.8
Egypt	39.6	33.5	78.2	61.0
Sudan	28.1	31.5	34.0	31.3
Tunisia	—	49.2	86.0	74.6
Algeria	78.4	51.5	69.0	45.6
Morocco	45.8	39.4	46.7	67.9
Liberia	89.6	125.4	125.6	84.6
Ghana	64.4	44.9	18.0	21.6
Senegal	82.5	60.9	77.9	79.7
Nigeria	34.9	26.1	57.0	29.5
Zaïre	107.6	92.5	82.9	78.9
Tanzania	57.5	52.6	36.6	23.2
Zambia	109.0	96.3	87.5	78.9
Kenya	67.0	62.8	69.8	56.3
Uganda	48.2	41.8	—	27.4

Source: World Bank, World Tables 1984, 1987

and imports in relation to GNP. Tables 3.15 and 3.16 cover the country variation in the degree of openness of the economy since 1960.

There is a quite substantial variation in the extent to which the economy of a so-called rich country is an open one. The small affluent countries in western Europe have considerably more open economies than the United States and Japan where the domestic market is very large. A very high degree of openness is characteristic of the Dutch, Belgian and Irish economies.

The so-called Third World countries differ even more in terms of openness of the economy.

Again we find that small countries tend to have a more open economy than large countries, all other things equal (Katzenstein, 1985). The very high score of Singapore must be pointed out, as it exemplifies how export led market capitalism may lead a country onto a path of staggering economic growth. Not all countries have augmented the openness of their economies, although the overall trend is a development towards increased openness in the economies of a dynamic world trade. The average impex score for all the countries included in our analysis was 53.0 in 1960, which by 1985 had increased to 63.7. A reduction in the impex index for a country indicates a less fortunate role in the world economy, which has expanded tremendously in volume since 1945.

An analysis of variance of the data indicate that there is hardly any special geographical dimension behind the impex data (Table 3.17). The average impex score for the OECD countries are somewhat higher than the average impex scores for the other country sets.

Table 3.17. Openness of the economy, 1985

	Mean	Max	Min	CV
OECD countries (N=24)	72.2	149.8	17.0	0.50
Communist countries (N=3)	60.2	85.4	35.6	0.41
Latin American countries (N=23)	61.0	150.7	20.1	0.58
African countries (N=31)	60.7	139.6	21.6	0.49
Asian countries (N=13)	60.6	146.2	16.1	0.65

Source: World Bank, World Tables 1984, 1987

Is there a clear relationship between the openness of the economy and basic indicators on economic growth and average level of affluence? On the one hand, Bela Belassa argues strongly for the existence of a causal connection between foreign trade and economic growth — see *Comparative Advantage Trade Policy and Economic Development*

(1989). One may speak of a so-called trade theory of economic growth, which argues that the trade pattern of a country is of decisive importance for its economic dynamism (Nurkse, 1961; Little, Scitovsky and Scott, 1970; Kreuger, 1978). On the other hand, there is the opposite argument that economic growth influences the trade pattern (Johnson, 1958, 1975; Södersten, 1964; Ros, 1987).

Table 3.18 presents surface correlation data about the relationship between socio-economic development and trade. A strict test of various alternative theories about the causal relationships and reciprocities between trade and growth would require a more sophisticated econometric analysis.

Table 3.18. Impex, affluence and economic growth

	Impex 1960	Impex 1970	Impex 1985
Real GDP/cap 1960	0.07 (N=94)	0.12 (N=102)	0.16 (N=95)
Real GDP/cap 1970	0.08 (N=96)	0.16 (N=104)	0.18 (N=97)
Real GDP/cap 1985	0.20 (N=96)	0.23 (N=103)	0.18 (N=96)
Growth real GDP/ cap 1965-1985	0.13 (N=84)	0.07 (N=92)	0.11 (N=88)

If one looks only at simple measures of association between indices that measure trade and affluence, then we note that there is no indication of any relationship at all. However, if one resorts to a regression analysis where more factors are taken into account, then the picture may look differently – a task that is beyond the aims of this volume.

The developmental process

Developmental theory designates some countries as developed and others as underdeveloped or the former as highly developed and the latter as less developed. The advanced industrial nations have passed through the process of social change, taking them out of agrarian poverty and into industrial affluence and the welfare state. Such a pattern of social change is considered the main objective for the poor countries according to the theory and practice of the modernization theme. The basic policy problem is to identify the strategy of modernization: planning- or market-induced change? The historical experiences of the market economies and the lessons from the Soviet Union and China suggest two ideal types which may be combined in practice in various ways. The Japanese development is often referred to as state-led market capitalism whereas China appeares to be moving towards so-called market socialism, at least up until the severe clash at Tiananmen Square in 1989.

Although there is considerable disagreement about the means and goals of development it can be stated that the zest for modernization may meet with success. Developing countries are not of one kind. Some have developed very quickly accomplishing vast social change whereas other countries have hardly modernized at all. Even if it is true that generally the gap between rich and poor countries has not been reduced it is also not the case that it is impossible for countries in the Third World to close that distance.

Development has a dynamic connotation. It singles out a set of countries that try to find the path from poverty to affluence. Developmental countries are those countries that are moving at varying rates of speed from a low level to a higher level of social welfare. Sometimes the ambition is high as the rich countries are depicted as models of what the developmental process should result in. Sometimes the modernization zeal is more realistic as the goal of the developmental process is only to move the countries out of poverty.

Let us consider an economic indicator, GNP growth per capita as measured by data collected by the World Bank (1982) (Table 3.19).

Table 3.19. Average growth rates in GNP/capita, 1960-80

OECD countries (N=22)	3.5
Communist countries (N=8)	5.3
Latin American countries (N=15)	2.7
Asian countries (N=12)	4.3
African countries (N=15)	1.7
Third World countries (N=43)	2.8
Sample (N=72)	3.3

Source: World Bank (1982)

Growth in the economy varies from one year to another and reflects a number of factors that are not related to development. What is of interest here is the average growth rates in different countries, i.e. the speed of the developmental process after accounting for economic fluctuations from one year to another. Countries differ substantially in so far as the long-term per capita growth rates between 1960 and 1980 are concerned.

Growth rates have in general been lower in Third World countries than in the rich countries. The exception is to be found among the Asian countries where the mean growth rate — about 4 per cent — exceeds that of the OECD countries — 3.5 per cent. The growth in the economies in Africa has been particularly weak — or a mean of less than 2 per cent — whereas the average growth rate in Latin America is not that low — or roughly 3 per cent. The mean growth rate of the communist systems studied here is quite high or 5 per cent, which seems an exaggeration. Had data for the 1980s been included the picture would not have been that bright for these countries. The severe pollution problems in eastern Europe are not captured by this measure which reveals that it is not a perfect indicator on development.

There are two possible explanations of the pattern in GDP growth per capita: output or population. Either the rate of increase in production in the Third World has been weak or the rate of population growth has been very strong. Let us look at some data that may shed light on this question. Table 3.20 presents information about the growth in aggregate GDP for the 1960s and the 1970s.

Table 3.20. Average growth rates in GDP, 1960-70, 1970-80

	1960-70		1970-80
(1) OECD countries (N=22)	5.3	(N=22)	3.3
(2) Socialist countries (N=2)	7.2	(N=7)	6.5
(3) Latin American countries (N=14)	5.2	(N=15)	5.2
(4) Asian countries (N=12)	6.5	(N=12)	6.8
(5) African countries (N=15)	4.2	(N=15)	3.8
(3-5) Third World countries (N=41)	5.2	(N=42)	5.2
(1-5) Sample (N=65)	5.3	(N=71)	4.7

Source: World Bank (1982)

It is not primarily the dynamism in the economies of the Third World that is at fault. Actually, the average increase in output in Third World countries is as good as that of the rich countries. With regard to the Asian world it may even be stated that the rate of economic growth is higher. What accounts for the low increase in income per capita in LDCs is the

Table 3.21. Average population growth rates, 1960-70 and 1970-80

	1960-70		1970-80
(1) OECD countries (N=22)	0.99	(N=22)	0.77
(2) Communist countries (N=9)	0.87	(N=9)	0.72
(3) Latin American countries (N=15)	2.53	(N=15)	2.34
(4) Asian countries (N=13)	2.65	(N=13)	2.45
(5) African countries (N=15)	2.65	(N=15)	2.81
(3-5) Third World countries (N=43)	2.60	(N=43)	2.57
(1-5) Sample (N=74)	1.91	(N=74)	1.81

Source: World Bank (1982)

rapid rise in the population (Bairoch, 1977). Table 3.21 reveals that the expansion of the population is almost as large as the increase in output, indicating that the overall change in level of affluence per capita will not be enough to bridge the gap between the rich countries and the poor, except in a few rapidly developing countries.

The economic development in Japan, South Korea, Singapore, Malaysia and Indonesia, with persistently high rates of economic growth each year, has meant a strong expansion in the level of affluence between 1960 and 1980. The figures for GDP per capita in these countries are comparable to those of some of the OECD countries. The level of affluence in Japan and Singapore is as high as that of the Netherlands or Finland, that of Malaysia, Taiwan and South Korea is comparable with Portugal and Greece, and that of Iran and Algeria with that of Turkey. Kuznets stated twenty-five years ago:

> It follows that the current international difference in per capita product, which is roughly between fifteen and twenty to one (based on the average for the developed countries and that for the populous Asian countries with per capita GDP in the early 1960's of below $100), results partly from differences in growth rates over the nineteenth and twentieth centuries, and partly from disparities in initial per capita product. Furthermore, since most countries that have enjoyed modern economic growth had initially high per capita product, international differences have grown wider and have continued to do so even in the post-World War II year (Kuznets, 1966:304-5).

This is hardly generally true any longer. Since 1960 the traditionally sharp distinction between poor and rich countries has lost its discriminating power. The well-known gap theory about development implies a pessimistic view of what future economic development may bring about. The gap theory argues that there was a sharp gulf between a set of rich countries and a set of poor countries at the end of the Second World War and that this gap has tended to increase during the post-war period.

It is believed that this separation between rich and poor countries coincides with the distinction between OECD countries and Communist countries, with the exception of China on the one hand and the Third World countries on the other, or with a divide between the north and the south. Looking at the real GDP data, we cannot confirm the gap theory as it is not true that this sharp gulf already existed in 1950 or that the gap between the OECD countries or the Communist countries and all sets of Third World countries continues to grow over time. Figure 3.3 shows the relation between level of affluence in 1970 and the average rate of economic growth between 1970 and 1985.

There is not the kind of relationship between level of economic affluence and average economic growth that the gap theory implies. There is an important set of Third World countries that have been able to close the gap to the OECD countries during the post-war period. Some

countries

Figure 3.3 Real GDP/capita 1970 and growth of real GDP/capita 1970-85 (in percentages)

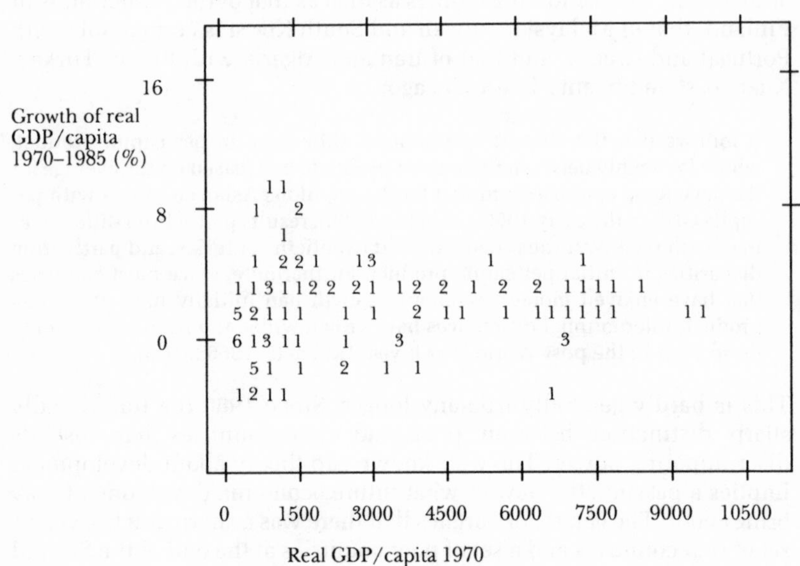

have moved out of poverty. It is not the case that the level of affluence in a country determines the average rate of economic growth which suggests that the development alternative is a real one.

Conclusion

It is a widely held belief that the distance between the rich OECD nations and the poor Third World countries is increasing: in spite of several decades of various kinds of efforts at development the gap has not been closed nor is it narrowing. It is true that there were substantial country differences in income per capita around 1960 reflecting a distinction between a rich Occident and a poor South, but it is not true that the same country differences are simply maintained or even increase.

To emphasize the major finding: There is no relation between level of affluence and rate of change in affluence on a per capita basis. This means that the development alternative is a real one. Several countries have moved out of poverty during the period 1960-90. The developmental process displays such considerable variation among the countries of the world that the traditional separation between rich and poor countries in terms of the distinction between industrialized OECD nations and non-industrialized Third World countries is inadequate.

Now, development may mean several things. If the concept of development refers to economic change in particular and social welfare in general, then it is possible to show that the developmental process may bring about considerable change in the country differences in affluence. Development is a major goal for most if not all Third World nations. It is believed to be the key to solving social problems and a necessary condition for not having to face even greater difficulties. Various methods have been tried in order to promote development, from central planning and coordination to the introduction of market capitalism. Usually development is interpreted as an economic target although one is reminded of the fact that development is more than GNP growth. What factors are conducive to economic growth? We will look at the major models of economic and social development by focusing on theories of economic growth. Before we embark on this task in Chapters 8 and 9 we will discuss the far more difficult concept of political development.

Appendix 3.1. Indicators and Sources

Real GDP/capita US dollar 1950, 1960, 1970, 1980, 1985 (1985 prices)	Summers and Heston, 1988
GNP/capita growth 1960-80	World Bank, 1982
GDP growth 1960-70	World Bank, 1982
GDP growth 1970-80	World Bank, 1982
GNP/capita growth 1965-85	World Bank, 1987
GDP/capita growth 1970-85	Summers and Heston, 1988
Population growth 1960-70	World Bank, 1982
Population growth 1970-80	World Bank, 1982
Life expectancy males 1975	Taylor, 1981
Literacy rates 1975	Taylor, 1981

School enrolment ratio 1st and 2nd level 1975	Taylor, 1981
Infant mortality rates 1975	Taylor, 1981
Number of physicians/million population 1975	Taylor, 1981
Calories/capita per diem 1974	Taylor, 1981
TV sets/1000 population 1975	Taylor, 1981
Energy consumption/per capita 1975	Taylor, 1981
Telephones/1000 population 1975	Taylor, 1981
Radios/1000 population 1975	Taylor, 1981
Gross domestic investment 1960-80: change	World Bank, 1982
Gross domestic investment 1980: level (per cent of GDP)	World Bank, 1982
Share of working age population 1975	Taylor, 1981
Agricultural population in percentage 1977	Taylor, 1981
Higher education enrolment 1975	Taylor, 1981
Impex index: import/GNP + export/GNP	World Bank, 1984, 1987
Gini-index	Taylor, 1981
Modernization, year of	Taylor and Lewis, 1972
Democracy 1975	Bollen, 1980
Human rights c. 1980	Humana, 1983
Socialist government	Delury, 1983
General government expenditure in per cent of GDP c. 1977	IMF, 1982
Share of adult population	Taylor, 1981
Population size	Taylor, 1981
Religious fragmentation	Taylor, 1981
Ethnic fragmentation	Taylor, 1981
Protestant and Catholic population	Taylor and Lewis, 1972

Countries included:

002 USA
020 Canada
040 Cuba
041 Haiti
042 Dominican Rep
051 Jamaica
052 Trinidad
053 Barbados
070 Mexico
436 Niger
437 Ivory Coast
438 Guinea
439 Burkina Faso
450 Liberia
451 Sierra Leone
452 Ghana
461 Togo
471 Cameroon

090 Guatemala
091 Honduras
092 El Salvador
093 Nicaragua
094 Costa Rica
095 Panama
100 Colombia
101 Venezuela
110 Guyana
130 Ecuador
135 Peru
140 Brazil
145 Bolivia
150 Paraguay
155 Chile
160 Argentina
165 Uruguay
200 UK
205 Ireland
210 Netherlands
211 Belgium
212 Luxembourg
220 France
225 Switzerland
230 Spain
235 Portugal
260 GFR
265 GDR
290 Poland
305 Austria
310 Hungary
315 Czechoslovakia
325 Italy
339 Albania
345 Yugoslavia
350 Greece
352 Cyprus
355 Bulgaria
360 Romania
365 Soviet Union
375 Finland
380 Sweden
385 Norway
390 Denmark
395 Iceland
432 Mali
433 Senegal
434 Benin
435 Mauritania
475 Nigeria
481 Gabon
482 Central African Republic
483 Chad
484 Congo
490 Zaïre
500 Uganda
501 Kenya
510 Tanzania
516 Burundi
517 Rwanda
520 Somalia
530 Ethiopia
540 Angola
541 Mozambique
551 Zambia
553 Malawi
580 Madagascar
600 Morocco
615 Algeria
616 Tunisia
620 Libya
625 Sudan
630 Iran
640 Turkey
645 Iraq
651 Egypt
652 Syria
660 Lebanon
663 Jordan
700 Afghanistan
712 Mongolia
713 Taiwan
731 North Korea
732 South Korea
740 Japan
750 India
770 Pakistan
775 Burma
780 Sri Lanka
790 Nepal
800 Thailand
811 Kampuchea
812 Laos
820 Malaysia
830 Singapore
840 Philippines
850 Indonesia
900 Austria
920 New Zealand

4 Political development

Introduction

Since political systems, whatever their basic characteristics, do change, we need theoretical notions about how political transformations take place. The literature on political change has focused much on political development, in particular some desired process of transformation of the Third World polities. The basic problem, however, is whether there exists an identifiable entity to be denoted by such a concept. A survey of various theories of political development provides a way to outline some conceptions of political change. As the theory of political development is in reality a set of theories of political and social change, an overview of the literature on political development provides a rich view of both the nature of political change and the interaction between economic and social development on the one hand and political development on the other.

Samuel Huntington describes the state of the concept of political development as one of confusion:

> Political development in general is of dubious usefulness in either of these ways. To the extent that political development is thought of as an umbrella concept encompassing a multiplicity of different processes...these often turn out to have little in common except the label which is attached to them.

However, it may be pointed out that the confusion may be a source of clarity; if one makes distinctions between various phenomena of political development and study their interrelationships by means of empirical methods, then insight into complexity may be the outcome. Huntington goes on:

> No one has yet been able to say of the various elements subsumed under the label of political development what Lerner, at a different level, was able to say

> about the broader processes subsumed under the label modernization: that they went together because 'in some historical sense, they had to go together'. (Huntington, 1971: 304)

When approaching the concept of political development one must relate it to the overall concept of development. A basic problem in the study of political development is how it relates to general processes of social and economic development. Some look upon political development as a function of social change whereas others penetrate the extent to which political change is conducive to economic development and social transformation. The literature on political development is amorphous in another sense, i.e. the wide variety of modes of presentation concerning the various phenomena of development. Some employ empirical indicators and statistical tools whereas others remain confident in only presenting a theoretical argument (Leftwich, 1990).

Starting from these deliberations we pose two problems that we will penetrate as far as possible given the present state of data; on the one hand, we wish to derive a set of indicators or ways of measuring the various dimensions in the concept of political development: to what extent does a particular definition or conception of political development have empirical implications in the sense of indices for measurement operations? On the other hand, we want to know whether or to what extent it is true that the concept of political development is truly multidimensional: given the derivation of a set of indicators, what is the co-variation between them? We will look at some of the major interpretations of political development and then proceed to identify a set of indicators.

Political development as democracy

If political development is some process of change that is also ethically appealing, then perhaps it is democratization? Some theories of political development explicitly state that the end of the change process is democracy, whereas other theories of change implicitly imply democratization.

The idea that political development would result in a democratic regime was first suggested in a succinct form by Seymour Martin Lipset in a famous 1959 article, 'Some social requisites of democracy: economic development and political legitimacy'. Criticizing the Lipset approach for its lack of measurement quality Bollen (1979) suggested an index of democracy which could be used in quantitative analyses of political development. And Bollen was successful in confirming the Lipset hypothesis about a close association between the introduction of democracy and high levels of socio-economic development. The famous

Cutright analysis of 1963 is a version of the same theme as is the work by Russett (1964) and Dahl (1971). The study of Adelman and Morris (1967) points in the same direction, but how valid are these findings if one looks at more recent data? It is recognized that the problem of the conditions for democracy is a complex one (Rustow, 1970).

The theory about an almost direct link between economic growth and the strengthening of democratic regimes was severely questioned in Guillermo O'Donnell's *Modernization and Bureaucratic-Authoritarianism: Studies in South American Politics* (1973). Contrary to the Lipset and Cutright hypothesis, O'Donnell showed that high levels of modernization in Latin America coincide with various types of authoritarian rule. In fact it has stimulated a whole new inquiry into the relationships between capitalism and right-wing authoritarianism searching for a theory explaining these unrecognized data (Collier, 1978).

The democracy approach looks upon the political system as the dependent variable whereas socio-economic development is considered as the independent variable. However, it is possible to reverse the relationship and consider in particular economic development as the dependent variable. And a number of attempts have been made to look for determinants of economic growth among political variables such as the introduction of a democratic regime (Weede, 1983) or the length of time of institutionalization (Olson, 1982).

The functional approach

One may question whether democratization is the only valuable form of political change. Perhaps a modern polity implies more than democracy or democratization reflects more valuable change processes? It is no exaggeration to state that *The Politics of Developing Areas* (1960) edited by Gabriel Almond and James S. Coleman is the basic book in the functionalist tradition. Since it was used as a textbook its view of political development and change became widely known and at times much accepted. This was presented in the introductory chapter by Almond. Almond started with a criticism of prevailing approaches:

> We have been talking of 'modern' and 'pre-modern', 'developed' and 'underdeveloped', 'industrial' and 'agrarian', 'Western and non-Western'; or the Parsonian syndromes of universalism-specificity-achievement-affective neutrality, versus particularism-diffuseness-ascription-affectivity. The universe of political systems is less tractable to simple contrasts than we have supposed. We need dualistic models rather than monistic ones, and developmental *as well as* equilibrium models, if we are to understand differences precisely and grapple effectively with the processes of political change. (Almond and Coleman, 1960: 25)

A multidimensional model of political development would start from the Almond conception of the political system as fulfilling functions in terms of structures. On the one hand, we have the input functions: political socialization and recruitment, interest articulation, interest aggregation and political communication. On the other hand, there is the set of output functions: rule-making, rule application and rule adjudication (Almond and Coleman, 1960: 17).

And political development is specified as the degree of specificity with which structures fulfil functions as well as the extent to which political structures are separated out of each other. Almond claims:

> In our presentation of the functional theory, we have continually stressed the point that all political structure is multifunctional, and all political culture is dualistic. The peculiar properties of 'modernity' of structure and culture are a particular mode of solution to the problems of multifunctionality and cultural dualism. (Almond and Coleman, 1960: 63)

One may reply that equating political development with such a general phenomenon as structural specificity amounts to very little. One may wish to know a little more about this structural specificity, what it looks like and how it comes about.

The answer was given in the major elaboration of the functionalist approach to politics in the Almond and Powell book on *Comparative Politics* (1966). It had the subtitle *A Developmental Approach* and it focused in particular on a special type of political change: the increase in system capabilities, in conversion processes and adaptation functions. The 1966 model, though basically functionalist, is different from the 1960 model as it incorporates a systems approach as well. Influenced by David Easton's *A Systems Analysis of Political Life* (1965), Almond and Powell speak of inputs and outputs as well as demand and support. Political systems have a varied capacity for handling inputs and outputs as conceptualized in the idea of system capacity:

> Thus we may speak of democracies as having a higher responsive capability. These concepts of regulative, extractive, distributive and responsive capability are simply ways of talking about the flows of activity into and out of the political system. (Almond and Powell, 1966: 28-9)

Moreover, political systems also vary with regard to the internal functioning of the system in terms of conversion processes. Almond and Powell state:

> The conversion processes, or functions, are the ways systems transform inputs into outputs. In the political system this involves the ways in which

> demands and supports are transformed into authoritative decisions and are implemented. (Almond and Powell, 1966: 29)

Lastly, we have the system maintenance and adaptation functions. Almond and Powell explain these in the following way:

> In a political system the incumbents of the various roles (diplomats, military officers, tax officials) must be recruited to these roles and learn to perform in them. New roles are created and new personnel 'broken in'. (Almond and Powell, 1966: 29-30)

Now, political development refers to the following basic functions: capabilities, conversion processes, system maintenance and adaptation functions. The concept of development has two modes: positive or negative development depending on the direction of change in these basic functions.

A significant addition to the 1960 framework was the elaboration in the 1966 volume of the conditions for and expressions of political development. Almond and Powell identify four types of challenge to a political system: state building, nation building, participation and distribution. And five factors are singled out as important in the analysis of political development. First, there is the nature of the problems that the political system faces, e.g. demands for participation or national unification or the nature of the pressures that a system faces. Second, we have the resources that a system can draw upon under various circumstances. Third, political development is conditioned by the developmental trends in other social systems, in the economy or in the international environment. Moreover, a fourth factor is the nature of the political system itself, and its capacity to handle demands and mobilize support. Fifth, there is the choice variable as determined by the response of political élites to various kinds of challenges.

In the concluding chapter Almond and Powell propose their theory of political development which has been the target of much criticism. The crucial notion of level of development refers to three aspects of structure: differentiation, autonomy and secularization. The basic theoretical proposition claims that the more modern or developed a polity is, the more it is characterized by differentiation, autonomy and secularization. Almond and Powell state:

> The basic theoretical statement here is that the development of higher levels of system capabilities is dependent upon the development of greater structural differentiation and cultural secularization. In a more specifically structural sense, it is predicted that higher capabilities depend upon the emergence of 'rational' bureaucratic organizations. (Almond and Powell, 1966: 323)

The 1966 theory aroused two kinds of reaction: an acceptance that sometimes led to dogma or a rejection that was sometimes sharp. The Almond conception of political development was much influenced by the general theory of structural-functionalism as interpreted, for example, by Frances X. Sutton in 'Social Theory and Comparative Politics' (1963) building on the several volumes of Talcott Parsons and his associates in the late 1940s and during the 1950s (Parsons and Shils, 1951, Parsons 1951; Levy, 1952; Parsons and Smelser, 1956). The general rebuttal of sociological functionalism contributed to the severe reaction against the Almond framework.

To sum up, the structural-functional approach to political development focused on the notion of system capacity and structural differentiation and its modes. Modern political systems are more developed because they have more differentiated structures. But this is all that the functionalist approach has to say about political development — and it is not terribly striking or surprising. Moreover, how is this concept of political development to be measured? There seem to exist a number of interesting change phenomena that fall outside the scope of the functionalist approach.

The idea that political development has something to do with system capacity and structural differentiation may be taken out of its functionalist webs. As a matter of fact there are a number of scholars who include these two concepts when defining the concept of political development without adhering to functionalism.

Indeed, the typical approach to political development has been to mention more than one defining characteristic while leaving it open as to whether or not the various definition properties covary or not. In his *Aspects of Political Development* (1966) Lucien Pye surveyed the literature to find no less than ten key properties: (a) the political prerequisites of economic development; (b) the politics typical of industrial societies; (c) political modernization; (d) the operation of a nation-state; (e) administrative and legal development; (f) mass mobilization and participation; (g) the building of democracy; (h) stability and orderly change; (i) mobilization and power; (j) one aspect of a multidimensional process of social change.

How could so many dimensions of a complex process of political change be reduced to manageable proportions? Pye states that '*capacity* of a political system...is related to the outputs of a political system and the extent to which the political system can affect the rest of society and economy' and that 'running through much of the discussion of political development is that of differentiation and specialization', implying that 'offices and agencies tend to have their distinct and limited functions, and there is an equivalent of a division of labor within the realm of government' (Pye, 1966: 46-47). It is easier to measure political system capacity than political system differentiation in terms of empirical indicators.

James S. Coleman singles out differentiation and capacity besides equality as typical of political development. He states:

> *political development* can be regarded as the acquisition by a political system of a consciously-sought and qualitatively new and enhanced, political capacity as manifested in the successful institutionalization of (1) new patterns of integration regulating and containing the tensions and conflicts produced by increased differentiation, and (2) new patterns of participation and resource distribution adequately responsive to the demands generated by the imperatives of equality. (Coleman, 1965: 15)

It seems obvious that the Coleman addition of equality and participation to capacity and differentiation implies a risk as it need not go together with the two other aspects of development. The tie between capacity and differentiation is far stronger than between the first two and the third: participation. However, even the association between capacity and differentiation may be doubted as the first refers more to the output side of the political system, whereas the second stands for some property of the structure of the system. In any case, it remains to be clarified how capacity and differentiation are to be measured empirically.

To identify political development with system capacity and system differentiation implies that political development is somehow a function of an increase in state involvement: the stronger the state the greater political development. However, when political development is identified with autonomy and system differentiation it seems as if it implies less state involvement. The less encompassing the nature of the state and the more subsystem autonomy there is, the more political development we have. To allow for this possibility of a contradiction in the concept of political development the set of indicators measuring the increase in state involvement should be separated from the set of indices measuring the decrease in state involvement or heteronomy.

If political development is identified with participation or equality one seems to move along a different line of argument than when one talks about state involvement. At the same time one should beware of a distinction between participation and equality as they need not go together. If political development does mean both state involvement and autonomy, this simply reflects that both processes of change may be considered valuable. If this is so, then perhaps what matters is modernization in general? We must take up the general approach to political development in the form of modernization, as Samuel Eisenstadt defined it, as a

> process of change towards those types of social, economic and political systems that have developed in western Europe and North America from the

seventeenth century to the nineteenth and have then spread to other European countries and in the nineteenth and twentieth centuries to the South American, Asian and African continents. (Eisenstadt, 1966: 1)

Social process approach

It is quite plausible to regard political development as a reflection of more general processes of social development. The theory of modernization states that political development is an offspring of more general developmental trends — industrialization, urbanization and mass literacy — moving a society from a traditional state to a modern one. There is a number of alternative versions of the modernization theme (Binder, 1986).

Marion J. Levy's *Modernization and the Structure of Societies* (1966) takes a broad approach to modernization and its modes. Levy states: 'A society will be considered more or les modernized to the extent that its members use inanimate sources of power and/or use tools to multiply the effects of their efforts' (Levy, 1966:1). Such a broad definition of modernization turns the theme into a general account of the evolution of culture and civilization. It is no wonder that Levy offers little in terms of middle-range hypothesis about the interaction between political change and more specific processes of socio-economic transformations. The modernization theme includes efforts to be more specific. Often the modernization theme was more oriented towards a static comparison of two kinds of society or polity — traditional or modern — than towards the process of change from one to the other.

One famous book on the modernization theme was *The Passing of Traditional Society: Modernizing the Middle East* by David Lerner (1958). Lerner presented a model distinguishing between three ideal type orientations — modern, transitional and traditional — on the basis of the following criteria: literacy, urbanism, media participation and empathy (Lerner, 1958: 71). The process of modernization is the movement away from traditional society which involves three basic phases: urbanization, literacy and media participation. The special contribution of Lerner to the modernization theme is the emphasis on communication mechanisms which mould the transition process. Political development refers to mass participation involving the use of modern media systems which have replaced the old, oral systems.

Lerner identifies four dimensions in modernization which are correlated to a considerable extent: urbanization, literacy, media participation and political participation. These findings refer to the 1950s and it may be questioned whether these phenomena really are interrelated today. It is an open question whether extensive political participation typical of democracies does indeed always follow from or is accompanied by high levels of literacy. Moreover, it is possible to look for expressions of modernization other than political participation. And we may regard other types of political change as equally basic.

In Lerner's work the concept of transitionals plays a major role. They stand between modern man and traditional man and they face the serious task of defining the process of modernization. They may constitute an élite that specifies the goals and means of the process of modernization — spokesman and administrator. For an interpretation reminiscent of the Lerner distinctions see Pye's separation between administrator, agitator and broker (1958).

The article by Karl Deutsch, 'Social Mobilization and Political Development' (1961) was an attempt to quantify the often diffuse concepts in the modernization theme. Frequently, modernization theory simply employs a pure distinction between two ideal types to portray the meaning of modernization. However, some authors adopting this approach attempted to model the modernization process by means of quantitative equations. Two different models were employed: one describing the general process of modernization or the coming of a Western-type society — industrialization, urbanization and mass mobilization. The other model placed the modern polity in a context where it was preceded by the process of social modernization. Typically, political development is looked upon as a reflection of more basic socio-economic transformations. Social mobilization denotes, as Deutsch writes:

> a concept which brackets together a number of more specific processes of change, such as changes of residence, of occupation, of social setting, of face-to-face associates, of institutions, roles, and ways of acting, of experiences and expectations, and finally of personal memories, habits and needs, including the need for new patterns of group affiliation and new images of personal identity. Singly, and even more in their cumulative impact, these changes tend to influence and sometimes to transform political behavior. (Deutsch, 1961: 493)

Whereas functionalism focused on the static differences between two types of society or two kinds of polity, the modernization approach emphasized the dynamic processes of change from one type of society to another. However, the exact implications of social change for political change remained to be specified. At this very point Deutsch was content to point out some possible political consequences of processes of broad social change but did not commit himself to something more definitive about such social processes.

The Politics of Modernization by David Apter (1965) elaborated on qualitative modernization theory by explicitly focusing on the variety of political system responses to the problems of the transformation from traditional to modern society characterizing Third World events. These polity-type responses include: a neomercantilist state, a mobilization state and a reconciliation state (Apter, 1965: 420).

Modernization

Some authors really tried to specify more definitely what modernization was all about. The problem involved basically two fundamental questions. On the one hand, there is the interpretation of the transformation of European society from feudalism to industrial life. On the other hand, we have the statement of the major differences between the industrialized world — the OECD countries as well as the Communist world — and the Third World LDC countries. A model was searched for that would solve these two different problems simultaneously. Sutton identified the following Parsonian characteristics of a traditional society versus a modern society (Figure 4.1):

Figure 4.1 Traditional versus modern society

Agricultural society:
1. Predominance of ascriptive, particularistic, diffuse patterns.
2. Stable local groups and limited spatial mobility.
3. Relatively simple and 'occupational' differentiation.
4. A 'deferential' stratification system of diffuse impact.

Modern industrial society:
1. Predominance of universalistic, specific, achievement norms.
2. High degree of social mobility.
3. Well-developed occupational system, insulated from other social systems.
4. Egalitarian class system based on generalized patterns of achievement.
5. Prevalence of associations, i.e. functionally specific non-ascriptive structures.

Source: Sutton (1963).

Modernization theorists argued that the transition from one kind of society to another kind implies a radically different polity. In *Political Modernization in Japan and Turkey* (1964) Rustow and Ward identified a list of properties of the so-called modern polity: (a) a highly differentiated and functionally specific system of governmental organization; (b) high degree of integration within this governmental structure; (c) the prevalence of rational and secular procedures for the making of political decisions; (d) the large volume, wide range and high efficacy of its political and administrative decisions; (e) a widespread and effective sense of popular identification with the history, territority and national identity of the state; (f) widespread popular interest and involvement in the political system, though not necessarily in the decision-making aspects thereof; (g) the allocation of political roles by achievement rather than ascription; (h) judicial and regulatory techniques based upon a predominantly secular and impersonal system of law (Rustow and Ward, 1964: 6-7).

Although the Rustow and Ward identification meant a substantial effort at making development theory more concrete and less abstruse, a number of questions remain unanswered. There is the problem of change: how is a modern polity typically introduced? There is also the problem of causality: is political modernization determined by socio-economic transformation? Moreover, there is the problem of classification: do communist systems have modern polities? In order to approach these problems development theory turned to comparative history.

Political development as institutionalization

What is truly modern? Are modernity and tradition always mutually exclusive? If modernization is what political change is all about, especially if it is conducive to a morally appealing predicament — political development — then we need to know what a modern society or polity amounts to. Capitalism or socialism? Public sector expansion or market values? Occidental rationalism or oriental rejection of mechanistic atomism? Since it is difficult to identify what change is truly development-conducive to modernity, then perhaps political development is the capacity to cope with processes of development whatever modernism may amount to? Samuel Huntington broke the spell of the modernization theme by equating valuable political change with growth of order or of political institutions whatever their value (O'Brien, 1972).

The idea that institutionalization is basic to political development has been advanced by Huntington in a number of articles. Let us follow the presentation in Huntington's article on 'Political Development and Political Decay' (1965). He states:

> For this purpose, it is useful to distinguish political development from modernization and to identify political development with the institutionalization of political organizations and procedures. Rapid increases in mobilization and participation, the principal political aspects of modernization, undermine political institutions. Rapid modernization, in

> brief, produces not political development, but political decay. (Huntington, 1965: 386)

This is a straightforward criticism of the modernization theme, but we must take a close look at what Huntington puts in the place of modernization: what is institutionalization? Huntington writes:

> Institutionalization is the process by which organizations and processes acquire value and stability. The level of institutionalization of any political system can be defined by the adaptability, complexity, autonomy and coherence of its organizations and procedures. (ibid.: 394)

These defining concepts — adaptability, complexity, autonomy and coherence — are very abstract and we need more information about how they are measured and then how these measures may be added together into a single index of institutionalization as political development. Is it really the case that increased institutionalization must result in more of adaptability or autonomy? Huntington states about adaptability and complexity:

> Adaptability can be measured by chronological age, leadership successions, generational changes, and functional changes. Complexity can be measured by the number and diversity of organizational subunits and by the number and diversity of functions performed by the organizations. (ibid.: 404-5)

To measure autonomy is more difficult, states Huntington, but it can be measured by the distinctiveness of the norms and values of the organization and by the personnel controls — cooptation, penetration, purging — between the organization and other groups and by the extent to which the organization controls material resources. Also coherence seems to be complex as Huntington requires lots of information to be available. It could be measured by the number of contested successions in relation to total successions, by the number of cleavages among leaders and members, by the occurrence of alienation and dissent within the organization as well as by the loyalty of organization members. (Huntington, 1965: 404-5)

Following this suggestion as to the measurement of political development as institutionalization, it is no exaggeration to state that this entails a complex procedure. And we still need more information about how these four measures are to be combined into a single measure: simple addition or perhaps some other mathematical procedure.

Reviewing the literature on political development in 1975 (Huntington and Dominguez, 1975), Huntington seems to have become aware of the difficulties with the proposed approach to political development. He declares:

> On subsequent reflection, however, there did not seem to be much gained by trying to identify one rather diffuse, controversial, and value-laden concept (like political development) with a somewhat more specific, analytical and value-free concept (like institutionalization). (Huntington and Dominguèz, 1975: 47)

Instead Huntington formulates a number of hypotheses about the linkages between socio-economic modernization and political development. The process of modernization is assumed to have an impact on the:

1. level of institutionalization;
2. degree of modernity or tradition of the organization, procedure or political system; and
3. concentration or pluralism in the distribution of power.

Huntington here comes close to a repetition of some of the basic ideas of the modernization approach. The emergence of a modern polity implies the rationalization of authority, the expansion of political participation and the differentiation of structures. However, Huntington also argues that socio-economic modernization implies the destruction of the traditional political system, meaning that we have to recognize both political decay and political birth. Institutionalization is but one pattern of political change and Huntington is clearly aware of the possibility that political change may imply the failure to develop proper institutions. He states:

> Thus, as socioeconomic modernization takes place, either the existing political institutions adapt to meet the new needs, or the political institutions are themselves changed into or replaced by new political institutions more capable of meeting those needs, or the modernization of the political system grinds to a halt and severe stresses develop as a result of the gap between continuing socioeconomic modernization and aborted political modernization. (Huntington and Dominguez, 1975: 54)

Huntington still conceives of political development as related to modernization. Instead of looking at political development as a derivative of socio-economic modernization or as functionally related to modernization, Huntington approaches modernization as presenting a set of major challenges to the political system. And successful modernization requires some basic transformations of the political system, namely institutionalization of the patterns of behaviour that introduce a modern polity replacing a traditional one. The idea that political development is related to crisis phenomena has stimulated a so-called crisis approach to political development.

The crisis approach

Political development may not be interpreted as deterministic change towards some desirable end state, but as the successful path to some temporary predicament. Basic social change means unrest and reorientation; perhaps political development is the polity's response to these various crisis phenomena as Almond argues in *Crisis, Choice and Change: Historical Studies of Political Development* (1973).

This novel theory of political development was elaborated by Leonard Binder in *Crises and Sequences in Political Development* (1971), summarizing some of the volumes of a major research project on political development conducted by the American Social Science Research Council in the 1960s. He states:

> If we re-examine these five areas of critical change, or these five crises of political development, the crisis of identity, the crisis of legitimacy, the crisis of participation, the crisis of distribution, and the crisis of penetration, we will find that all five types of change may occur without any concomitant strengthening of the political institutions of the country affected. (Binder, 1971: 65)

Thus political development may not be order or institutionalization *per se*, but it is related to a successful institutional response — élites coping with challenges maintaining the valuable entity of order whether rightist or leftist — to various crises.

Binder points out in a 1986 article that the concept of political development tends to differ as a function of how one perceives the institutional response to crisis. He separates between:

1. the liberal theory of development: democracy and equality as systems response;
2. the state theory: increased control, planning and technology;
3. the revolutionary theory: mobilization of the masses and socialist transformation;
4. the dependence theory: increased centre-periphery dependency.

Some identify the concept of political development with democracy, others with étatism, and still others with revolution and socialism.

Independently of each other, Almond and Rustow suggested a new approach to political development underlining choice and response by actors. It also involved a much broader perspective on political change as the concept was removed from the grand social theory approach of modernism versus traditionalism. Instead Almond and Rustow identified various kinds of processes of change involving political unrest and the conscious response to political instability by leaders and institutions (Almond et al, 1973; Rustow, 1970).

Brunner's and Brewer's *Organized Complexity: Empirical Theories of Political Development* (1971) belongs to the search for an alternative approach to the outdated versions of functionalism and modernization. Attempting to explain processes of change in modern Turkey and the Philippines, Brunner and Brewer introduced a number of partial models including factors which the political élite could manipulate, again underlining choice and response to political system crisis.

Development as stability or instability

There are two main implications arising from the consequences of socio-economic changes such as modernization of the society for the stability of the polity. One popular theme implies that political development leads to more stability as political systems adapt to the new exigencies. Thus we find attempts to measure political development by various indicators of political stability (Sigelman, 1971: 36-7): government stability, political participation by the military, interest articulation by anomic groups, political leadership, interest articulation by associational groups, and the character of bureaucracy.

Alternatively, another major theme implies that typical of political development is instability as there is a search for indicators of political development in phenomena of political instability: coups d'état, major constitutional changes, cabinet changes, and changes in effective executive (Banks, 1972). No doubt the state of the concept of political development is bewildering. No less conspicuous is the 180-degree reversal of development as conducive to underdevelopment.

The radical approach

If political development is the outcome of processes of change that present real challenges to political élites, then could it be that these social and economic change processes result in undesirable outcomes? Perhaps the overall movement is one towards political underdevelopment?

In *Capitalism and Underdevelopment in Latin America* (1967), André Gunder Frank introduced a quite novel paradigm for interpreting broad processes of social, economic and political change — partly inspired by earlier marxist interpretations by Baran and Sweezy, among others. The crucial distinctions in the Frank framework are the ones between undeveloped and underdeveloped and between centre and periphery. The transition from traditionalism to modernism is one of movement from an undeveloped stage towards underdevelopment — the opposite theme to that of the modernization theorists. The process of underdevelopment is governed by the logic of the interaction between a world capitalist centre and Third World periphery in terms of which the predicament of the so-called developing nations become worse. How do we test this new radical theory of development as underdevelopment? Does it imply something more specific about political change?

According to the theory of world system analysis proposed by Immanuel Wallerstein (1974, 1979), processes of change in various parts of the world are interdependent in terms of a more or less zero-sum game. The centre of the capitalist world, including the East European countries, are the winners in this world system interaction where the poor Third World countries are the losers. The basic criterion of change is the increase in inequality between these nations and within the peripheral countries. Wallerstein looks upon development as being determined by commodity production for profit in a world market which is characterized by various forms of labour exploitation based on asymmetrical power relations between powerful states and peripheral areas.

Thus development results in inequality, inflation and unemployment in the Third World. What are the implications for political development? Although the radical approach to development has resulted in an abundant literature about capitalism and the Third World (Chilcote and Johnson, 1983), there is perhaps not a distinct radical theory about political development. In it we still find the same hope for some kind of desirable political change process.

Thus far, the radical theory of development as the underdevelopment of an undeveloped area has offered little in terms of suggestions about the political implications of this process of underdevelopment. The Frank-Wallerstein theme is mainly a socio-economic theory. When political development is discussed along the lines of this theme the approach is exclusively normative. Ocampo and Johnson, on the other hand, define political development in the following way without tying it to ideas about how to reverse the trend towards development: 'Development involves the liberation of man from condition of exploitation and oppression. Politics is the means of human liberation' (Ocampo and Johnson, 1972: 424).

Underdevelopment theory has been criticized as being too deterministic and general in describing everything with the centre-periphery concepts as well as too little action-oriented (Phillips, 1978; Taylor, 1987). What would a real test of the radical theory of development amount to? First, the theory predicts that poor nations or peripheral regions will score low on various economic indicators: inequality, inflation, unemployment and public sector deficit spending. Second, it would claim that real political development is a function of the power of the left in state and society, because the right would only defend the status quo of underdevelopment. Since we are focusing on the political aspects of development, we will only discuss the last mentioned implication. The interaction of social, economic and political development will be treated separately.

Variety of dimensions

It may be stated that the concept of political development appears to be ambiguous. It remains to be asked whether it is multidimensional, what the various dimensions are and how these could be employed for further inquiry into political change. It may refer to both social and political phenomena or to only political phenomena. Rich in a value-loaded sense, it may refer to some desirable pattern of political change, e.g. towards democracy. Or it may mean some general institutional pattern or institutional response. It may cover both successful institutional change and institutional failure. More neutrally it may refer to both political stability and political instability. How the radical approach to development is to be handled in terms of indicators is an open question.

It may be worthwhile to introduce some distinctions and then try to elaborate on how these distinctions relate to each other at the measurement level. Thus we have a large number of variables related to the five aspects of development derived from the literature:

1. Democratic development:
   - democracy score
   - human rights
   - political role of the military
   - party system fractionalization or pluralism
   - political or economic discrimination
   - party system functions

2. Capacity:
   - government consumption
   - general or central government expenditure
   - military personnel and military expenditure
   - war involvement post-Second World War

3. Institutionalization:
   - institutional sclerosis
   - modern leadership, year of introduction
   - modern leadership, year in effect
   - State status

4. Stability:
   - political strike

- violence
- protest

5. Radical orientation:
   - left strength
   - left in government

These variables may be measured by means of a large number of indicators, which in turn may reduced to a set of measurement indices by means of a standard data reduction technique — factor analysis. Testing a theory implies a search for those implications which may refute the theory if the data fail to corroborate the implications. What does a serious test of the political development theme amount to in terms of feasible empirical research strategies?

Data for the variables listed above are available for some seventy countries in a cross-section referring roughly to the 1970s. We refrain from including any Communist systems, since the focus is on the nature of the overall political change involved in moving from an undeveloped to a developed situation as this is conceived in the analysis of the Third World countries. Some empirical propositions may be derived from the theoretical literature:

1. The country variation on the various dimensions of political development in this period are unrelated to each other.
2. There is a substantial variation between countries or categories of countries on each of the different political development dimensions.

The countries covered as well as the indicators employed are rendered in Appendix 4.1. The analysis of the data is mainly an analysis of variance based on standard data reduction techniques, factor analyses of indicators of the various concepts identified above.

Dimensions of political development

Since there is much ambiguity as well as controversy surrounding the concept of democracy, stating a proper set of indicators for the measurement of various levels of democracy is no easy task. In the literature there are several attempts at deriving indices measuring various aspects of the democratic nature of a polity. They range from discrimination indices over human and civil rights indices to party system indices, including also a measure of the overall role of the military establishment in national politics (Table 4.1). In order to reduce the amount of information about this aspect of political development we resort to a standard data reduction technique.

Table 4.1. Factor analysis of democracy indicators

Indicators	Factor loadings		Communality
	Factor 1	Factor 2	
Political discrim.	−0.01	0.94	0.88
Economic discrim.	0.08	0.92	0.86
Human rights c. 1980	0.81	−0.05	0.66
Democracy c. 1965	0.87	0.05	0.76
Democracy c. 1960	0.81	0.07	0.65
Party system functions	0.81	0.03	0.66
Role of military	−0.71	0.21	0.54
Political rights	−0.91	−0.13	0.85
Civil rights	−0.92	−0.12	0.86
Party syst fract '70s	0.66	0.17	0.46
Party syst fract '60s	0.68	0.42	0.64
Explained variance	53.6%	17.5%	

Most of the indicators on the extent of democracy of a political system identify one single dimension. The exceptions are the discrimination indices which appear to vary somewhat independently of the democracy scores. The explanation is that the political as well as the economic discrimination indices measure the intensity of discrimination, which means that countries with large immigrant groups will score high on these indices though they may also score high on the amount of political and human rights for the citizens of these countries. In the subsequent analysis we employ a general democracy index based on those indicators which go together in Table 4.1.

Political system capacity is expressed in various actual ways or it may constitute a potential that may be drawn upon in times of exceptional events. Different factors in a society may be conducive to polity strength or state capacity. The indicators on political capacity range from the size of the population — a source of great power ambitions — over actual involvement in war activities — one traditional expression of political ambitions to display strength — to ordinary measures of the size of the state or the public sector. Since small states and peaceful societies that are welfare states have big governments we should expect to find that the capacity indicators do not co-vary (Table 4.2).

As expected, capacity in a political context may mean two very different things: welfare spending or military effort as war involvement.

Thus we include two different capacity indices: a big government index versus a war experience index.

Table 4.2. Factor analysis of capacity indicators

Indicators	Factor loadings		Communality
	Factor 1	Factor 2	
Military personnel	0.16	0.65	0.45
Military expenditure	0.28	0.80	0.72
War involvement	0.05	0.79	0.62
Central gov exp. 70s	0.79	0.45	0.83
Central gov exp. 70s	0.83	0.45	0.89
General gov exp. 70s	0.92	0.09	0.85
Public consumption	0.88	0.05	0.78
Explained variance	55.5%	18.1%	

The concept of institutionalization may appear to be abstract, but the truth is that it is generally agreed that the measurement of the concept refers to state consolidation and nation building (Rokkan et al., 1970; Tilly, 1975). On the one hand, there is the introduction of modernized leadership at a crucial point of time in the history of a country. On the other hand, we have the official recognition of the state in international affairs. The general index of institutional sclerosis is a recent attempt to measure the period of time of uninterrupted organizational growth in a society suggested in order to tap the strength of so-called distributional coalitions or special interest organizations (Olson, 1982) (Table 4.3).

Table 4.3. Factor analysis of institutionalization indicators

Indicators	*Factor loadings* *Factor 1*	*Communality*
Modernized leadership: introduction	0.94	0.88
Modernized leadership: in effect	0.84	0.71
Institutional sclerosis	0.93	0.87
Qualified as a state	0.82	0.68
Member of international system	0.84	0.71
Explained variance	76.9%	

The finding is that institutionalization would seem to cause no problem at the measurement level. Thus we employ an institutionalization score.

Political development would necessarily imply political change, but the opposite is not true. And where there is polity change there may also be the typical expressions of political instability: protest or violent protest as well as the occurrence of violence in state and society in general. Of course, the first type of phenomenon may be accompanied by the second kind and vice versa (Table 4.4).

Table 4.4. Factor analysis of stability indicators

Indicators	Factor loadings		Communality
	Factor 1	Factor 2	
Protest demonstrations	0.73	0.30	0.62
Riots	0.83	0.27	0.76
Political strikes	0.82	−0.06	0.67
Armed attacks	0.54	0.72	0.81
Assassinations	0.03	0.87	0.76
Deaths from domestic violence	0.18	0.83	0.72
Explained variance	52.4%	20.3%	

The various indicators on protest and violence are both interrelated and independent to some extent. We may distinguish between two rather distinct factors: non-violent protest, on the one hand, and the occurrence of violence on the other. Thus we derive a protest index and a violence index both of which will be employed for further analysis.

The last-mentioned dimension is theoretically somewhat dubious, but it refers to the hypothesis central to the underdevelopment theme that social and economic development can only take place if the polity is a radical one. Various indicators may be used to tap the strength of the left in a country — from election outcomes over trade union-organization to leftist participation in government (Table 4.5). For the purposes of this analysis it is enough to single out one radical orientation index.

Table 4.5. Factor analysis of radical orientation indicators

Indicators	*Factor Loadings* *Factor 1*	*Communality*
Communist party support	0.84	0.71
Socialist-communist support	0.94	0.88
Tradition of socialist government	0.71	0.51
Explained variance	70.1%	

Interrelationships between dimensions

To what extent are the indices now derived really independent in relation to data about some seventy countries for the 1970s? Table 4.6 presents some clues as to the answer of the problem of multidimensionality of the political development concept.

Table 4.6. Correlation matrix for derived political development dimensions

	(1)	(2)	(3)	(4)	(5)	(6)	(7)
Democracy (1)	1.00	0.44	−0.35	−0.62	0.06	0.09	−0.22
Polity capacity (2)		1.00	0.03	−0.26	0.30	−0.07	−0.17
Military involvement (3)			1.00	−0.02	−0.11	0.16	0.22
Institutionalization (4)				1.00	−0.08	−0.41	−0.14
Radical orientation (5)					1.00	−0.01	0.09
Protest (6)						1.00	0.48
Violence (7)							1.00

The overall finding is that it is striking how little the seven indices on various aspects of political development correlate. There is hardly any evidence of the notion of some general concept of political development that would constitute the common core of the various polity characteristics listed as development in the literature. This means that one faces the decision whether or not 'political development' as a key term should not be replaced by a whole set of different words, one for each of the separate dimensions identified. Actually, there are one or two cases of moderate interaction: violence and protest on the one hand, as stated above, and on the other democracy and institutionalization reflecting the long lifetime of the regimes of the Western political systems that survived the authoritarian challenge during the Second World War.

We will now go on to look at the variation in the scores on democracy, big government, war involvement, institutionalization, protest and violence, as well as on radical orientation in four subsets of nations: the OECD world, the Latin American world and the sets of African and Asian countries. How do the country scores on these seven dimensions vary between and within these sets?

Comparative analysis of political development

Any interpretation of the concept of political development may combine the factual and the normative elements. To some scholars political development means a desirable predicament whatever the likelihood of its occurrence, for example, a dominant position of the left as the starting point for real development of an undeveloped or underdeveloped country. To others there is a balance between feasibility and desirability as, for example, in the argument that democracy is the result of true political development. Or such a balance identifying recurrent matters of fact with political ideology values may be expressed in the notion that political development implies increased state involvement in the form of big government or strength in military ventures. Finally, the conception of political development may be almost exclusively oriented towards factual matters whatever their intrinsic value may be, for example, the institutionalization interpretation or the instability — stability theme.

The mix of fact and value in the concept of political development may appear troublesome but it does not preclude that the various dimensions included in the umbrella idea of political development may be used to point out some pertinent country differences. Table 4.7 reports on an analysis of variance of the first of the seven political development indices.

Table 4.7. Average democracy scores (1)

Latin America (N=15)	48.6
OECD countries (N=24)	60.1
Africa (N=15)	40.7
Asia (N=13)	43.7
E^2= 0.65	

Note: The democracy score is based upon the following indicators: human rights; democracy, 1960, 1965; party system; role of the military; political and civil rights as well as party system fractionalization, 1960s, 1970s.

Politically developed countries in the sense of democratic regimes are not unsurprisingly to be found in the set of OECD countries. The experience of democracy is particularly low in the sets of African and Asian countries whereas some Central and Latin American countries hover between authoritarianism and democracy in a circular time frame. The high eta-coefficient indicates that the differences between these categories of countries are larger than the differences within the same categories. Let us take a closer look at the occurrence of democractic regime characteristics in the world around 1980 (Table 4.8).

Countries that score low on the democracy index within the OECD set of nations are the ones that have recently experienced the dismantling of an authoritarian regime: Spain in 1975, Portugal in 1974 and Greece in 1974. The status of democratic institutions in Turkey is still precarious, to say the least. In Asia there are a few countries which have a democratic

Table 4.8. Democracy scores (2)

OECD		*Asia*		*Latin America*	
USA	60.54	Iran	37.57	Dominican Rep	47.81
Canada	62.53	Iraq	29.65	Mexico	49.43
UK	61.91	Egypt	41.33	El Salvador	47.29
Ireland	60.98	Jordan	34.30	Costa Rica	60.34
Netherlands	63.62	Korea Rep	45.68	Panama	45.44
Belgium	63.19	India	56.59	Colombia	54.25
Luxembourg	62.48	Pakistan	38.57	Venezuela	59.10
France	61.44	Sri Lanka	58.48	Ecuador	48.22
Switzerland	63.67	Thailand	37.69	Peru	46.85
Spain	44.07	Malaysia	52.16	Brazil	51.06
Portugal	47.90	Singapore	47.91	Bolivia	40.22
FRG	60.59	Philippines	48.81	Paraguay	40.11
Austria	61.97	Indonesia	39.97	Chile	48.47
Italy	61.65			Argentina	41.62
Greece	53.36	Mean	43.7	Uruguay	49.12
Finland	62.07				
Sweden	62.89			Mean	48.6
Norway	63.37	*Africa*			
Denmark	63.46				
Iceland	63.18	Senegal	44.84	Madagascar	45.72
Turkey	51.83	Liberia	41.20	Morocco	43.87
Japan	61.52	Ghana	35.91	Algeria	34.66
Australia	61.59	Cameroon	42.61	Tunisia	42.77
New Zealand	61.97	Nigeria	42.28		
		Zaïre	35.18	Mean	40.7
Mean	60.1	Kenya	42.67		
		Tanzania	41.48		
		Ethiopia	30.66		
		Zambia	46.45		
		Malawi	39.84		

Note: The democracy score is based on the following indicators: human rights; democracy, 1960, 1965; party system; role of the military; political and civil rights as well as party system fractionalization, 1960s, 1970s. The Z-scores order the countries from a low degree of democracy to a high degree of democracy.

tradition though not a long one: India, Sri Lanka and Malaysia. There is hardly any country in Africa that could qualify as a democracy whereas there are a few cases in Central and Latin America: Costa Rica, Venezuela and Colombia.

The hypothesis that political development is political system capacity implies that countries with large public sectors are the developed

Table 4.9. Average polity capacity scores (1)

Latin America (N=15)	42.2
OECD countries (N=24)	57.4
Africa (N=15)	49.3
Asia (N=13)	47.5
E^2= 0.36	

Note: The polity capacity score is based upon the following indicators: central government 1970s; general government expenditures 1970s; public consumption.

nations (Table 4.9). Extensive public expenditure patterns are to be found in either welfare states providing citizens with the public provision of several services including social security or in those Leviathan states where for one reason or another military expenditures are the reason for comprehensive public budgets. Let us look more closely at the country variation (Table 4.10).

Table 4.10. Polity capacity scores (2)

OECD		*Asia*		*Latin America*	
USA	51.87	Iran	61.16	Dominican Rep	38.46
Canada	65.41	Iraq	52.40	Mexico	40.06
UK	64.08	Egypt	70.35	El Salvador	40.16
Ireland	62.07	Jordan	57.79	Costa Rica	47.33
Netherlands	65.80	Korea Rep	41.96	Panama	50.09
Belgium	59.06	India	36.46	Colombia	32.91
Luxembourg	56.43	Pakistan	40.50	Venezuela	49.52
France	55.74	Sri Lanka	44.76	Ecuador	42.61
Switzerland	52.02	Thailand	39.77	Peru	44.59
Spain	41.60	Malaysia	55.09	Brazil	41.84
Portugal	45.79	Singapore	42.92	Bolivia	41.19
FRG	61.07	Philippines	35.02	Paraguay	32.05
Austria	59.83	Indonesia	39.59	Chile	48.18
Italy	57.05			Argentina	40.11
Greece	47.66	Mean	47.50	Uruguay	44.22
Finland	61.92				
Sweden	75.98			Mean	42.20
Norway	65.13	*Africa*			
Denmark	69.08				
Iceland	51.75	Senegal	47.34		
Turkey	45.67	Liberia	42.33		
Japan	43.60	Ghana	44.49		

Table 4.10 continued

OECD		*Africa*	
Australia	58.00	Cameroon	44.93
New Zealand	60.33	Nigeria	43.54
		Zaïre	53.26
Mean	57.40	Kenya	47.64
		Tanzania	49.39
		Ethiopia	41.81
		Zambia	61.64
		Malawi	45.22
		Madacasgar	51.85
		Morocco	56.69
		Algeria	54.29
		Tunisia	55.70
		Mean	49.30

Note: The polity capacity score is based on the following indicators: central government expenditure, 1970s; general government expenditures, 1970s; public consumption. The Z-scores order the countries from low to high according to extent of polity capacity.

Not surprisingly Sweden scores highest in the OECD set, sometimes considered the OECD model for a future welfare state. The Scandinavian countries score high generally whereas southern European nations score rather low. The countries on the other side of the Atlantic also come out high on this dimension but for different reasons. The high score of the United States reflects its military commitment whereas the high scores of the other nations indicate high welfare spending. As we move on to consider political system capacity in the Third World it must be recognized that the cause of big budgets as a percentage of overall national resources is without exception military spending: Egypt, Iran, Iraq, Jordan, Morocco, Tunisia, Algeria, Zambia and Zaïre (Table 4.11).

Table 4.11. Average military involvement scores (1)

Latin America (N=15)	46.2
OECD countries (N=24)	49.1
Africa (N=15)	46.1
Asia (N=13)	62.8

$E^2 = 0.32$

Note: The military involvement score is based upon the following indicators: military personnel; military expenditures; war involvement.

Table 4.12. Military involvement scores (2)

OECD		*Asia*		*Latin America*	
USA	77.72	Iran	69.78	Domican Rep	47.17
Canada	40.94	Iraq	74.78	Mexico	42.45
UK	57.14	Egypt	90.58	El Salvador	47.34
Ireland	41.32	Jordan	81.19	Costa Rica	39.68
Netherlands	48.17	Korea Rep	63.90	Panama	42.95
Belgium	52.67	India	60.29	Colombia	47.01
Luxembourg	37.03	Pakistan	64.31	Venezuela	43.96
France	56.78	Sri Lanka	39.62	Ecuador	46.56
Switzerland	43.18	Thailand	55.45	Peru	50.77
Spain	49.74	Malaysia	55.05	Brazil	43.59
Portugal	71.87	Singapore	58.41	Bolivia	48.68
FRG	44.70	Philippines	50.22	Paraguay	48.40
Austria	41.62	Indonesia	52.89	Chile	52.31
Italy	45.64			Argentina	46.88
Greece	63.33	Mean	62.80	Uruguay	45.39
Finland	43.97				
Sweden	42.77			Mean	46.20
Norway	45.16	*Africa*			
Denmark	41.63				
Iceland	35.93	Senegal	42.16		
Turkey	63.69	Liberia	42.72		
Japan	43.60	Ghana	54.91		
Australia	47.69	Cameroon	41.00		
New Zealand	42.11	Nigeria	51.34		
		Zaïre	52.89		
Mean	49.10	Kenya	41.20		
		Tanzania	45.29		
		Ethiopia	52.05		
		Zambia	38.28		
		Malawi	40.61		
		Madagascar	40.07		
		Morocco	55.67		
		Algeria	46.87		
		Tunisia	45.84		
		Mean	46.10		

Note: The military involvement score is based on the following indicators: military personnel; military expenditure; war involvement. The Z-scores order the countries from a low to a high war involvement.

One may raise objections in relation to the interpretation of state capacity as war experience. However, states may use their capacity to mobilize resources and employ modern techniques in warfare in order to promote various state-related objectives, including, for example, national aggrandizement. The war involvement index differentiates both between the four categories of nations as well as within these subsets (Table 4.12).

Among the OECD nations the United States is really the only country with a high score on this political development dimension. Notice the very low scores for Iceland, Luxembourg and Switzerland. Outside the OECD framework the situation is very different, as in Asia in particular but also in Africa as we find a large number of countries with an extensive experience of war: India, Egypt, Iran, Iraq, Pakistan, Indonesia, Zaïre, Morocco, Ethiopia.

Table 4.13. Average institutionalization scores (1)

Latin America (N=15)	46.8
OECD countries (N=24)	40.9
Africa (N=15)	61.0
Asia (N=13)	57.7

$E^2 = 0.71$

Note: The institutionalization score is based on the following indicators: modernized leadership, introduction, effect; institutional sclerosis; qualification as state; member of the international system.

The institutionalization index is scored in such a way that low scores mean a lengthy time period of institutionalization and high scores stand for recent institutionalization (Table 4.13). Politically developed in this interpretation of the concept are those countries where a modernized leadership or a process of nation-building was introduced in the late nineteenth or early twentieth century. Let us look more closely at the country variation within the four categories of countries (Table 4.14).

The developed nations in this interpretation are to be found in the rich world, in Central and Latin America. Very low scores are to be found for the United Kingdom, the United States, Switzerland, France, Belgium and Denmark, as well as for Uruguay, Mexico and Brazil. Less

Table 4.14. Institutionalization scores (2)

OECD		*Asia*		*Latin America*	
USA	32.79	Iran	47.40	Dominican Rep	51.15
Canada	39.64	Iraq	56.63	Mexico	42.98
UK	23.98	Egypt	58.57	El Salvador	54.06

Table 4.14 continued

OECD		*Asia*		*Latin America*	
Ireland	50.47	Jordan	58.29	Costa Rica	50.59
Netherlands	33.02	Korea Rep	58.05	Panama	53.91
Belgium	34.37	India	58.01	Colombia	45.79
Luxembourg	38.56	Pakistan	57.96	Venezuela	46.18
France	33.36	Sri Lanka	58.18	Ecuador	47.63
Switzerland	32.99	Thailand	53.37	Peru	46.12
Spain	39.85	Malaysia	63.59	Brazil	42.12
Portugal	39.93	Singapore	64.49	Bolivia	46.75
FRG	45.53	Philippines	56.37	Paraguay	46.13
Austria	48.84	Indonesia	58.99	Chile	43.06
Italy	39.39			Argentina	43.67
Greece	43.63	Mean	57.7	Uruguay	41.84
Finland	49.87				
Sweden	43.75			Mean	46.8
Norway	43.98				
Denmark	34.86	*Africa*			
Iceland	52.24				
Turkey	45.97	Senegal	63.37	Zambia	64.42
Japan	46.51	Liberia	47.68	Malawi	64.38
Australia	43.45	Ghana	62.75	Madagascar	63.37
New Zealand	45.72	Cameroon	63.43	Morocco	60.49
		Nigeria	63.95	Algeria	54.50
Mean	40.9	Zaïre	64.13	Tunisia	59.36
		Kenya	64.04		
		Tanzania	63.83	Mean	61.0
		Ethiopia	55.72		

Note: The institutionalization score is based on the following indicators: modernized leadership, introduction, effect; institutional sclerosis; qualification as state; member of the international system. The Z-scores order the countries in such a way that a low score indicate a high degree of institutionalization whereas a high score indicate a low degree of institutionalization.

institutionalized are the countries in Asia and Africa. Several of these nations date their birth to the post-Second World War period: Zambia, Malawi, Zaïre, Kenya and Madagascar in Africa, as well as Singapore and Malaysia in Asia.

Underdevelopment theory implies that a radical government is a prerequisite for a process of 'real' development interpreted as human liberation from the capitalist oak. Politically developed in this interpretation would be those countries where according to the theory a rejection of the centre-periphery interaction system of world

Table 4.15. Radical orientation scores (1)

Central and Latin America (N=15)	45.8
OECD countries (N=24)	53.0
Africa (N=15)	52.7
Asia (N=13)	46.1

$E^2 = 0.12$

capitalism would most likely be initiated, i.e. in the periphery. The findings, however, indicate a somewhat different pattern as the countries in the OECD set and in Africa tend to be more radical on average than those in Latin America or in Asia (Table 4.15). Let us look at the specific country scores (Table 4.16).

Table 4.16. Radical orientation scores (2)

OECD		*Asia*		*Latin America*	
USA	41.00	Iran	41.00	Dominican Rep	53.17
Canada	43.28	Iraq	79.59	Mexico	50.39
UK	54.56	Egypt	44.82	El Salvador	41.00
Ireland	46.95	Jordan	41.00	Costa Rica	53.96
Netherlands	54.73	Korea Rep	41.00	Panama	41.00
Belgium	53.67	India	47.92	Colombia	41.62
Luxembourg	52.32	Pakistan	44.82	Venezuela	51.65
France	55.11	Sri Lanka	48.64	Ecuador	45.56
Switzerland	49.23	Thailand	41.00	Peru	46.37
Spain	48.34	Malaysia	42.52	Brazil	44.82
Portugal	54.92	Singapore	44.82	Bolivia	45.58
FRG	55.17	Philippines	41.00	Paraguay	41.00
Austria	60.36	Indonesia	41.00	Chile	44.82
Italy	57.32			Argentina	44.82
Greece	48.51	Mean	46.1	Uruguay	41.00
Finland	58.31				
Sweden	60.53			Mean	45.8
Norway	60.38	*Africa*			
Denmark	56.60				
Iceland	51.91	Senegal	57.27		
Turkey	51.65	Liberia	41.00		
Japan	48.20	Ghana	45.12		
Australia	55.17	Cameroon	41.00		
New Zealand	54.71	Nigeria	41.00		
		Zaïre	41.00		
Mean	53.0	Kenya	41.00		

Table 4.16 continued

Africa

Tanzanaia	79.59
Ethiopia	75.77
Zambia	44.82
Malawi	41.00
Madagascar	69.58
Morocco	41.00
Algeria	83.40
Tunisia	48.64
Mean	52.7

Note: The radical orientation score is based on the following indicators: communist party support; socialist-communist support; tradition of socialist government. The Z-scores order the countries in such a way that a low score indicates a weak position for the strength of the left in society whereas a high score implies a strong position.

Politically developed in this interpretation are some countries in Western Europe: the Scandinavian nations, Austria and Italy. In Africa we have periods of a radical government in Algeria, Tanzania, Ethiopia and Madagascar. Only Iraq scores high in Asia in our data set. Orthodox Marxist theory states that political development as the radicalization of government or as increased trade-union power in society is not only possible in rich countries but also necessary there as the crucial step towards human betterment. There is some truth to this claim in the data, but the hypothesis does not fit, generally speaking, as one rich country — the United States — scores very low whereas some nations in poor Africa score high.

Table 4.17. Average protest scores (1)

Latin America (N=15)	50.9
OECD countries (N=24)	54.6
Africa (N=15)	45.0
Asia (N=13)	46.3

$E^2 = 0.16$

Note: The protest score is based on the following indicators: protest demonstrations; riots; political strikes.

Table 4.18. Average violence scores (1)

Latin America (N=15)	54.1
OECD countries (N=24)	48.8
Africa (N=15)	46.1
Asia (N=13)	51.9

$E^2 = 0.08$

Note: The violence score is based on the following indicators: armed attacks; assassinations; deaths from domestic violence.

The hypothesis that political instability is a typical concomitant event to political change follows from the interpretation of development as crisis-conducive processes. However, the overall finding is that the variation in the two main expressions of political instability hardly follows the variation in the extent of political development as democracy, big government, war involvement or institutionalization. Even more interesting is the finding that political instability is a highly country-specific characteristic. Let us look at each country separately (Table 4.19 and 4.20).

Table 4.19. Protest scores (2)

OECD		*Asia*		*Latin America*	
USA	49.80	Iran	41.81	Dominican Rep	42.62
Canada	47.74	Iraq	46.59	Mexico	47.14
UK	71.79	Egypt	45.84	El Salvador	54.09
Ireland	61.72	Jordan	44.33	Costa Rica	51.58
Netherlands	50.49	Korea Rep	58.09	Panama	65.09
Belgium	44.23	India	42.50	Colombia	55.60
Luxembourg	38.50	Pakistan	51.60	Venezuela	40.40
France	61.19	Sri Lanka	49.06	Ecuador	56.49
Switzerland	51.64	Thailand	53.62	Peru	59.13
Spain	79.42	Malaysia	45.43	Brazil	42.52
Portugal	87.53	Singapore	38.50	Bolivia	65.51
FRG	47.26	Philippines	45.56	Paraguay	38.50
Austria	45.46	Indonesia	39.48	Chile	40.66
Italy	60.38			Argentina	57.71
Greece	72.49	Mean	46.3	Uruguay	46.01
Finland	43.79				
Sweden	47.10			Mean	50.9
Norway	48.95				
Denmark	52.75	*Africa*			
Iceland	52.99				

Table 4.19 continued

OECD		*Africa*			
Turkey	52.52	Senegal	38.50		
Japan	42.17	Liberia	51.84		
Australia	49.09	Ghana	49.06	Ethiopia	60.41
New Zealand	50.49	Cameroon	45.59	Zambia	43.61
		Nigeria	49.27	Malawi	38.50
Mean	54.6	Zaïre	38.50	Madagascar	41.58
		Kenya	51.00	Morocco	40.20
		Tanzania	43.00	Algeria	38.50
				Tunisia	45.54
				Mean	45.00

Note: The protest score is based on the following indicators: protest demonstrations; riots; political strikes. The Z-scores order the countries according a low to a high extent of occurrence of protest.

Table 4.20. Violence scores (2)

OECD		*Asia*		*Latin America*	
USA	44.54	Iran	54.32	Dominican Rep	58.83
Canada	40.38	Iraq	66.67	Mexico	55.22
UK	69.30	Egypt	50.84	El Salvador	64.97
Ireland	75.25	Jordan	52.11	Costa Rica	47.33
Netherlands	49.92	Korea Rep	43.74	Panama	45.94
Belgium	44.70	India	43.95	Colombia	56.46
Luxembourg	38.67	Pakistan	53.96	Venezuela	45.48
France	56.34	Sri Lanka	52.36	Ecuador	52.64
Switzerland	43.56	Thailand	57.01	Peru	50.77
Spain	61.56	Malaysia	57.40	Brazil	40.00
Portugal	58.65	Singapore	43.49	Bolivia	55.77
FRG	47.79	Philippines	58.58	Paraguay	49.91
Austria	48.99	Indonesia	39.69	Chile	50.80
Italy	57.51			Argentina	84.19
Greece	57.26	Mean	51.90	Uruguay	53.52
Finland	38.67				
Sweden	45.42			Mean	54.1
Norway	38.67	*Africa*			
Denmark	41.78				
Iceland	38.67	Liberia	38.67	Zambia	50.29
Turkey	50.44	Ghana	39.97	Malawi	38.67
Japan	42.60	Cameroon	38.67	Madagascar	58.65

Table 4.20 continued

OECD		*Africa*			
Australia	43.02	Nigeria	44.53	Ethiopia	76.53
New Zealand	38.67	Zaïre	49.71	Senegal	38.67
		Tanzania	40.10		
		Kenya	51.58	Mean	46.10
Mean	48.8	Morocco	42.46		
		Algeria	44.51		
		Tunisia	38.67		

Note: The violence score is based on the following indicators: armed attacks; assassinations; deaths from domestic violence. The Z-scores order the countries from a low to a high extent of occurrence of violence.

We find high protest scores in countries as different as: Bolivia, the United Kingdom, Portugal and the Republic of Korea. And a high violence score is displayed in countries from all the four subsets: Argentina, Spain, Ethiopia and Iraq.

Conclusion

The theme of political development aroused interest among political scientists in the late 1950s who were moving away from a particularistic concern with occidental political systems on the basis of a mainly legalistic approach. The new theme soon generated a vast literature. So many were the attempts at interpreting desirable political change stemming from the grand socio-economic transition from agraria to industria (Riggs, 1957), and so shifting the variety of theoretical models, that there had to come a final statement fitting all the hypotheses into the theory of political development (Pye, 1987). It would provide political science with what economic growth theory had given to economics. We all know that this was not what happened. The theme fell apart, rejected as methodologically flawed due to its unrecognized Western value biases (Leftwich, 1990).

However, whatever the scientific value of the set of theories of political development may be, it is impossible to disregard vital phenomena of political change. A fresh start may be found where the elusive concept of political development was left off. Recognizing the crucial part played by so-called value premises (Weber, 1949; Myrdal, 1970), the political development concept may be unpacked into manageable dimensions. Explicit multidimensionality is substituted for implicit ambiguity. And the derivation of different aspects of political development may be substantiated in the interpretation of data for a selection of countries of the world, thus validating the theoretical distinctions derived. The use of clear-cut indices for the seven dimensions identified does discriminate between categories of countries as well as between countries within the sets of OECD, Central and South American, African and Asian countries at present. The next step in a political economy perspective would be to look for interaction between the different dimensions of political development and economic phenomena.

Whether each and any of these dimensions constitute political development in a real sense is an open question to be resolved by normative argument. But having recourse to some measurable aspects of political development is a necessary condition for moving ahead to analyse the causes and effects of political development. Let us proceed to an analysis of the social and economic sources of one prominent type of political development: democratization. How valid is the hypothesis that there is a close connection between economic development and democracy as a political regime? In order to take a closer look at the theory about economic causes of political system institutions we need to consult the discipline of comparative politics. What are the main lessons in the field of comparative politics for the new political economy school?

Appendix 4.1. Indicators and sources

1. *Democratic development*

Political discimination: intensity	Taylor and Jodice, 1983
Economic discrimination: intensity	Taylor and Jodice, 1983
Human rights c. 1980	Humana, 1983
Democracy c. 1965	Bollen, 1980
Democracy c. 1960	Bollen, 1980
Party system functions	Estes, 1984
Role of the military in politics	Estes, 1984
Political rights index	Taylor and Jodice, 1983
Civil rights index	Taylor and Jodice, 1983
Party system fractionalization 1970s	Taylor and Jodice, 1983
Party system fractionalization 1960	Banks, 1971

2. *Capacity*

Military personnel 1975	Taylor and Jodice, 1983
Military expenditure 1970s	Sivard, 1980
War involvement after 1945	Weede, 1984
Central government expenditure 1970s	Sivard, 1980

Central government expenditure 1970s	Taylor and Jodice, 1983
General government expenditure 1970s	IMF, 1982
Public consumption	World Bank, 1980-87

3. Institutionalization

Modern leadership: year of introduction	Taylor and Hudson, 1972
Modern leadership: year in effect	Taylor and Hudson, 1972
Institutional sclerosis	Based on Choi, 1983
Year qualified as state	Banks, 1971
Year member of the international system	Banks, 1971

4. Stability

Protest demonstrations per capita log	Taylor and Jodice, 1983
Riots per capita log	Taylor and Jodice, 1983
Political strikes per capita log	Taylor and Jodice, 1983
Armed attacks per capita log	Taylor and Jodice, 1983
Assassinations per capita log	Taylor and Jodice, 1983
Deaths from domestic violence per capita log	Taylor and Jodice, 1983

5. Radical orientation

Communist party support	Staar, 1981
Socialist-communist support	Day and Degenhardt, 1980
Tradition of socialist government	Based on Schmidt, 1983

Countries included:

002 USA
020 Canada
040 Cuba
042 Dominican Rep
070 Mexico
092 El Salvador
094 Costa Rica
095 Panama
100 Colombia
101 Venezuela

305 Austria
325 Italy
350 Greece
375 Finland
380 Sweden
385 Norway
390 Denmark

630 Iran
640 Turkey
645 Iraq
651 Egypt
663 Jordan
732 South Korea
740 Japan
750 India
770 Pakistan

130 Ecuador
135 Peru
140 Brazil
145 Bolivia
150 Paraguay
155 Chile
160 Argentina
165 Uruguay
200 UK
205 Ireland
210 Netherlands
211 Belgium
212 Luxembourg
220 France
225 Switzerland
230 Spain
235 Portugal
260 GFR
395 Iceland
433 Senegal
450 Liberia
452 Ghana
471 Cameroon
475 Nigeria
490 Zaïre
501 Kenya
510 Tanzania
530 Ethiopia
551 Zambia
553 Malawi
580 Madagascar
615 Algeria
616 Tunsia
780 Sri Lanka
800 Thailand
820 Malaysia
830 Singapore
840 Philippines
850 Indonesia
900 Australia
920 New Zealand

5 Economic development, democracy and performance

Introduction

The theory that the economic predicament of a country has a decisive impact on its politics comes in two different versions. Firstly, there is the *regime hypothesis* claiming that the extent to which a country displays stable democratic institutions is conditioned by the general level of affluence in the country. Democratic regimes will be sustained only in rich economic environments, the GDP per capita predicting the longevity of democracy. Secondly, there is the *policy hypothesis* stating that the public policy profile of a country is determined by its level of affluence. In particular, welfare state spending is only feasible in a rich economic environment, the GDP per capita predicting the policy configuration of a country. The policy hypothesis will be tested in Chapters 6 and 7; whereas here we focus on the regime hypothesis by looking more closely at the implications of the comparative theory of democracy for the kind of political economy theory we are aiming at in this volume.

The study of democratic polities belong to the field of comparative politics, which has attracted a growing interest in recent decades as reflected in the number of publications and journals. New study programmes dealing with different areas of the world have emerged. Area specialists claim that cross-national studies are a legitimate concern although area studies are more oriented towards case-study analysis than the use of the comparative method. At the same time the interest in genuine comparative analysis has grown substantially, as modern comparative politics is clearly different from what used to be designated 'the traditional approach' (Sigelman and Gadbois, 1983), which is very relevant to the concerns of the new political economy.

In the 1950s the case against the traditional approach was stated affirmatively as it was rejected as being non-comparative, descriptive, parochial, static and monographic (Macridis, 1955). With some notable exceptions — Max Weber, John Bryce and Herbert Finer — comparative politics used to focus on rules or constitutions, displayed a heavy bias towards the major Western countries and lacked any methodology for the conduct of systematic empirical inquiry. The rejection of the traditional approach was too overwhelming not to change the course of comparative politics. A number of developments within political science reinforced the search for new approaches in the comparative analysis of political systems (Bill and Hardgrave, 1973; Cantori and Ziegler, 1988; Bebler and Seroka, 1989; Diamond, Linz and Lipset, 1988, 1989a, 1989b).

The behavioural revolution implied that behaviour was more important than rules, thus necessitating the systematic collection of large amounts of data about politics in various countries. As data without theory would be *blind*, the behavioural revolution implied the explicit elaboration of concepts, models and hypotheses. Political sociology carried the claim that the politics of a country could be better understood if its institutions were related to social forces. The emergence of the Third World stimulated a whole new approach to the explanation of the differences between politics and society in rich and poor countries — *the modernization theme*. The attack on the traditional approach was no doubt successful. The reorientation of comparative politics resulted in an expansion of comparative politics in terms of theoretical depth and empirical scope, as attempts were made to integrate a growing but disparate body of knowledge by means of theory. Since theory without data would be *empty*, genuine comparative theory was put to more severe tests as a result of an abundance of new data.

Comparative approaches

Generally speaking, comparative politics covers three major concerns: (1) the interpretation of the relationship between society and politics, (2) the identification of the major types of political systems, and (3) the understanding of the impact of politics on society. Comparative politics first focused on the input side, political sociology claiming that basic properties of political systems were to be understood against background information about structure and processes in society; thus it was claimed that political conflict dimensions were structured according to cleavage dimensions in the social structure (Rokkan et al, 1970).

This reductionist approach offset a reaction arguing for the autonomy of politics in relation to social and economic factors. The second stage in modern comparative politics aimed at institutional analysis of the variation of political systems and their constituent parts, such as parties and party systems in their own right (Lijphart, 1968; Sartori, 1969, 1976).

Central to this were crucial distinctions between different types of democracy, authoritarian rule and modernizing polities (Dahl, 1971; Lijphart, 1977, 1984). Finally, the growing interest in the output side of politics within political science also affected comparative politics. Why study different political systems if it was not the case that politics matters for policies?

The third stage implied a merger of comparative politics with public policy and political economy, attempting to understand what different political systems do (policy outputs) and actually accomplish (policy outcomes) — this is the focus of comparative public policy (Groth, 1971; Heady, 1979; Heidenheimer, Heclo and Adams, 1983; Wildavsky, 1986).

Those who emphasize the input side typically refer to the impact of social cleavages, the basic problem being the extent to which the environment determines the polity. The cleavage approach which reduces politics to cleavage dimensions in the social structure, seems as exaggerated as institutionalism or the hypothesis that there is no relationship whatsoever between social and economic factors and the political system. But how does one strike a balance between social or economic determinism and political indeterminism?

How, in the comparative analysis of the political systems in various countries, can one identify crucial concepts with which to identify major system differences and similarities? As the attempt to separate traditional, developing and modern polities failed as a result of the value-loaded nature of these concepts (Almond and Powell, 1966), the distinction between democratic and authoritarian regimes became the fundamental one (Blondel, 1969; Dahl, 1971). However, even if there is unanimity as to the meaning and applicability of the term 'democracy' — some thirty polities in the world — there is disagreement about the properties or indicators that identify a democratic regime. Two very different types of democractic models have been recognized: the Westminster-type democracy versus the consensus or the so-called consociational-type democracy (Lijphart, 1984).

But how about the far larger set of non-democratic systems? There are 'between 150 and 200 sovereign states in the world today, the number varying according to how the word sovereign is defined' (Derbyshire and Derbyshire, 1989:viii) but there is no agreement how they are to be classified. And there is no taxonomy of Third World politics available (Clapham, 1985). No doubt, much future comparative research will focus on the set of non-democratic regimes in order to set out how they vary along a few basic dimensions (Perlmutter, 1981). The study of subsystems such as political parties or party systems and legislatures are truly comparative in this sense (Janda, 1980; Loewenberg and Patterson, 1979). However, much too little has been done in order to come up with some sort of typology of non-democratic systems (Linz, 1975).

The emergence of political economy has added a new dimension to comparative politics (Rose, 1973; Frey, 1978; Alt and Crystal, 1983; Hedström, 1986; Whiteley, 1986). The basic puzzle regarding the output or outcome side is whether politics in a broad sense matters for citizen welfare (Castles, Lehner and Schmidt, 1988). Granting the profound structural differences between various states in terms of governmental structures, citizens' rights and political party or trade union operations, are these vital distinctions also relevant for the understanding of allocational and redistributional differences? It has been argued that what matters for the scope and character of the welfare system — health, education and social care — is not politics but affluence (Galbraith, 1962, 1969; Tinbergen, 1967; Pryor, 1968; Wilensky, 1975).

The counter-argument is that the strength of the right or the left does mean a difference to the size of the welfare system or policy outcomes such as the rates of unemployment and inflation (Castles, 1982; Schmidt, 1982). Or the historical evolution of the state matters, institutional sclerosis affecting the rate of economic growth causing the decline of nations (Olson, 1982). The intersection between comparative politics and public policy is the focus on the state or national government. Do characteristics like regime properties matter for policies and outcomes? More specifically, here we take a closer look at one widely debated theme in comparative politics that is at the heart of the new political economy. We want to inquire into the relation between the socio-economic structure and the polity, testing claims about social conditions for democracy.

The polity

The concept of a democratic regime is used to distinguish it among political systems. Sometimes a dichotomy between democratic and non-democratic systems is employed. At other times stable and unstable democratic regimes are referred to. R. Wesson speaks of stable, insecure and partial democracies versus limited authoritarianism and absolutism (Wesson, 1987). Dahl makes a distinction between fully inclusive polyarchies and near-polyarchies. The countries in Table 5.1 are typically listed as the democratic ones.

The reduction in the number of democracies reflects both real world developments and disagreement about classification. A true development towards a democratic regime has taken place in Spain since 1975, Portugal as of 1974 and Greece since 1974. The existence of democratic political institutions in Mexico, Venezuela, Colombia, India and The Philippines has been interpreted differently. The basic problem is the somewhat blurred dividing line between stable and insecure democracies, as the classification of Greece in 1967 and 1987 exemplifies.

Table 5.1. Countries classified as stable democracies

	Rustow (1967)	Dahl (1971)	Wesson (1987)
USA	x	x	x
Canada	x	x	x
Jamaica		x	
Trinidad		x	x
Barbados			x
Mexico	x		
Costa Rica	x	x	x
Colombia	x		x
Venezuela			x
Chile	x	x	
Uruguay	x	x	
United Kingdom	x	x	x
Ireland	x	x	x
Netherlands	x	x	x
Belgium	x	x	x
Luxembourg	x	x	x
France	x	x	x
Switzerland	x	x	x
Spain			x
Portugal			x
Germany FR	x	x	x
Austria	x	x	x
Italy	x	x	x
Greece	x		
Finland	x	x	x
Sweden	x	x	x
Norway	x	x	x
Denmark	x	x	x
Iceland	x	x	x
Lebanon	x	x	
Israel	x	x	x
Japan	x	x	x
India	x	x	
Sri Lanka	x		
Philippines	x	x	
Australia	x	x	x
New Zealand	x	x	x
N =	31	30	28

Note: The order follows the ICPSR (Ann Arbor) country code.

It is now widely recognized that a more precise modelling of the conditions and consequences of democracy requires quantitative indicators measuring the extent of democracy. There are a number of measurement indices, applied to a different number of countries:

1. Cutright's index of political development: legislative branch of government; executive branch of government (N = 77)

2. Smith's index of aggregate degree of political democracy: Cutright's index; composite index of nineteen variables (N = 110)

3. Neubauer's index of democratic political development: Percentage of adult population eligible to vote; equality of representation; information equality; electoral competition (N = 23)

4. Jackman's index of democratic performance: Number of adults voting; competitiveness of party system; electoral irregularity; freedom of the press (N = 60)

5. Bollen's index of political democracy: Press freedom; freedom of group opposition; government sanctions; fairness of elections; executive selection; legislature selection (N = 113)

6. Vanhanen's index of democratization: Competitiveness of party system; electoral participation (N = 119)

7. Humana's index of human rights: (N= 96; 98)

8. Gastil's index of freedom: political rights; civil rights; freedom status (N = 167).

The existence of so many indicators of democracy reflects the contested nature of the concept of democracy. However, even if standard indicators on democracy differ conceptually, they co-vary to a considerable extent in reality. Table 5.2 presents a correlation matrix for indicators measuring the degree of democracy around the 1960s. The different indices refer to different periods of time, some covering a longer time period, whereas others refer to a more specific time reference.

With the exception of Cutright's and Neubauer's indices there is a high correlation indicating that roughly the same countries are placed in the same way around 1960. Whereas we have seven indices for the 1960s, there are only two genuine indices for the 1970s, one referring to human rights and the other to political participation and competition. They correlate considerably: r = 0.86. With regard to the 1980s there are three indices measuring, basically, human rights. Again, the substantial intercorrelations between the indices means that the countries are measured in a roughly similar way (Table 5.3).

Table 5.2. Correlation between different measures of democracy (c. 1960)

	(1)	(2)	(3)	(4)	(5)	(6)	(7)
Neubauer 1940-60s (1)	1.00						
Cutright 1940-60s (2)	0.15	1.00					
Smith 1960s (3)	0.57	0.88	1.00				
Jackman 1960s (4)	0.63	0.64	0.80	1.00			
Bollen 1960 (5)	0.57	0.70	0.83	0.84	1.00		
Bollen 1965 (6)	0.46	0.74	0.83	0.84	0.93	1.00	
Vanhanen 1960s (7)	0.58	0.66	0.82	0.79	0.80	0.76	1.00

It must be acknowledged that there is no perfect correlation between the indices, neither within the same time period or between the time periods. This reflects again both real world changes and differences in the measurement of the concept. We may disregard the Cutright and Neubauer indices; Cutright's index has been criticized as involving a stability bias (Bollen, 1979) whereas Neubauer's index only covers twenty-three countries.

Table 5.3. Correlation between different measures of democracy (c. 1980)

	(1)	(2)	(3)
Gastil 1980s (1)	1.00		
Humana 1980s I (2)	0.90	1.00	
Humana 1980s II (3)	0.92	0.92	1.00

Summing up, we may say that even though there are differences between the indices the concept of a democratic regime is empirically unambiguous. When indices are applied to the different time periods, there is a strong correlation, suggesting that change in real world democracy is not very large (Table 5.4). We focus on democracy in the 1980s and its social and economic sources and policy consequences. We may, therefore, with some confidence employ one index of the extent to which a political system has a democratic regime, because even if it may be pointed out that there are other equally justifiable indices, it would not make any practical difference to shift to another.

Table 5.4. Correlation between measures of democracy for different periods

	(1)	(2)	(3)
(1) 1980s (Humana)	1.00		
(2) 1970s (Gastil)	0.82	1.00	
(3) 1960s (Bollen)	0.71	0.77	1.00

The conditions for democratic persistence

It is a basic tenet of political sociology that the structure of society or the dynamics of society has a profound impact on the polity. The similarities and differences of political systems are determined by background factors such as level of affluence, rate of economic development, overall socio-economic development, social cleavages and inequality. Economic and social conditions are said to stand in a causal connection with polity properties such as democracy versus authoritarianism or type of democracy and political stability. The basic problem is to model the relationships between environmental variables and political system variables and to estimate the strength of the relationships in a body of data. How are we to draw causal inferences about the social and economic sources of political systems given the existence of a set of correlations in a comparative context?

The test of models of the sources of a democratic regime has attracted the interest of a number of scholars who point out the methodological difficulties inherent in an inquiry into the causes of political systems in general and democracy in particular. These difficulties involve the selection of indicators, time slices and countries (Neubauer, 1967; Olsen, 1968; Coulter, 1971; Bollen, 1979; Bollen and Grandjean, 1981); moreover, they also include causal modelling problems (Smith, 1969; Rustow, 1970; Jackman, 1974; Huntington, 1984) and the choice between cross-sectional and longitudinal interpretations.

Taking these difficulties into account, we present correlations from a data set that covers some 120 countries at the following points of time: 1960s, 1970s and 1980s. We focus on the conditions for the *persistence* of a democracy, not the conditions for the *genesis* of a democratic regime in the first place (Rustow, 1970). Is it true that the institutionalization of a democratic regime is strongly affected by the environment of the political system: economic, social, cultural or political?

The occurrence of democratic regime properties may be tapped by means of the indices introduced above. Table 5.5 shows the average scores of the extent of democracy in various subsets of countries.

The democratic regime type prevails among the OECD countries, occurs often in the set of Central and South American countries and not so often in the set of Asian countries. As expected, the extent of democracy is low in the African set and in the Communist world. An analysis of variance indicates that this country pattern is fairly stable (Eta-squared > 0.5). Thus we face one of the fundamental puzzles of comparative politics: why is it the case that democracy as a set of regime characteristics occurs so differently in the countries of the world? Or what conditions are conducive to the institutionalization of stable democratic regime characteristics? A number of factors have been suggested in order to explain this fact.

Table 5.5. The world of democracy (average values, E^2)

	OECD	Latin America	Africa	Asia	Comm-nist	E^2	Min	Max
1980s (Gastil)	95.2	59.9	19.8	36.5	10.3	.72	0	100
1980s	92.0	66.1	47.3	44.1	31.0	.68	13	98
1980s (Humana)	89.2	59.4	53.5	48.0	35.5	.58	17	96
1970s (Gastil)	92.4	51.3	18.7	34.2	6.8	.72	0	100
1970s (Vanhanen)	27.2	7.1	0.5	5.7	0.1	.69	0	42.3
1960s (Vanhanen)	24.2	9.1	1.6	5.9	0.7	.59	0	40.7
1960s (Bollen)	89.8	71.0	56.8	54.6	23.1	.45	10.7	100
1960s (Bollen)	90.2	65.8	44.2	49.9	21.3	.48	5.2	100
1960s (Jackman)	77.0	62.4	41.2	64.2	—	.30	18	90
1960s (Smith)	120.7	105.5	90.8	87.2	94.4	.50	55.8	137.7
1960s (Cutright)	58.0	53.1	—	41.7	47.5	.53	33	66

Note: The indices are explained in Appendix 5.1. The Eta-squared statistic is higher the less the within group variation.

The Lipset *affluence model* points to the state of the economy (Lipset, 1959). The level of affluence is said to be a crucial determinant in the occurrence of democratic regime characteristics. As countries grow more affluent, their social and political structure becomes more diversified, making a dictatorship impossible. The affluence model attracted considerable attention as several attempts at empirical validation were made (Cutright, 1963; Smith, 1969; Jackman, 1974) until Guiermo O'Donnell questioned the whole approach (O'Donnell, 1973, 1988). What could a theoretical argument making affluence a sufficient or necessary condition for democracy look like (Usher, 1981)? Let us look at the correlations depicted in Table 5.6.

Although there is an overall statistical association between level of affluence measured in terms of real GDP per capita and various indices of democracy, it hardly confirms the claim of the affluence model. First, the association is not that strong as a correlation of about 0.70 means that roughly 50 per cent of the variation remains to be explained (r-squared = .49).

Table 5.6. The affluence model: democracy and wealth (real GDP/cap.) (Pearson's r)

	Total	OECD	Latin America	Africa	Asia
1980s (Gastil)	0.67	0.62	0.39	0.15	0.28
1980s (Humana)	0.66	0.61	0.53	0.04	0.27
1980s (Humana)	0.60	0.68	0.29	0.13	0.11
1970s (Gastil)	0.70	0.67	0.31	0.25	0.33
1970s (Vanhanen)	0.78	0.54	0.50	0.29	0.57
1960s (Vanhanen)	0.72	0.45	0.73	−0.00	0.63
1960s (Bollen)	0.47	0.57	0.47	0.20	0.39
1960s (Bollen)	0.55	0.52	0.56	−0.02	0.42
1960s (Jackman)	0.60	0.52	0.43	−0.21	0.57
1960s (Smith)	0.72	0.63	0.52	0.32	0.43
1960s (Cutright)	0.72	0.74	0.39	—	0.37

Note: The Pearson's correlations have been computed using the standard indices on democracy

Figure 5.1. Level of affluence and degree of democracy around 1980

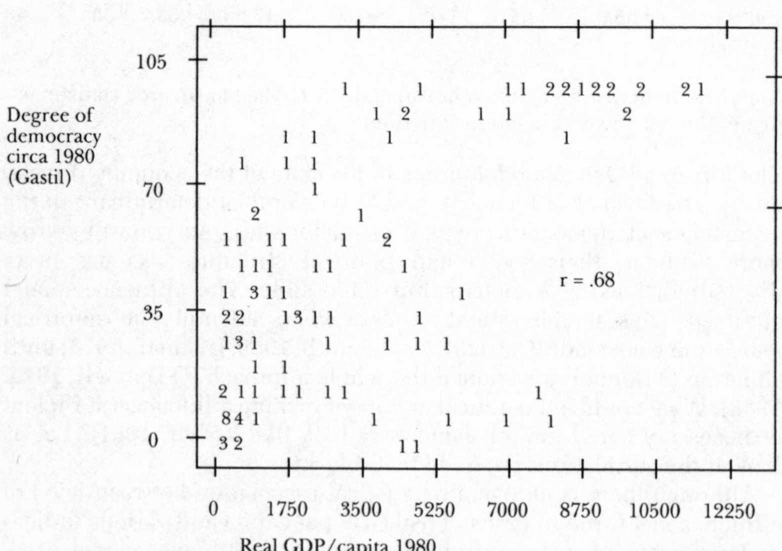

Second, the statistical association is not stable in various country subsets. The relationship is particularly strong in the set of OECD countries, not in other country subsets. In the set of Latin American countries it hovers considerably as some of these countries move back and forth between different types of regimes. Let us turn to Figure 5.1 where level of affluence has been combined with extent of democracy around 1980.

Although the variation in democracy tends to follow the variation in economic affluence, it seems premature to conclude that there is a *causal connection* between the economy and the polity as suggested by the affluence model (O'Donnell and Schmitter, 1986). If affluence is a necessary condition for democracy, then why is there democracy in India? If affluence is a sufficient condition for democracy, then why is there not democracy in Saudi Arabia? If this is the negative finding in the data in Table 5.6, affluence not explaining democracy, then what accounts for the occurrence of democratic regime characteristics?

The *modernization model* argues that a decisive condition for the persistence of a democratic regime is a so-called modern social structure (Lerner, 1958; Deutsch, 1961). Although it is far from obvious what a 'modern' social structure amounts to — modernity being a value-loaded concept — the implication of the modernization theme is that processes of industrialization and urbanization are conducive to democracy. However, since modernization is strongly correlated with level of affluence we would not expect that the modernization models fit the data better than the affluence model. The correlations in Table 5.7 corroborates this conjecture.

Social structure involves more than economics and its derivatives. It has been suggested that a more general *culture model* accounts for the extent of democracy. One theory focuses on religion, or more specifically on the position of protestantism in the country (Schumpeter, 1944; Lenski, 1963). The model states that the stronger the position of Lutheranism or Calvinism in its various forms, the more stable would be the democratic institutions of a country. Another religious model emphasizes homogeneity in the religious structure of a country predicting that heterogeneity would enhance democratic instability or strengthen an authoritarian regime. Diversity in the social structure may pertain to characteristics other than religion, namely language or cultural tradition. Ethnic heterogeneity would make democracy very difficult according to this theory due to the explosive nature of ethnic cleavages (de Schweinitz, 1964; Moore, 1966; Wallerstein, 1977). The correlations in Table 5.7 provide some confirmation of these hypotheses.

An alternative model type — a *political model* — looks for the determinants of democracy among more specific political factors. One theory points out the length of experience of a democratic regime and another theory emphasizes the length of the period of so-called modernized leadership. In general, a segmented social structure would be conducive to democratic instability (Eckstein, 1966; Rustow, 1970; Dahl, 1971). The status of a democratic regime is a function of how long modern institutions have persisted without interruption. Or a democratic regime is a function of time, the longer the time period since the genesis of democracy the more persistent the democratic polity. Again, there is empirical support for these models (Table 5.7).

Table 5.7. Conditions for the persistence of democracy

	Humana 1980s	Gastil 1970s	Bollen 1960s
Protestantism	0.45	0.48	0.44
Ethno-linguistic structure: fractionalization	−0.28	−0.29	−0.30
Religious structure: fractionalization	−0.14	−0.12	−0.03
Religious and ethno-linguistic fractionalization	−0.23	−0.23	−0.11
Cultural pluralism	−0.43	−0.42	−0.29
Agricultural employment 1965	−0.58	−0.52	−0.65
Agricultural employment 1980	−0.50	−0.44	−0.57
Introduction of modernized leadership	−0.57	−0.40	−0.60
Effective modernized leadership	−0.47	−0.39	−0.54
Qualified as member of the international system	−0.38	−0.25	−0.43
Period of democratic rule (Hewitt)	0.56	0.30	0.56
Period of democratic rule (Muller)	0.59	0.68	0.64

Note: the table reports on correlations (Pearson's r) between the democracy indices and indicators on some explanatory factors in various democracy models.

However, all correlations are of such a moderate strength that much more research is needed in order to arrive at a theory about the conditions for democratic continuity. Thus, whichever factor we emphasize, there will be deviant cases requiring *ad hoc* explanations. Take the religious models: if a protestant culture is important, then why stable democracy in Japan, India or Italy and France; when religious homogeneity is pointed out, then how about Switzerland and The Netherlands? Or if ethnic homogeneity or cultural diversity matters, then why democracy in Spain, the United States, Canada or India? Moreover, if a modern social structure, i.e. a small agricultural population, is crucial, then why is there democracy in India and not in Algeria? If an early nation-building process is a necessary or sufficient condition for stable democracy, then why democracy in Greece and Portugal and not in Bolivia? These correlations do not suffice for the derivation of either sufficient or necessary conditions.

Democratic performance

Political systems may be valued for their own sake or for their value as instruments for the accomplishment of social goals. Thus democracy may be emphasized because it embodies certain values in itself or because its operation leads to social outcomes considered desirable. There are a number of models that offer explanations of the consequences of government operations. These effects of the operation of a polity may relate to either general performance dimensions like polity durability, civil order, legitimacy and decisional efficacy (Eckstein, 1971; Gurr and McClelland, 1971), or to specific policy outputs or policy outcomes. We focus here on the theme of democratic performance before we enter a more thorough discussion in the next chapters of the determinants of policies in a comparative perspective.

The equality model claims that the more democratic a polity is, the greater will be the extent of equality in the distribution of affluence (Lenski, 1966). The economic growth model states that the more democratic a polity is, the lower will be the rate of growth in the economy. The soft state model ties into this model, predicting that a more authoritarian regime will be conducive to rapid economic development (Myrdal, 1968). So does the sclerosis model: the longer the time period of institutionalization, the stronger the distributional coalitions and the lower the rate of growth in the economy (Olson, 1982).

The inflation model implies that the higher the level of democracy in a country, the higher the rate of inflation (Tufte, 1978). The political violence model argues that the more repressive a regime tends to become, the higher will be the levels of occurrence of political violence (Muller, 1985). Finally, the convergence model implies that political systems, whether communist or democratic, tend towards the same pattern of state activities: the welfare state. This is a hypothesis about variation in policy outputs which denies that policies differ as a function of the type of regime that rules the country (Tinbergen, 1967; Galbraith,

1969). Finally, there is a war model that states that democracy is conducive to peace (Weede, 1984).

A test of these various models presents serious methodological difficulties concerning data, model specification and estimation techniques (Banks, 1972a; Jackman, 1973; Dick, 1974; Hewitt, 1977; Rubinson and Quinlan, 1977; Weede, 1983, 1984b; Bollen and Jackman, 1985). Recognizing these technical problems we arrive at the correlations presented in Table 5.8.

Table 5.8. Democratic performance

	Humana 1980s	Gastil 1970s	Bollen 1960s
GNP/capita growth 1965-1980	0.17	0.19	0.01
General government expenditures circa 1977	0.05	0.07	−0.02
Welfare effort 1970's (Estes, 1984)	0.53	0.53	0.41
Education 1970's (Estes, 1984)	0.47	0.52	0.43
Education 1980's (Estes, 1984)	0.46	0.53	0.40
Health 1970's (Estes, 1984)	0.52	0.59	0.45
Health 1980's (Estes 1984)	0.49	0.59	0.43
Inequality: Gini-index	−0.43	−0.40	−0.33
Inequality: Ward (1978)	−0.47	−0.51	−0.37
Inflation 1965-1980	−0.08	−0.10	0.10
Inflation 1980-85	−0.09	−0.05	−0.05
War	−0.14	0.02	−0.07

Note: the table reports on correlations (Pearson's r) between the democracy indices and some indicators on policy outputs and outcomes.

A democratic regime means a difference towards an authoritarian polity in two ways. First, in a direct sense democracy offers human rights as a part of the democratic procedures themselves. Second, there is empirical support for the theory that a democratic regime is different from an authoritarian polity in terms of its policy outputs. Democracies have a more pronounced welfare effort than other types of regimes. Although it is far from true that all democracies have a similar policy output configuration, Table 5.8 shows that there is a clear trend that democracies spend more on education and health or welfare items in general. This finding has a bearing on the well-known convergence hypothesis.

The hypothesis that political systems would converge towards a similar pattern of welfare expenditures is not supported. The welfare efforts in non-democratic polities have not been enough to match those in several democracies, particularly as the Communist welfare system has lagged behind during the last twenty years (Castles, 1986). It also seems to be the case that there is a better likelihood of more equality in the distribution of resources in a democracy. On the other hand, the hypotheses that argue that democracy has an impact on the level of inflation or the duration of peace receive little empirical support.

The wealth theory of democracy states not only that affluence determines democratic longevity, but it also implies that the institutionalization of democratic political institutions will have a considerable positive impact on the average rate of economic growth (Pourgerami, 1989). However, we find no evidence of any impact of democracy on economic growth. In addition, we find no influence of democracy on factors like size of the state, inflation or war experience.

It remains to be asked whether it is really the factor democracy that counts for some of the performance indicators reported on in Table 5.8, or whether some other political variable is more significant. Comparative political economy analyses the problem of policy determinants both within the set of democracies — the variation within the set of rich countries — and between democracies and non-democracies — the variation between rich and poor countries, to which we turn now.

Conclusion

As the traditional approach to comparative politics was abandoned in the 1960s as a result of both substantial and methodological criticism, the volume of cross-national studies has risen sharply, particularly the number of area studies. And the efforts at more genuine comparative analysis have increased (Przeworski and Teune, 1970; Przeworski, 1987). As comparative politics is moving more towards comparative public policy and comparative political economy, the trend is towards quantitative modelling of the causes and consequences of the political system. There is still a bias towards examining democratic regimes, though democracy is by no means the prevailing regime among the political systems today. The focus on the conditions for democracy and democratic performance has given away to a broader perspective on the policy variation in different kinds of political regimes, to the analysis of which the next chapters are devoted.

The chief finding in this chapter is that the so-called wealth theory of democracy must be questioned. First, it is not the case that affluence accounts for the variation in regime types. A high level of economic affluence is neither a necessary nor sufficient condition for the persistence of a democratic regime, although there is considerable statistical association. Second, there is little support for the hypothesis that democracy as a factor has an impact on the average growth of the economy in a country. Let us move on to another version of economic determinism in political economy. If affluence and democracy were causally related, then perhaps affluence also could explain the pattern of policy variation between countries?

The hypothesis that politics does not matter for policies was launched in regional and local government research (Dye, 1966; Sharkansky, 1969; Hofferbert, 1974). The so-called *demographic model* pointed out policy determinants among non-political factors such as affluence, urbanization and industrialization. If the policy variation between subnational governmental units could be accounted for by means of socio-economic structure, then how about the explanation of national public policy variations?

Appendix 5.1. Indicators and sources

Democracy

Indicator	N	Source
1980s Gastil's index	N=120	Gastil, 1987
1980s Humana's index	N=112	Humana, 1986
1980s Humana's index	N=102	Humana, 1983
1970s Gastil's index	N=120	Gastil, 1987
1970s Vanhanen's index	N=111	Vanhanen, 1984
1960s Vanhanen's index	N=111	Vanhanen, 1984
1960s Bollen's index	N=110	Bollen, 1980
1960s Bollen's index	N=120	Bollen, 1980
1960s Jackman's index	N=58	Jackman, 1975
1960s Smith's index	N=109	Smith, 1969
1960s Cutright's index	N=74	Cutright, 1963
1960s Neubauer's index	N=23	Neubauer, 1967

Input dimensions

Indicator	N	Source
Real GDP/capita 1960	N=112	Summers and Heston, 1984
Real GDP/capita 1970	N=112	Summers and Heston, 1984
Real GDP/capita 1980	N=112	Summers and Heston, 1984
Protestantism	N=121	Taylor and Hudson, 1972
Religious fragmentation	N=120	Taylor and Hudson, 1972
Ethno-linguistic fragmentation	N=121	Taylor and Hudson, 1972
Religious and ethnic fragmentation	N=120	Taylor and Hudson, 1972

Pluralism	N=107	Haug, 1967
Agricultural employment 1965	N=114	World Bank, 1987
Agricultural employment 1980	N=111	World Bank, 1987
Modernizing leadership introduced	N=121	Taylor and Hudson, 1972
Modernizing leadership in effect	N=121	Taylor and Hudson, 1972
Qualified as member of the international system	N=121	Banks, 1971
Period of democratic rule	N=24	Hewitt, 1977
Period of democratic rule	N=66	Muller, 1988

Output dimensions

GNP/capita growth 1965-80	N=94	World Bank, 1987
General government expenditures 1977	N=77	IMF, 1982
Welfare effort	N=104	Estes, 1984
Education 1970s	N=104	Estes, 1984
Education 1980s	N=104	Estes, 1984
Health 1970s	N=104	Estes, 1984
Health 1980s	N=104	Estes, 1984
Inequality: Gini index	N=81	Taylor and Jodice, 1983
Inequality: Ward index	N=97	Dye and Zeigler, 1988
Inflation 1965-80	N=95	World Bank, 1987
Inflation 1980-85	N=92	World Bank, 1987
War experience	N=106	Weede, 1984

6 Policy determinants in western Europe

Introduction

Few themes have aroused so much interest and contention in modern political economy as the search for so-called determinants or explanatory factors of public policy. The major problem in this debate concerns the identification of the *independent* variables accounting for the cross-country variation in public policies or expenditures as the *dependent* variables. The literature on how and why public policies vary between countries both in terms of *levels of expenditure* and *growth in expenditures* is large, particularly with regard to so-called rich countries or the capitalist democracies in Western Europe (Tarschys, 1975; Larkey, Stolp and Winer, 1981; Wildavsky, 1985; Lybeck and Henrekson, 1988; Paldam, 1990).

We will try to look at the problem of accounting for public policy patterns from a somewhat new angle. It is important to recognize the possibility of structural *variability*, because the standard independent variables may operate differently on the key dependent variables in various subsets of countries. If we abandon the idea of identifying *stable* structures that describe the relationships between independent and dependent variables in an invariant way in all sets of countries, we can identify policy determinants in Western Europe that may not be relevant when we look at both rich and poor countries.

The findings in comparative policy research shows that it is difficult to arrive at stable estimates of relationships between dependent and independent variables; if one cross-sectional slice is chosen then we get one finding; if another slice is taken then we get a different result. Below we attempt to detach whatever structural stability exists and to pin down the structural variability typical of the data. Instead of searching for universal relationships between policy variables and environmental factors, we will try to locate when and where such relationships exist (Westlund and Lane, 1983).

Public sector growth theory

A seminal trend in the development of the politico-economic regimes in the so-called Western world is the growth of the state, particularly since 1945. In all so-called market regimes or advanced capitalist countries there is a seminal process of government budget expansion measured in terms of resources mobilized by the public sector as a percentage of GDP. The growth of the welfare state has been particularly strong in the major West European countries (Table 6.1).

Table 6.1. General government: current receipts as a percentage of GDP

	1950	1955	1960	1965	1970	1975	1980	1985
Austria	27.9	29.5	31.4	36.1	39.7	42.9	46.0	47.7
Belgium	24.2	24.0	26.7	30.7	35.2	40.4	43.2	46.5
Denmark	21.7	25.7	27.6	31.4	41.7	46.2	52.2	57.0
Finland	30.3	30.2	31.6	33.5	34.9	38.8	37.8	40.5
France	32.6	33.0	34.1	37.7	39.0	40.3	45.6	48.5
GFR	31.6	34.7	36.0	36.2	38.5	42.7	44.6	45.4
Greece	15.5	18.2	20.4	23.4	26.8	27.4	30.5	34.9
Ireland	23.4	23.8	24.6	28.0	35.3	35.2	41.7	44.3
Italy	21.0	26.2	29.8	31.6	30.4	31.2	37.4	37.5
Netherlands	33.0	28.9	33.4	36.8	44.5	53.2	55.0	54.4
Norway	29.6	30.8	34.5	37.7	43.5	49.6	54.0	56.1
Portugal	20.0	19.1	17.6	20.4	24.3	24.8	31.5	—
Spain	—	—	18.1	19.3	22.5	24.4	30.0	33.2
Sweden	26.2	32.7	35.0	42.0	47.0	50.7	56.7	59.4
Switzerland	25.5	24.0	25.4	25.4	26.5	32.1	32.8	34.4
UK	33.5	30.4	29.6	32.8	40.7	40.8	40.9	43.7
Luxembourg	31.7	30.0	32.5	35.2	35.0	49.0	51.5	53.0
Iceland	27.6	26.9	36.4	29.0	31.8	35.6	32.1	33.4
Turkey	—	—	—	19.9	23.7	—	—	—
Canada	24.1	26.0	28.0	30.6	35.2	36.9	37.2	38.8
US	24.0	25.0	27.5	27.3	30.3	30.5	32.8	31.1
Japan	21.9	19.9	20.7	20.8	20.7	24.0	28.0	31.2
Australia	—	—	25.4	27.3	27.8	31.0	33.4	33.7
New Zealand	—	—	—	—	—	—	—	—

Sources: 1950-1965: OECD (1968) *National accounts 1950-1968*; OECD (1979) *National accounts 1960-1977*; 1970-1980: OECD (1983) *National accounts 1964-1981*; 1985: OECD (1987) *National accounts 1973-1985*.

Note: Current receipts consist mainly of direct and indirect taxes, and social security contributions paid by employers and employees. General government consists of all departments, offices, organization and other bodies which are agents or instruments of the central, state or local public authorities.

The public sector in the OECD countries has grown from a level of about 20 per cent of the GDP at the end of the Second World War to roughly 50 per cent or more in some countries in 1985, when the exceptional growth process was brought to a halt. Why? There are two problems involved in the theories explaining public sector expansion in the OECD countries. On the one hand, we want to know why there is this general growth in the tax state in the rich advanced capitalist countries. On the other hand, we need to explain why the public sector has grown in such a different manner in various countries. Whereas the tax state has expanded from 26 per cent to 60 per cent in Sweden, the increase in the tax state in Switzerland is only from 25 per cent to 34 per cent. Why?

Demand-side approaches

The first attempts to account for the tremendous public sector growth in rich countries took the form of *demand* theories suggesting that socio-economic development of necessity requires public resource allocation (Wagner's law), that increasing affluence implies larger budgets (Wilensky's first law), that the dominance of the left in society or government means budget expansion replacing market mechanisms (Schmidt's law), that a strong position for the right in government is a negative determinant (Castles' law), that collectivist ideologies promote public sector expansion (Wilensky's second law), that sudden social shocks necessitate budgetary shift-points towards much higher levels of public spending (Peacock's and Wiseman's law), that technological development pushes industrial societies more towards the public sector to balance the private sector (Galbraith's law), that welfare spending by the neighbouring state implies a demand for welfare programmes at home (Tarschys' law), that the increasing openness of the economies of the rich countries of the world create a demand for budgetary stabilization of the erratic fluctuations of markets (Cameron's law) and that all political systems whether capitalist or socialist face the same policy demands for public programmes (Pryor's law).

Supply-side approaches

The second stage in the debate about public sector growth was *supply*-oriented. Here we find the hypothesis that budget-making must mean oversupply (Niskanen's law), that public spending involves bureaucratic waste (Tullock's law), that public sector growth is a function of bureau size maximization (Downs' law), that public sector productivity is negative, claiming more resources every year for the 'same' output (Baumol's law), that budget-making rests upon fiscal illusions about the relation between cost and benefit (Oates' law), that budget-making is asymmetrical meaning that those benefiting from public sector expansion are strategically stronger than those that have to pay (Kristensen's law), that public officials whether politicians or bureaucrats are motivated by a private interest function tied to the size of the budget (Breton's law), and that it is difficult to close the gap between benefit and cost in the public sector (Wicksell's law).

Table 6.2. General government: current disbursements as a percentage of GDP

	1950	1955	1960	1965	1970	1975	1980	1985
Austria	21.2	23.0	25.4	28.9	33.1	38.6	42.7	45.2
Belgium	25.5	23.8	27.8	29.8	33.0	41.2	48.1	52.3
Denmark	18.0	21.4	21.7	25.9	34.6	43.5	52.2	56.7
Finland	19.7	20.7	21.9	25.8	28.9	32.2	34.3	37.7
France	26.7	29.8	30.2	32.9	34.7	39.2	43.1	49.4
GFR	28.3	27.0	28.2	30.4	32.6	43.4	42.8	43.4
Greece	19.6	16.3	17.8	21.3	22.4	26.7	30.4	45.3
Ireland	22.9	23.4	24.5	27.6	34.2	42.0	48.3	50.4
Italy	20.7	24.6	26.6	30.9	30.2	38.3	41.4	44.1
Netherlands	23.9	25.5	28.0	33.0	40.2	51.1	54.2	55.2
Norway	21.9	24.4	28.0	31.9	36.5	41.8	45.1	44.0
Portugal	16.3	15.9	15.2	17.7	19.5	27.2	33.8	—
Spain	—	—	13.7	15.8	18.8	21.2	29.4	34.7
Sweden	23.5	26.4	28.7	31.9	37.2	44.9	57.1	60.8
Switzerland	19.4	18.5	19.1	21.3	21.3	28.8	29.3	30.9
UK	30.1	28.8	29.3	30.5	33.2	41.0	42.3	44.9
Luxembourg	22.5	26.9	25.5	29.7	28.6	41.3	45.7	47.8
Turkey	—	—	—	15.5	16.4	—	—	—
Iceland	19.9	20.0	23.4	20.6	21.7	28.3	25.0	28.3
Canada	19.2	23.4	26.6	26.4	32.2	36.8	37.7	43.8
USA	20.0	22.5	25.0	25.2	30.3	33.6	33.5	35.3
Japan	14.6	15.5	13.6	14.7	14.0	20.9	25.4	26.9
Australia	—	—	18.9	21.6	21.8	27.6	30.4	35.5
New Zealand	—	—	—	—	—	—	—	—

Sources: 1950-1965: OECD (1968) *National accounts 1950-1968*; OECD (1979) *National accounts 1960-1977*; 1970-1980: OECD (1983) *National accounts 1964-1981*; 1985: OECD (1987) *National accounts 1973-1985*.

Note: Current disbursements consist of final consumption expenditure, interest on the public debt, subsidies and social security transfers to households. General government consists of all departments, offices, organization and other bodies which are agents or instruments of the central, state or local public authorities.

The purpose of this chapter is to evaluate some of these public policy theories suggesting factors that explain the cross-sectional and longitudinal variation in the size and growth of the public sector in various West European nations. We concentrate here on sixteen major countries in western Europe. These countries are welfare states with a rather similar background, but they differ with regard to the levels and growth rates in total government expenditures (Table 6.2). Why?

'Does politics matter?'

Although research in the various social sciences has been interested in identifying the sources of variation in welfare spending for quite some time, there is as yet no agreement as to which determinants explain the growth of the tax state (Rose, 1984). Some scholars point to the role of demographic factors and affluence (Wilensky, 1975), whereas others mention more specific economic variables like openness of the economy (Cameron, 1978). An incremental approach, last year's expenditure determining this year's outlay, has been propounded (Alt and Chrystal, 1983), but it has also been suggested that culture is a determinant (Wildavsky, 1986). Some argue that political factors play a significant role in shaping patterns of expenditure (Wilensky, 1976; Whitely, 1980, 1986; Hibbs and Fassbender, 1981, Castles, 1982; Schmidt, 1982; Hibbs, 1987; Paldam, 1990).

The test of public policy hypotheses concerning the causes of public sector expansion has not resulted in any specific and generally valid findings. It is argued that the lack of any true general comparative results about the forces that lead to the growth of the state implies that we should resort to a more institutional approach focusing on country specific factors (Anckar and Ståhlberg, 1980; Lybeck and Henrekson, 1988; Olsen, 1988). No doubt it is important to analyse the expansion of the public sector in each country — conditions, decisions, implementation — but this does not exclude efforts at a comparative understanding of similarities and differences. Let us take a comparative look at the policy data once more, but recognize that conditions for policy-making may differ when it comes to the variation between the rich welfare countries in Western Europe and the much larger differences in public policies when the set of countries studied include both rich and poor, north and south, communist and non-communist.

Testing policy hypotheses

It is important to emphasize the implications of the choice of the dependent variables for the evaluation of the environmental theory that economic, political or social factors determine levels or growth rates in public finance systems. If one argues that politics is important for policy outputs in a public finance setting, then it may make a difference which public expenditure or revenue item is chosen. However, the test of the environmental theory is not to be dependent on the choice of expenditure or revenue item in a completely arbitrary fashion; conceivably, we might get one answer if one type of public expenditure item is selected and another if some other type is chosen. Should the analysis focus upon revenue items or expenditure items, upon total outlays or some subaggregations, upon variables of the total public sector or on variables of different public bodies at various levels of government?

No satisfactory solution to this problem has been suggested in the literature on policy determinants. The indeterminacy typical of the problem of selecting the dependent variables may account for the inconclusiveness that characterizes the finding concerning public expenditure determination. In order to resolve some of the inconclusiveness concerning the policy determination problem, we suggest an approach which draws theoretically upon the public finance tradition (Musgrave, 1959; Musgrave and Peacock, 1967; Buchanan and Flowers, 1980) and employs empirical techniques which allow us to draw upon as much of the variation in the data as possible when testing the theory that socio-economic forces are a major determinant of public finance variations.

In order to take the possibility of structural variability into account we make two policy analyses; one refers to only the West European democracies, on which so much of the debate has focused due to their combination of markets and huge welfare state spending; the other covers a much larger set of countries including various kinds of politico-economic regimes, rich market systems, Communist countries and Third World nations in Chapter 7.

Dependent Variables

In a public finance perspective, public policy or public expenditure belongs, of course, to the public household. The set of public expenditure items is potentially very large depending on the aggregation level chosen; the public budget has a set of variables which may be approached in terms of a simple input — output model of the political budgeting process (Figure 6.1). National patterns of public spending are typically described by means of some monetary indicator adjusted according to the size of the population of the country. Other indicators for public policies sometimes supplement per capita measures or percentage indices of GDP, but we will use only monetary indices. The public finance data have been taken from the OECD statistical publications, which are fairly comprehensive for our set of countries. What are the dependent variables? B. Guy Peters and Martin O. Heisler have emphasized the difficulties in conceptualizing and measuring what the government and public sector stand for (Peters and Heisler, 1983).

Figure 6.1. Structure of public finance systems

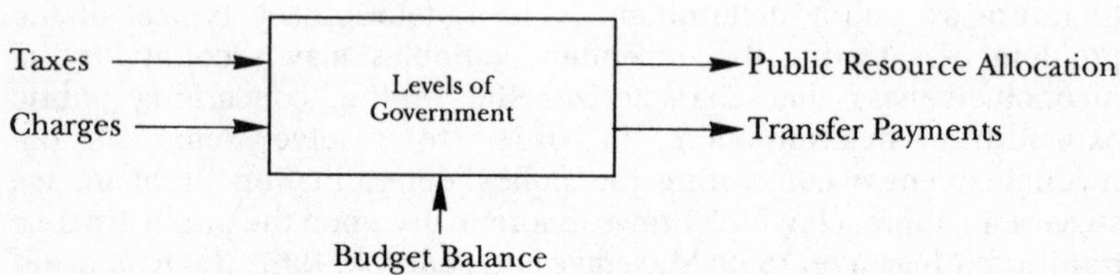

For purposes of analysis, the variables of the model may be broken down in various ways. In comparative research on the properties of political budget-making systems, the availability of data on various public finance items constrains the choice of variables to be covered. Since our purpose is to analyse the relationships between policy determinants and public finance variables, we have included only those public finance items for which there is information for most of the years and most of the countries the structural analysis aims to cover. Although the focus chosen means that some interesting categories could not be included in the analysis, we still faced a real choice when picking a set of dependent variables from the fairly large set for which the OECD publications contain data. Roughly fifteen revenue or expenditure items may be included, given the choice of such a long time period and such a large number of nations (Appendix 6.1).

There are two possible strategies for maximizing the number of years covered and the number of countries studied; either we analyse each of the public finance items for which there are data in accordance with our criteria, or we try to reduce the number of dependent variables by the identification of communalities. If the first strategy is chosen, we run into the addition problem, meaning that there is no natural method for summing up the separate findings from the regression analysis of each item into an overall judgement about environmental determinism. We suggest that the second strategy is the better one, following Peacock and Wiseman that factor analysis is a suitable tool in the present state of public finance knowledge (Peacock and Wiseman, 1979). If we could identify a few latent variables among the manifest variables chosen, then the search for determinants would have a clearer objective, and the findings in the structural analysis would be more easily interpretable.

Table 6.3. Factor analysis of the dependent variables (Varimax rotation)

	Factor 1	*Factor 2*	*Factor 3*
General government:			
Current disbursement/GDP	0.77	0.60	−0.09
Current receipts/GDP	0.75	0.58	0.28
Taxes/GDP	0.87	0.16	0.33
Budgetary balance/GDP	−0.00	−0.02	0.97
Social security contributions/GDP	0.17	0.94	0.01
Social security expenditures/GDP	0.39	0.84	−0.11
Government final consumption/ GDP	0.79	0.30	−0.08
Central government:			
Current disburements/GDP	0.94	0.07	−0.20
Current receipts/GDP	0.95	0.03	0.93
Taxes/GDP	0.93	0.03	0.00
Budgetary balance/GDP	0.04	−0.13	0.93
GDP (log)	−0.07	0.81	−0.11
Explained variance per cent	53.4	19.7	14.8

First, we make a distinction between input-output items and properties that refer to internal transactions within the public finance systems, like fiscal centralization and the transfer of grants. We will treat the distribution of the expenditure 'cake' between various levels of governments as an independent variable of potential relevance in explaining the size and growth of the public sector (Tarschys, 1975; Oates, 1972). Secondly, we employ an explanatory factor analysis to find out whether the public finance variables for which there are comparable data are reducible to a manageable set of dimensions. A special type of factor analysis must be resorted to: 'super P factor analysis' (Park, 1973), which combines cross-sectional and longitudinal data, covering the entire time and space variation. Had we resorted to factor analysis of some cross-sectional slice we would have run into the very difficulty that we were trying to avoid — the dependence of the findings on the arbitrary choice of one or other space or time slice.

The factor analysis of the indicators on the dependent variables is presented in Table 6.3 which shows that data reduction is a real possibility. It appears from the factor analysis that three dimensions catch roughly 90 per cent of the variation in the data; moreover, these three dimensions allow an interesting theoretical interpretation on the basis of traditional conceptual distinctions in the public finance literature.

The first dimension would constitute the allocation branch — measured by the indicator government final consumption — made up of a set of pure and impure public goods as well as merit goods in the Musgravian terminology (Musgrave, 1959). The indicator selected does not display the highest factor loading on this dimension, but it is more specific than the general revenue variables which belong to the same dimension (taxes, current disbursements, current receipts). The analysis of structural determinants would not be different had we selected instead of final government consumption some other indicator such as current receipts.

The second dimension would cover the distribution branch — still following Musgrave's concepts — where the main items are transfer payments of various kinds (social security expenditures). Interestingly, the second dimension includes no central government finance variables, but some general public finance variables correlate with the societal expenditure variables. The fact that current disbursement and current receipts also load on the second latent variable supports the theoretical interpretation suggested here. Transfer payments must, of course, be paid for through the public finance system, but several nations use mechanisms other than the central government budget to deal with these items, thus accounting for the pattern of factor loadings.

Third, the factor analysis separates out data concerning budgetary balance as a separate dimension. If revenues and expenditure do not match, the public sector resorts to deficit spending. Obviously, we have here a variation that is independent of the variation in public resource allocation and public transfers; not surprisingly, the two main indicators on budgetary balance — total public sector surplus and central government budget deficit — go together, which means that we can select one of them — central government surplus — as our indicator. It is difficult to argue convincingly for the selection of either of the two indicators — general government or central government budgetary balance.

Most of the attention which focuses upon the budgetary balance of the public sector tends to concentrate on the relation between central government revenue and expenditure. Actually, total government balance is more important, as a large central government deficit may be covered by financial transactions within the public finance system, the central government borrowing from surpluses elsewhere in the system. However, since the two budgetary balances go together we select the variable which is usually employed when deficit spending is discussed.

Independent Variables

When it comes to the specification of the variables in the set of independent variables, it seems natural to follow the debate on the 'Does politics matter' theme (Peacock, 1979; Schmidt, 1983; Alt and Chrystal, 1983). The number of variables that pertain to the political background of the public finance system (Appendix 6.1) is maximized given the constraints that follow from the comparative ambition to cover sixteen nations over a longer time span. We have added economic variables to the set of independent variables, as the literature also contains hypotheses about the implications for public spending of the level and growth of the economy, of the openness of the economy, industry, unemployment and inflation. A large list of independent variables may be identified, which is of potential interest in an explanation of policy patterns in a comparative expenditure perspective.

The set of independent variables thus arrived at is of course much too cumbersome; it has to be reduced in some way. The first step is to classify the set of independent variables according to the traditional trichotomy: economy, polity and society. The next step would be to select on a theoretical basis a few variables that pertain to each of these major categories. The third step is to employ again the so-called super P factor analysis in order to cover as much as possible of the variation during the time period selected for our cases.

The factor analysis of the indicators on the large set of independent variables allows us to identify six dimensions in the set of independent variables. The six dimensions may be interpreted in a determinate manner (Table 6.4)

1. *Modernization*: this dimension is tapped by two variables which are inversely related, age structure and size of agricultural employment. This is hardly surprising as the development of a post-industrial economy has implied both a continued reduction of the population engaged in agriculture and a steady growth in the number of retired people.

Table 6.4. Factor analysis of independent variables (Varimax variation)

	Factors					
	1	2	3	4	5	6
Centralization	0.55	−0.02	−0.32	0.57	0.06	−0.01
Impex index	0.02	−0.14	0.10	0.89	0.08	−0.11
Agricultural emp	−0.90	−0.06	−0.24	−0.07	−0.08	−0.09
Age structure: 65-	0.32	−0.05	0.56	−0.23	0.43	−0.04
Unemployment	−0.62	0.30	−0.04	0.09	0.48	0.09
Inflation rate	0.03	−0.11	0.05	0.13	0.78	0.20
GDP real growth	−0.14	0.22	0.17	0.02	−0.62	0.46
Trade-union density	0.02	−0.23	0.86	0.24	0.02	−0.01
Socialist vote	0.25	−0.22	0.71	−0.07	−0.26	−0.37
Conservative vote	0.13	0.80	−0.07	−0.21	−0.13	−0.23
Socialist cabinet	0.19	−0.75	0.32	−0.01	0.00	−0.06
Conservative cabinet	0.04	0.91	−0.03	−0.14	−0.09	0.13
Government change	−0.03	0.04	−0.01	−0.09	0.05	0.64
Volatility	0.22	−0.14	−0.32	−0.01	0.02	0.66
GDP (log)	0.74	0.07	0.13	−0.11	0.16	0.31
Population (log)	0.45	0.45	−0.18	−0.66	−0.01	0.06
Explained variance (%)	21.7	16.9	11.8	8.8	8.4	6.4

2. *Conservative strength*: some crucial measures of the partisan character of government and parliament go together such as conservative vote, conservative cabinets and socialist cabinet (negative). There is here some support for the contention of Castles that the conservative dimension in the political environment of the public household is *sui generis* and should not be identified with a general political party dimension (Castles, 1982).

3. *Left-wing strength*: as Schmidt has emphasized, the power of the left in a society is not only a matter of the political position of socialist and communist parties; of equal importance is the access to power of the trade-union movement which is partly a function of its organizational density. It appears that measures of the position of the trade-union movement and the position of the socialist parties go together and constitute a dimension separate from that of the position of the conservative camp in a society.

4. *Openness of the economy*: the index on economic interaction between nations belongs to the same factor as the size of a nation measured by the number of inhabitants. It seems as if the extent of openness in an economy depends on how large a nation is in terms

of population. The larger the nation the less openness there is, indicating that we may expect to find openness among the smaller European democracies.

5. *The economic dimension*: GDP growth, level of unemployment and inflation rate have been singled out as a separate dimension. It appears that all three major economic variables go together to a great degree. This is particularly true for inflation rate and GDP growth, which are naturally inversely related.

6. *Political stability*: the level of change in government turnover as well as in voter alignments constitutes a separate dimension, which is of potential interest in explaining public finance patterns. It has been argued that changes in expenditure depend not only on the partisan character of government, but also upon the rate of change in government, higher rates being conducive to expenditure growth.

The findings of the factor analysis in Table 6.4 indicate that a compromise between a maximum and a minimum strategy is called for with regard to the set of independent variables. It is neither necessary to include whatever variable one may find, nor to go to great lengths in trying to reduce the number of variables to two or three dimensions. The analysis of structural connections between the dependent variables and the independent variables is based on a combined cross-sectional and longitudinal file. The research strategy includes two steps. First, we look for invariant relationships. Second, we try to locate relationships that only hold true for some time period and some countries. The analysis consists of two separate sections, one focusing upon *levels* of public expenditure on the other on *changes* in public expenditure. It could be the case that there are structural connections between political factors and public finance items in a dynamic perspective when a major change is implemented in the expenditure pattern. Such a finding does not necessarily imply that political factors are relevant statistically for the explanation of variations in expenditure levels.

The policy variation in expenditure levels

It is a classic theory in the public finance tradition (Buchanan, 1967, 1980; Musgrave and Peacock, 1967) that the provision of a minimal level of public goods is a necessary condition for social order and the peaceful operation of exchange in various markets. The implication is that we should not expect any extensive variation in one indicator — final government consumption between the nations studied — at least during the first decade covered. However, the expansion of the welfare state means, in a public finance conceptual framework, that the public sector has moved into the provision of semi-public goods or merit goods such as education and health care. The implication is then the opposite, i.e. we may expect a growing variation between our nations as we move into the next few decades, because preferences may vary considerably as regards merit goods and semi-public goods.

There is no consensus as to the nature of the public expenditure variation, some arguing in favour of the *convergence hypothesis* — that the variation between nations with a mixed economy is decreasing — and others denying any such seminal trend (see Castles, 1982). We have to test two hypotheses, one stating that the country variation will tend to increase as the government increasingly allocates semi-public and merit goods; the second — the convergence hypothesis — argues that country differences in preferences for allocation patterns will decrease over time as all nations tend to regard the provision of certain goods as citizens' rights, the richer a nation becomes and the more visible the welfare state in any one nation becomes for all the other nations. The convergence hypothesis is based on a variety of assumptions about the development patterns of the post-industrial state (Galbraith, 1967; Bell, 1973).

The purpose here is limited as we wish to analyse how large the variation in public finance system is and how it has developed over time. We focus upon two statistical measures of the variation, the coefficient of variation (CV) and the Eta-squared statistic (E^2) in relation to data for the 1950's, 1960's and 1970's when the West European welfare state was built up in order to reach a steady state in the 1980s. The CV score is obtained by dividing the standard deviation by the mean value:

$$CV = s/\bar{X}$$

where a higher score than some arbitrary 0.20 indicates a variation that warrants an analysis; the larger the CV score the more the variation. The eta squared statistic is arrived at in the following way:

$$E^2 = \frac{TSS - WSS}{TSS}$$

where TSS equals the total sum of squared deviation and WSS stands for the within group sum of squares; the larger the eta statistic the more the variation between the groups than within the groups. Table 6.5 reports on average values for the three dimensions in the public finance data.

Table 6.5. Variation in levels in public finance dimensions

	Final government consumption			*Social security expenditures*			*Central government budgetary balance*		
	1950s	1960s	1970s	1950s	1960s	1970s	1950s	1960s	1970s
Austria	13.1	13.6	16.2	9.7	11.5	12.3	2.5	2.8	1.2
Belgium	12.1	13.2	15.7	9.5	12.0	17.4	−0.4	0.00	−1.1
Denmark	12.0	15.6	22.6	6.8	9.3	12.9	—	—	0.1
FRG	13.8	15.1	18.8	12.0	11.0	12.4	2.6	1.5	1.3
Finland	11.6	14.6	16.7	—	5.9	6.9	—	4.5	4.8
France	13.6	13.2	14.0	12.5	14.3	17.3	2.1	3.0	1.6
Greece	12.1	12.0	13.9	5.1	6.9	7.8	0.2	1.4	−0.2
Ireland	12.5	13.1	18.3	5.8	7.1	11.9	0.4	0.8	−1.6
Italy	11.8	14.5	15.7	9.5	11.3	15.4	0.5	1.8	−2.2
Netherlands	13.6	15.2	17.3	7.8	13.1	20.7	3.1	3.8	2.8
Norway	11.2	14.1	16.8	5.7	9.5	13.7	4.7	4.7	5.1
Portugal	10.0	12.7	14.2	2.4	3.2	5.8	1.5	0.7	0.5
Spain	8.9	8.2	9.2	—	4.6	9.3	—	2.8	2.3
Sweden	14.9	18.0	24.6	6.2	8.5	13.5	2.3	3.3	1.5
Switzerland	9.6	10.2	11.7	5.6	5.9	8.7	2.1	2.1	1.5
UK	17.5	17.1	19.7	5.9	7.0	9.0	1.6	2.5	1.2
Total	12.5	13.8	16.6	7.5	8.8	12.3	1.8	2.4	1.2
E^2	0.86	0.84	0.83	0.93	0.87	0.83	0.65	0.64	0.54
CV score	0.17	0.18	0.24	0.38	0.38	0.36	0.96	0.72	2.31

Note: Data for 1985 is presented in Table 6.13.

The data indicate that in the post-war decade we find little variation between the nations as they focus on classical public goods (CV = 0.17). The high eta scores indicate clearly that the between country differences are stable during the 1950s. The second major finding is also in accordance with the public finance framework: the expansion of government during the 1960s and the 1970s has resulted in increased country variation, because spending on impure public goods implies greater freedom for governments at various levels to take action as regards goods and services when it is considered that markets do not perform adequately. Thus we find that the CV score is up considerably during the 1970s and the decreasing values of the Eta-squared indicate that the between-nation differences are not as stable as they used to be. For the 1970s we find a CV value of 0.24 to be compared with the figure for the 1950s.

Concerning final government consumption, the conclusion is that there is no support in the data for the convergence theme. The spread between nations has increased and the pattern of between nation-differences is not stable. The size of public transfers expresses equity considerations according to public finance theory. The national ambition in this field of public expenditure is bound to vary as a function of the prevailing political preference function.

In nations where equality has a firm basis in the political machinery we would expect high levels of transfer payments as a percentage of GDP. Naturally we expect to find higher levels of redistribution effort as the welfare state matures over time. The data in Table 6.5 support our expectations. The variation in the redistributive ambitions is quite large for all the three decades, CV = 0.38 in the 1950s, 0.38 in the 1960s, 0.36 in the 1970s. The high eta values indicate that the variation between the nations is larger than the variation within the nations over time. The fact that the convergence hypothesis receives some support in relation to social security expenditures may be explained by different arguments: increasing affluence tends to bring about insurance action, an intense welfare effort in one nation calls for similar levels of spending in other nations (the demonstration effect), or similar organizations or age groups may be strong enough effectively to demand more transfer payments, at least for their own groups.

It is a well-known fact that the effect of the development in the world economy during the 1970s was that nations faced growing difficulties in matching expenditure with revenues. The data concerning the budgetary balance of the central government in Table 6.5 confirm the general impression as the average net surplus is down considerably (from 2.4 per cent in the 1960s to 1.2 per cent in the 1970s). Not surprisingly we find a lot of variation both between the countries and within the countries as regards budgetary balance.

To sum up, if the various systems of public finance are analysed in terms of three dimensions — final government consumption, transfer payments and budgetary balance — we may establish that there is a clear pattern of variation that calls for a search for determinants of various kinds. It appears that the transfer payments vary more extensively between the nations than public resource allocation, and that the pattern of variation in budgetary balance is much less stable countrywise than the variation in the other two dimensions. Finally, the data does not confirm the convergence hypothesis, not even as regards transfer payments. If there is a pattern of variation in the levels of these public finance dimensions that is stable over time in terms of between-nation differences, then we ask if there are political, economic or institutional traits in these nations that explain the pattern derived.

In looking for determinants of levels of final government consumption, public transfer payments and budgetary balance we have two objectives:

— to identify time invariant structures, and
— to unravel whatever structural connections may obtain during certain time periods.

Let us begin by looking at simple correlations for final government consumption (Appendix 6.2). We find a few stable correlations in the post-war period that account for the variation in final government consumption; the level of public resource allocation is affected by agricultural employment (r=-0.55), age structure (r=0.53), centralization (r=0.52), trade-union density (r=0.45), socialist vote and cabinet (r=0.33) and openness of economy (r=0.29). If we allow for structural variability it is also possible to identify other determinants: GDP growth (1961-2 and 1971-2), conservative vote (1951-2), (1977-8), conservative cabinet (1951-2 and 1977-8), government stability (1961-2) and party system change (1971-2).

The correlation analysis does not support statements to the effect that political variables are the essential explanatory factors. However, trade-union strength and the position of the socialist parties appear to have a stable impact upon final government consumption together with two demographic variables and one variable of the public finance system. It may be the case that other variables have an impact upon government final consumption, but the causal pattern is not invariant; sometimes these variables do have an impact, sometimes they do not. As suggested above, focusing on only some cross-sectional slice may lead to findings that have a limited validity. Turning to regression analysis we must ask how the factors that appear to have a lasting impact upon final government consumption relate to each other. Table 6.6 has the answer.

Table 6.6. Regression analysis of general government final consumption/GDP (pooled data)

	OLS			Pseudo-GLS*		
	Coefficient	t-statistic	R^2	Coefficient	t-statistic	R^2
Centralization	0.11	7.14	0.48	−0.86	−2.60	0.72
Trade-union density	0.04	4.50		0.08	2.28	
Age structure	0.44	4.87		−0.26	−0.30	
Impex index	−0.03	−4.86		−0.09	−0.47	
Socialist cabinet	0.01	3.82		−0.01	−0.34	
Agriculture emp	−0.04	−2.36		−0.31	−4.41	

Note: * Kmenta, 1971:511; Pindyck and Rubinfeld, 1981:259

Employing the OLS technique supplemented by the GLS technique, we find that three variables are of causal importance: agricultural employment, trade-union density and centralization. Thus the analysis of partial effects does not corroborate any general statement about the impact of political parties on public resource allocation. The positive finding is that trade-union strength does seem to have a lasting impact on final government expenditure. Most interestingly, the effect of age structure vanishes when the other variables are kept constant. So much for the invariant relationships, i.e. relations between the dependent variable and the set of independent variables that are structurally stable over time and space.

Let us look at various cross-sectional slices on the basis of two-year periods in order to locate time periods in which we have stronger connections between government final consumption and environmental factors. We tested a political model for each of these cross-sectional slices explaining levels of government final consumption with trade-union density, socialist vote and socialist cabinet. The findings may be summarized in the following manner: the variation in goodness of fit is considerable, because for some time periods — roughly up until 1964 — the political model explains little, whereas for the time periods after 1965 the political model has some explanatory power. At most the political model explains about 60 per cent of the variation (in 1967-8), when the political model works at its best and where socialist cabinet is the strongest of the explanatory variables. However, it must be emphasized that there is no uniform trend towards an increase in the explanatory relevance of the political model: in 1977-8 the model only captures 27 per cent of the variation in the dependent variable.

The analysis of the various cross-sectional slices confirms the finding from the overall analysis that trade-union density is the best predictor of government final consumption when only a set of political variables are considered. Turning to a model with other independent variables included in a model with one political variable, we tested for the partial effect of the political variable over various time periods. The test is a partial confirmation of the 'politics matter' theme, as it appears that the political variable in a combined model is often the best predictor for those time periods when the combined model functions best — roughly 50 per cent of the variation.

There is thus an interesting finding: political factors appear to grow in importance as determinants of the country variation in the allocation branch of the public finance system. We suggest the following interpretation; at the end of the Second World War most European nations had to concentrate their public effort on more or less pure public goods, the provision of which is not so closely related to the partisan character of government. During the 1950s and the 1960s the expansion of the GDP meant that provision of semi-public goods and merit goods became possible to a much greater extent, which provided the opportunity for socialist groups to use government to correct for market outcomes. The conclusion is that politics matter in relation to the outputs of the allocation branch, but the relation is not an invariant one. We must allow for structural variability.

If politics matter for certain time periods in relation to the allocation branch, what is its impact on the redistribution branch? Here we would expect to find strong associations as the ideology of socialist parties causes these parties to emphasize transfer payments as a tool for achieving income redistribution. Let us first look at correlations for the whole time period (Appendix 6.3). We find a few invariant relationships with regard to the variation in levels of public transfer payments. The following factors appear to have a lasting impact on the redistribution effort: centralization ($r = 0.53$), age structure ($r = 0.52$), agriculture ($r = -0.47$), and conservative cabinet ($r = 0.30$) and conservative vote ($r = 0.15$).

We cannot find that trade union power or the position of the socialist parties exert a stable impact upon transfer payments. Surprisingly, the relationship between conservative party strength and social security expenditures is positive. This may reflect the uncertainty about how the large Catholic parties are to be classified. If the Christian Democratic parties are placed together with the main stream conservative parties as is done here, the positive correlation becomes more understandable. It has been argued that there is a strong positive connection between catholicism and welfare spending also at the level of politics (Wilensky, 1976; Flora and Heidenheimer, 1981).

Some variables seem to be relevant only for some time periods: openness of economy (1951-2), (1975-6 and 1977-8), unemployment (1953-4), inflation (1953-4) and GDP growth (1955-6), (1961-2), trade union density (51-52). Thus we are reminded again of the fact that the selection of the cross-section slice may affect the conclusions arrived at which are generalized to other time periods in which they may fail.

The analysis indicates that there may be one configuration between the independent variables and transfer payments and another configuration between the same independent variables and public resource allocation. We find that other factors are relevant for the explanation of transfer payments. How do these factors relate to each other? Let us look at a pooled regression (Table 6.7).

The regression estimates do not corroborate the standard assumptions about the factors that are conducive to differences in ambition with regard to redistribution. Only centralization in the public finance system has an impact if a model including age structure, conservative vote and conservative cabinet in addition to centralization is tested.

Perhaps we can find a stronger impact during some of the time periods. Again, we tested two models on a series of cross-sectional data

Table 6.7. Regression analysis of social security expenditure/GDP (pooled data)

	OLS			*Pseudo-GLS*		
	Coefficient	t-statistic	R^2	Coefficient	t-statistic	R^2
Centralization	0.13	8.67	0.43	0.09	4.56	0.79
Conservative vote	−0.41	−2.35			0.00	0.52
Age structure	0.77	9.31			0.01	1.98
Conservative cabinet	0.04	7.79			0.10	3.95

covering the various two-year periods in order to locate any structurally variant determinant on levels of social security expenditure. The findings are not as positive as in the case concerning government final consumption. A political model explains little most of the time. Surprisingly, it is best during the first decade. In the 1960s and the 1970s the model lacks virtually any explanatory power. A combined model performs better. When such a combined model does well (1953-4, 1977-8), it appears that the political variable included is outweighed by the non-political ones, particularly age structure, industry and impex.

The third dimension — budgetary balance — remains to be considered. We found a few invariant relationships (Appendix 6.4). The level of budgetary surplus appears to be a function of: unemployment ($r = -0.51$), socialist vote ($r = 0.30$) and conservative vote ($r = -0.21$). The relation between level of unemployment and budgetary deficit is not difficult to account for, but how do we explain that the strength of the socialist parties is positively related to budgetary balance whereas the strength of conservative parties is negatively related to budgetary balance? It seems as if budgetary balance may be affected by other variables as well, but their impact varies in both strength and direction with the time period selected. A pooled regression singles out unemployment as a crucial determinant of budgetary balance. The rise in unemployment since the oil crises appears in Table 6.8.

Trying a combined model on the various two-year periods we established that politics matters little for the determination of levels of budgetary balance in public finance systems on a national level. Central government budgetary deficits vary more often as a function of variables such as unemployment during the 1970s, GDP growth in the early fifties and inflation in 1967-8 and 1971-2. When a political model works — between 1957 and 1964 — we get the same surprising result that a socialist cabinet positively affects the level of budget surplus.

Table 6.8. Unemployment as a percentage of total labour force: average

	1950 −54	1955 −59	1960 −64	1965 −69	1970 −74	1975 −79	1980 −84
Austria	5.2	3.6	2.1	1.9	1.3	1.7	2.9
Belguim	4.9	3.2	2.2	2.2	2.1	6.2	11.1
Denmark	4.4	4.4	1.8	1.7	1.9	6.6	9.5
Finland	1.4	1.9	1.4	2.5	2.2	5.0	5.1
France	1.3	1.1	1.2	1.6	2.1	4.9	8.0
Germany, Federal Republic of	6.7	3.1	0.7	0.9	1.1	3.8	6.2
Greece	—	—	—	5.2	2.7	1.9	5.7
Ireland	6.1	5.9	5.0	4.9	5.9	8.1	11.6
Italy	7.4	6.9	3.1	3.6	3.2	6.8	8.6
Netherlands	2.4	1.5	0.9	1.4	2.1	5.3	9.9
Norway	0.8	1.2	1.1	0.9	0.8	1.9	2.5
Portugal	—	—	—	2.5	2.3	6.8	7.9
Spain	1.2	0.8	1.2	1.6	2.5	5.9	15.2
Sweden	2.3	2.1	1.3	1.6	1.8	1.9	2.9
Switzerland	—	—	—	—	—	0.4	0.6
UK	1.2	1.2	1.5	1.7	2.5	4.6	9.5

Source: 1950-74: Madsen and Paldam (1978); 1975-84: OECD (1988) *Labour Force Statistics*.

To sum up, politics matters for the level of public finance dimensions, but not in a uniform manner over all time periods or in the same way for the three basic dimensions. Political variables are relevant from an explanatory point of view with regard to levels of government final consumption for several periods of time, mainly since the mid-1960s. The direction of the impact is clear: the stronger the socialist side or the trade-unions the larger the allocation branch. The variation in trade-union strength is indicated by the extent of labour force trade-union membership, or how encompassing the trade-union movement is. Table 6.9 has some relevant data.

As regards the two other dimensions, social security expenditures and budgetary balance, the findings do not support the hypothesis that environmental factors in general or political variables in particular account to any considerable extent for the variation. There are hardly any stable relationships and not even for short time periods is it possible to locate strong impacts.

Table 6.9. Estimates of percentage of work force unionized 1950-1980.

	1950	1955	1960	1965	1970	1975	1980
Austria	62	63	63	63	62	59	58
Belguim	52	53	57	55	61	66	71
Denmark	53	59	62	62	67	67	—
Finland	33	31	32	36	57	75	—
France	32	25	22	21	23	25	—
Germany, Federal Republic of	33	34	33	32	32	33	33
Greece	—	—	—	—	—	—	—
Ireland	—	—	—	—	—	—	—
Italy	34	—	—	32	41	47	—
Netherlands	40	38	39	37	39	40	38
Norway	52	54	63	64	64	61	65
Portugal	—	—	—	—	—	—	—
Spain	—	—	—	—	—	—	—
Sweden	67	68	68	71	73	82	85
Switzerland	—	—	—	—	—	—	—
UK	44	44	44	43	47	51	54

Source: Kjellberg (1983); Matheson (1979) for Finland

The policy variation in growth rates

One finding from the analysis of the variation in levels of public finance effort — final government consumption and social security payments — is stability. The between-country differences are substantial but not extreme; moreover, the country differences are larger than the intra-country differences over time. Stability does not imply lack of change. Actually, we expect to find a great deal of one type of change; growth, as the post-war period contains the expansionary years of the welfare state. Table 6.10 presents a picture of the variation in growth rates in our public finance dimensions.

Table 6.10. Variations in growth rates in public finance dimensions (percentages)

	Final government consumption			*Social security expenditures*			*Central government budgetary balance*		
	1950s	1960s	1970s	1950s	1960s	1970s	1950s	1960s	1970s
Austria	7.0	6.2	6.2	9.2	6.6	5.8	34.0	8.8	−3.2
Belgium	2.6	5.8	6.7	4.5	7.6	8.1	59.2	−350.5	−118.2
Denmark	5.5	10.3	5.6	6.0	12.4	6.9	—	—	−49.0

Table 6.10 continued

	Final government consumption			*Social security expenditures*			*Central government budgetary balance*		
	1950s	1960s	1970s	1950s	1960s	1970s	1950s	1960s	1970s
FRG	5.6	6.7	5.8	8.6	3.5	5.9	1.6	−29.5	13.1
Finland	6.1	7.4	6.0	—	6.1	7.2	—	5.0	0.8
France	6.5	5.4	5.6	7.0	7.2	7.6	49.3	10.8	−137.7
Greece	6.1	8.2	8.3	7.9	11.1	7.3	−19.0	40.3	27.7
Ireland	0.7	5.9	14.3	1.7	8.3	14.5	18.9	−179.7	3.4
Italy	6.4	7.8	4.5	11.5	8.8	5.7	−5.4	−0.6	15.9
Netherlands	—	7.1	5.3	—	10.4	8.8	—	0.3	−8.0
Norway	6.6	7.2	6.2	9.3	8.7	8.0	7.5	7.5	−2.1
Portugal	6.4	8.4	6.1	7.1	7.8	28.5	10.4	−1.4	132.7
Spain	3.6	7.1	7.3	—	27.7	10.3	—	3.4	−2.3
Sweden	6.4	7.0	5.7	6.9	7.9	8.1	10.0	19.4	−533.9
Switzerland	3.8	5.9	3.6	6.0	6.6	7.6	−14.2	52.1	3.5
UK	0.7	3.5	4.3	5.2	4.7	5.6	21.4	46.2	−31.3
Total	5.1	6.9	6.3	7.0	9.0	8.9	13.9	−25.7	−46.3
E^2	0.13	0.12	0.15	0.10	0.13	0.31	0.07	0.21	0.17
CV score	1.1	0.6	1.0	1.0	1.6	1.0	6.0	8.9	7.3

The overall expansion rates hardly require extensive comment; of course, final government expenditure and transfer payments grow whereas the budgetary balance moves the other way. The average growth rate is somewhat larger for social security payments than for public resource allocation; in the 1950s we have 7 per cent versus 5.1 per cent, in the 1960s 9 per cent versus 6.9 per cent and in the 1970s we have 8.9 per cent versus 6.3 per cent. The drastic change in economic conditions for public finance appears in the reversal of the growth rates in budgetary balance from the 1950s and the 1960s to the 1970s (14, -26 and -46 per cent). The findings concerning the CV scores and the eta values are more interesting.

The variation in growth rates is very different from the pattern of variation in the levels of the public finance dimensions. Growth rates fluctuate considerably both in time and space. The country variation is quite substantial for all three dimensions and all three periods of time. Moreover, the within-nation differences over time are also large, which implies that we cannot expect a unique set of nations that persistently display high growth rates in all the years studied. What factors account for the extensive fluctuations in the growth rates in the public finance dimensions? If politics does not matter that much in relation to levels of public finance dimensions, then perhaps political variables are more relevant in relation to change? Before we jump to any conclusions about the conditions for growth in public finance systems we must call to mind

Table 6.11. Correlation Matrix: Final Government Comsumption (Growth)

	Centra-lization	Impex index	Agricult. employm.	Age struc.	Unem-ployment	Infl. rate	GDP growth	Trade un.dens.	Soc vote	Con vote	Soc cabi	Con cabi	Govern change	Partysyst. instability
Total period	.05	.13	.10	−.08	.02	.08	.14	.02	−.07	−.03	−.00	−.01	−.03	.11
Austria	−.05	−.02	.11	.03	.01	.47	.18	.01	−.19	.22	−.06	.06	−.07	.09
Belgium	.22	.30	−.52	.54	−.28	.31	−.17	.54	−.45	−.29	−.63	.63	−.05	.19
Denmark	.49	−.18	.03	.05	−.52	−.01	.10	−.03	.01	.37	−.21	—	−.27	−.17
F R Germany	.08	−.33	.03	−.11	−.48	.17	.01	−.18	.04	−.13	−.07	.07	.27	.12
Finland	−.35	−.21	.28	.10	−.31	−.27	−.23	−.09	−.17	−.06	.01	—	−.32	.10
France	−.26	.06	−.19	−.03	−.05	.32	.02	−.01	−.01	−.20	.23	.22	.29	.02
Greece	.15	.19	.60	.02	−.17	.24	−.25	—	.20	−.13	—	−.29	.17	.58
Ireland	.44	.87	−.47	−.01	.22	.15	.42	.57	.05	.07	—	−.12	−.11	−.01
Italy	−.44	−.37	.32	−.35	−.22	−.41	.11	−.44	.39	.48	—	—	−.01	.03
The Netherlands	−.60	.12	.55	−.24	−.56	−.28	.28	−.18	−.31	.58	−.31	.31	−.24	−.31
Norway	−.14	−.12	.02	−.04	.13	.02	.22	.04	−.08	.05	.17	—	−.15	.01
Portugal	−.34	−.00	−.05	−.07	—	−.10	.27	—	—	—	—	—	—	—
Spain	.23	.24	−.17	.18	.15	−.06	.19	—	—	—	—	—	—	—
Sweden	.20	−.23	.49	−.13	−.29	−.04	−.01	−.14	.19	−.16	.05	—	−.14	−.20
Switzerland	−.28	.13	−.41	−.00	−.30	.27	.31	−.08	−.09	.18	—	—	—	−.10
United Kingdom	.35	−.06	−.26	.49	.03	.24	.01	.11	−.28	−.12	.08	−.08	−.10	.31

the methodological distinction between invariant structures and structural variability over space and time.

First we focus on stable relations over time and space and then we look for structural connections within each country. Table 6.11 has the data for the first public finance dimension: final government consumption. Although the finding concerning the existence of invariant conditions for final government consumption growth is negative, it is an important one; there is no factor in the set of independent variables that is a condition for change in final government consumption for all countries for all the years studied. Let us then proceed to inquire into the existence of relations that may explain each country's pattern of growth. Focusing on final government expenditure we find a number of country specific connections, several in some countries.

We first consider the political variables. In some nations conservative vote and conservative cabinet have a positive impact, whereas in others the impact is negative; the same applies to socialist vote and cabinet. Trade-union strength does affect growth rates in some nations, but the direction of the relation varies, not simply the magnitude. If politics does not uniformly affect public finance growth, then perhaps GDP growth or other economic variables operate more clearly? It is not true that the higher the GDP growth the higher the rate of expansion in final government consumption. For some nations there is such a relation: Ireland, the Netherlands, Portugal and Switzerland. But in some nations the reverse relation holds: Belgium, Finland and Greece. The same kind of variation in the direction of the relation appears with regard to inflation, unemployment and openness of the economy. Also, it seems as if age structure may have a positive impact in some nations (Belgium, The United Kingdom) but quite the opposite in other nations (Italy and The Netherlands).

If the search for invariant determinants of the growth in public resource allocation is an abortive one, then perhaps we will succeed in the attempt to find a set of conditions that uniformly affects change in social security expenditure in a clear way. Table 6.12 has the correlations, which offer a crude picture. Again, we may establish that there are no general factors operating which affect the change in transfer payments uniformly in the different countries and during the various periods of time. The correlations between this public finance dimension and the set of independent variables are very low in a combined cross-sectional and longitudinal data set. Looking at the country specific-patterns, we can identify a number of connections which are sometimes positive, sometimes negative, depending on the country studied. The standard idea of socialist cabinets raising transfer payments is hardly corroborated in the data; nor is it always the case that the stronger the

Table 6.12. Correlation Matrix: Social Security Expenditures (Growth)

	Centra-lization	Impex index	Agricult. employ	Age struc	Unem-ployment	Infl. rate	GDP growth	Trade union d.	Soc vote	Con vote	Soc cab	Con cab	Govern change	Partysyst. instability
Total period	−.10	.02	.13	−.09	.02	.05	−.02	.03	−.03	−.07	.03	−.04	.06	−.03
Austria	−.31	−.37	−.38	−.36	.33	.49	−.28	.02	−.39	.05	−.21	.21	−.19	−.16
Belgium	.15	.13	−.26	.39	−.20	.23	−.21	.25	−.32	−.22	−.40	.40	.11	.06
Denmark	−.38	−.04	.06	.02	−.06	.11	−.46	.05	.04	.03	.01	—	−.24	−.08
F R of Germany	.10	.25	.06	.12	.32	.19	−.29	.11	.01	−.06	.04	−.04	.13	−.13
Finland	−.03	−.02	.41	.11	−.03	−.02	.03	.05	.22	.10	.03	—	.07	−.00
France	−.50	−.59	.37	−.28	−.68	−.45	.50	−.37	−.70	.29	−.10	.08	−.16	−.23
Greece	.08	−.04	−.71	.03	.28	−.27	−.22	—	.09	.05	—	−.16	.17	−.35
Ireland	.39	.82	−.48	−.13	.16	.20	.40	.51	.12	.15	—	−.13	−.14	−.08
Italy	.02	−.26	.15	−.15	−.06	−.26	.15	−.27	.17	.09	—	—	−.12	−.00
The Netherlands	−.16	−.06	.23	.08	−.37	−.05	.13	−.21	−.29	.30	−.21	.21	.29	−.11
Norway	−.01	−.52	.07	−.06	−.05	−.24	−.36	.10	.30	.08	.05	—	−.20	−.02
Portugal	.82	.20	−.47	.60	—	.65	−.24	—	—	—	—	—	—	—
Spain	−.40	−.31	.22	−.37	−.20	−.13	−.00	—	—	—	—	—	—	—
Sweden	.19	.02	−.08	.17	.24	−.33	−.01	.13	−.00	.03	−.00	—	−.24	−.06
Switzerland	.12	.07	−.33	.15	−.20	.23	.12	−.08	−.29	−.14	—	—	—	.02
United Kingdom	.16	.04	−.16	.14	.29	.03	−.14	.09	−.07	−.21	.30	−.30	−.16	.04

conservative side in society (conservative vote and conservative cabinet), the lower the redistribution effort.

In order to test whether growth rates may be explained by a set of environmental factors, we resorted to a time series analysis of the growth pattern of each nation covering the whole time period. Two models were estimated for each of the two dependent variables, growth rates in governmental final consumption and social security expenditure. The political model performs poorly as regards explanation of the growth in social security expenditure, but displays some explanatory relevance for the changes in government final consumption, particularly for Belgium, Ireland and Italy. However, there is no single political variable that has the same impact when a political model is relevant.

By resorting to a model that includes non-political factors it is possible to explain parts of the variation in growth rates. For some nations a combined model is relevant with regard to social security expenditure: Finland, Ireland, Norway and Portugal, but the factors vary from case to case. The same finding recurs with relation to the explanation of change in government final consumption. In nations like Austria, Belgium, Denmark and West Germany, we are able to detect some environmental impact, but there is no factor that operates the same way in all these cases.

To sum up, the findings concerning the relevance of environmental factors in general and political variables in particular for explaining the quite substantial variation in growth rates for the three public finance dimensions are hardly impressive. It is not the case that economic, political or institutional variables have a uniform effect upon change in public finance systems. The standard idea that the strength of the socialist side in society affects the rate of change in social security expenditure is falsified. In order to understand change in public finance systems in Western Europe we must look for other casual mechanisms than those traditionally specified in the 'Does politics matter-theme'.

Conclusion

As the welfare states in western Europe have matured at a steady-state level in the 1980s, there remains some interesting differences between the sixteen countries studied here with regard to the three basic categories employed above. Table 6.13 presents a perspective on the country variation in general government public finance items: final consumption, general government transfer payments and budgetary balance. It includes the other OECD countries for the purpose of comparison.

Table 6.13. General government public finance data, 1985

	Final consumption as a percentage of GDP	*Social security transfers as a percentage of GDP*	*Deficit as a percentage of GDP*
	1985	1985	1985
Austria	18.7	20.1	2.5
Belgium	17.7	22.0	−5.8
Denmark	25.4	16.5	0.3
Finland	20.3	11.6	2.8
France	16.3	26.6	−0.9
GFR	19.9	16.6	2.0
Greece	20.3	15.0	−10.5
Ireland	19.2	18.2	−6.1
Italy	16.6	16.9	−6.6
Netherlands	16.3	28.5	−0.8
Norway	18.6	14.8	12.1
Portugal	—	—	—
Spain	13.7	16.0	−1.5
Sweden	27.4	19.3	−1.4
Switzerland	13.2	13.7	3.5
UK	21.1	14.6	−1.2
Iceland	18.2	5.2	5.1
Luxembourg	16.6	23.2	5.2
Turkey	—	—	—
Canada	20.1	12.3	−5.0
USA	18.3	11.0	−4.2
Japan	9.7	11.5	4.3
Australia	19.2	10.8	−1.8
New Zealand	—	—	—

Sources: OECD (1987) *National accounts 1973-1985.*

Note: Government final consumption consist of expenditures on goods and services for public administration, defense, health and education. Social security transfers consist of social security benefits, social assistance grants, unfunded employee pension and welfare benefits, and transfers to private non-profit institutions serving households. The deficit is current receipts minus current disbursments.

In the expanding literature on the determinants of policy outputs and policy outcomes there is as yet no consensus on how the pattern of variation in public finance variables in the major West European countries is to be causally interpreted. It is necessary to allow for structural variability or the fact that the policy determinants may have differential impacts in different time periods and different countries. Any general statements to the effect that public sector growth is crucially dependent on the strength and position of the left is not corroborated if the whole time period is covered.

We find that the convergence theme has limited validity as it is not the case generally that public finance systems are becoming more similar. Political variables — various indicators of the strength and position of socialist parties, conservative parties and the trade unions — have a sharply delimited impact on public finance dimensions. We cannot talk about these variables as essential determinants of all aspects of public finance. There is a relationship between the level of final government consumption and trade-union density, and there is a negative relationship between deficit spending and the level of unemployment — but that is all if we are looking for invariant relations. A clear but negative finding is that levels of transfer payments and change or growth rates in public finance items cannot be accounted for by any general factors.

Could it be the case that Western Europe is different due to a seminal process of depoliticization resulting in widespread support for big government? What happens to these findings from the analysis of policy data in the set of West European countries with a rather similar cultural and political background when we move to a much broader analysis of policy determinants in a large set of countries covering the whole world in Chapter 7? Perhaps politics matter after all when we focus on the fundamental choice between market and state among all kinds of countries, rich and poor as well as communist and non-communist.

Appendix 6.1. Indicators and sources

Variables	*Sources*
General government:	
Current disbursements: final consumption expenditures, interest on public debt, subsidies, social security transfers.	OECD: Table 9: line 23
Current receipts: direct and indirect taxes, social security contributions	OECD: Table 9: line 12
Budgetary balance: current receipts minus current disbursements	OECD: Table 9: line 5 and 6
Taxes: indirect taxes plus direct taxes	
Social security contributions	OECD: Table 9: line 8
Social security expenditures	OECD: Table 9: line 17 and 18
Government final consumption: current	OECD: Table 9:

Variable	Source
purchases of goods and services for public administration, defence, health and education, excluding all transfer payments	line 13
Central government:	
Current disbursements	OECD: Table 10:
Current receipts	line 23 and 12
Taxes	OECD: Table 10:
Budgetary balance	line 5, 6, 12, 23
Centralization: central government transfers to subsectors of general government/current disbursements	OECD: Table 10: line 21.1/23
Impex index: Imports plus exports/GDP	
Agricultural employment: Agricultural employment as percentage of civilian employment	Labour force statistics: OECD Observer
Age structure: Proportion of population 65 year and over	Labour force statistics
Unemployment:	OECD Economic Outlook; Yearbook of Labour statistics
Inflation	OECD Economic Outlook; UN Statistical Year-book; Madsen
GDP real growth	OECD Economic Outlook; UN Statistical Year-book; Madsen
Trade-union density: Membership of trade-union in relation to potential membership	Kjellberg, Bain and Price among others
Socialist vote: socialist and/or social democratic parties	Mackie and Rose
Conservative vote: conservative and/or christian democratic parties	Mackie and Rose
Socialist cabinet: socialist prime minister	Beyme

Conservative cabinet: conservative prime minister	Beyme
Government change: number of governments	Beyme among others
Party system volatility: net changes for all the parties within a party system between two elections	Mackie and Rose

Appendix 6.2. Correlation matrix: final government consumption levels

	Centra-lization	Impex index	Agricult. employ	Age struc	Unem-ployment	Infl. rate	GDP growth	Trade union d.	Soc vote	Con vote	Soc cab	Con cab	Govern change	Partysyst. instability
Total period	.52	.29	−.55	.53	.10	.23	−.28	.45	.33	−.10	.33	−.12	−.03	.10
1951/52	.30	−.16	−.57	.52	.06	−.04	.08	.07	.14	.52	.08	.33	.03	.19
1953/54	.33	.12	−.64	.55	−.03	−.12	−.09	.23	.43	.36	.09	.25	−.17	.11
1955/56	.23	.21	−.64	.09	−.03	.16	−.22	.19	.33	.26	.14	.18	.04	.10
1957/58	.38	.25	−.70	.47	−.06	−.13	−.17	.27	.49	.17	.25	.08	.04	.09
1959/60	.32	.14	−.60	.45	.02	−.02	.16	.33	.42	.24	.18	.24	−.00	.03
1961/62	.39	.11	−.71	.12	−.10	.20	−.58	.32	.49	.09	.28	.16	−.14	−.05
1963/64	.63	.18	−.70	.31	−.13	−.22	−.33	.34	.51	.09	.29	.19	.09	−.27
1965/66	.62	.18	−.45	.41	−.12	−.26	−.47	.47	.61	−.09	.64	−.14	−.11	−.09
1967/68	.54	.15	−.46	.38	−.08	.12	−.32	.62	.65	−.23	.66	−.25	−.02	.27
1969/70	.39	.19	−.46	.43	−.11	.16	−.26	.69	.57	−.27	.44	−.21	.01	.05
1971/72	.47	.17	−.48	.46	.06	.02	−.37	.65	.49	−.30	.39	−.15	.06	.45
1973/74	.47	.23	−.47	.47	.08	−.15	−.31	.61	.44	−.30	.39	−.29	−.12	.13
1975/76	.53	.28	−.46	.52	.11	−.04	.06	.62	.44	−.28	.68	−.38	−.06	.01
1977/78	.34	.42	−.34	—	.05	−.17	−.16	.58	.22	−.38	.16	−.46	.05	−.02

Appendix 6.3. Correlation matrix: social security expenditure

	Centra-lization	Impex index	Agricult. employ	Age struc	Unem-ployment	Infl. rate	GDP growth	Trade union d.	Soc vote	Con vote	Soc cab	Con cab	Govern change	Partysyst. instability
Total period	.53	.26	−.47	.52	.14	.17	−.14	.00	−.03	.15	−.08	.30	.05	.14
1951/52	.53	−.34	−.20	.62	.28	.00	.36	−.51	−.15	.26	−.47	.68	.13	.16
1953/54	.70	−.23	.03	.71	.33	−.53	.13	−.43	−.09	.33	−.35	.12	.59	.75
1955/56	.48	−.28	.06	.33	.18	−.07	.37	−.37	−.09	.12	−.08	−.01	.13	.69
1957/58	.57	−.13	−.10	.48	−.10	.16	.24	−.25	.04	.34	−.01	.17	.41	.60
1959/60	.46	.08	−.45	.55	−.04	.31	.18	−.08	.10	.58	−.22	.60	.15	.46
1961/62	.39	.19	−.52	−.29	−.06	−.05	−.34	.03	.16	.42	−.17	.60	.11	.45
1963/64	.41	.23	−.47	.51	−.15	−.18	−.29	.11	.15	.42	.01	.56	−.22	.09
1965/66	.48	.13	−.47	.49	−.11	−.29	−.07	.00	−.03	.54	−.37	.81	.20	.28
1967/68	.45	.12	−.49	−.51	−.14	−.23	−.12	.10	−.18	.56	−.48	.86	.27	.17
1969/70	.38	.26	−.47	.46	−.10	.05	−.04	.03	−.19	.48	−.29	.69	−.02	.11
1971/72	.35	.31	−.42	.36	.05	−.16	−.28	−.01	−.14	.24	−.11	.59	.11	.16
1973/74	.41	.44	−.43	.23	.20	−.21	.00	−.05	−.09	.02	.01	.11	.21	−.08
1975/76	.42	.51	−.43	.13	.14	−.30	.08	−.04	−.05	.05	.11	.21	−.28	−.18
1977/78	.40	.42	−.41		.02	−.30	−.03	.03	−.01	.04	−.23	.21	.14	−.23

Appendix 6.4. Correlation matrix: central government budgetary balance

	Centra-lization	Impex index	Agricult. employ	Age struc	Unem-ployment	Infl. rate	GDP growth	Trade union d.	Soc vote	Con vote	Soc cab	Con cab	Govern change	Partysyst. instability
Total period	−.04	.00	.00	−.10	−.51	−.20	.16	.08	.30	−.21	.24	−.21	−.08	.−11
1951/52	.27	.47	.16	−.58	−.43	.12	−.03	.57	.79	−.52	.08	.33	.03	.19
1953/54	−.01	−.08	.42	−.03	−.29	−.13	.34	.21	.31	−.34	.14	−.05	−.15	.00
1955/56	−.02	.25	−.03	.23	−.45	−.05	.41	.30	.47	−.22	.09	−.18	−.13	−.36
1957/58	.07	.39	.09	−.02	−.38	.20	.10	.17	.39	−.21	.40	−.24	−.38	−.15
1959/60	.07	.33	−.10	−.10	−.63	.43	.26	−.07	.27	−.37	.33	−.33	.04	−.10
1961/62	.35	.15	−.12	−.26	−.60	.08	−.09	.13	.33	−.42	.44	−.27	.09	−.39
1963/64	.30	.08	−.04	.03	−.62	.23	−.02	.01	.21	−.35	.48	−.19	.10	−.60
1965/66	−.02	.08	.07	.04	−.25	.15	−.10	.19	.20	−.35	.34	−.27	−.03	−.26
1967/68	.15	.16	−.02	−.14	−.19	.53	−.23	.01	.25	−.31	.43	−.41	−.12	.30
1969/70	.09	.01	−.27	.06	−.30	.13	−.32	.16	.48	−.10	.44	−.21	−.01	.05
1971/72	.13	.24	−.17	.03	−.36	.41	−.04	.29	.45	−.32	.39	−.34	.33	.42
1973/74	−.02	.12	−.08	−.28	−.46	−.30	.18	.24	.30	−.40	.40	−.51	−.30	.19
1975/76	−.12	−.04	−.25	−.01	−.59	−.23	.04	.28	.22	−.35	.34	−.48	.05	−.03
1977/78	−.17	−.30	−.22		−.49	−.06	−.27	−.03	.34	−.05	.34	−.24	−.04	−.07

7 State or market in the world

Introduction

State and market are the two principal methods for the allocation of scarce resources to human needs and wants. If a nation favours public resource allocation it will end up with a large public sector, whereas if it trusts the market the private sector will tend to be larger than the public sector (Hirschman, 1982). Nations differ quite considerably in their principal choice between state and market. How are we to account for the various ways of combining state and market as allocative mechanisms? This problem is related to the basic question in comparative public policy of how to explain the policy variation between various kinds of nations as measured by the amount of resources allocated by means of the public budget. Here we will take a broad look at the public finance variations between various countries all over the world.

Does politics matter?

It used to be considered that political structures mattered very much. The interest of political scientists was focused upon the structure of the state, classifying political systems as democratic, authoritarian, modern and traditional as in one popular scheme. The properties of the structure of the public organization of society had a value in itself because some structures were regarded as better than others. The reorientation of political science after the Second World War meant that outputs have been considered more interesting than structural properties. However, there remains the basic problem of how structure is related to output. The literature on comparative public policy has identified a number of determinants of policy outputs (Tarschys, 1975; Ashford, 1978; Dye and

Gray, 1980), but so far there is no agreement on the *relative weight* of politics or political institutions as a determinant of public policy in relation to, for example, economic factors (Borcherding, 1977, 1984; Wildavsky, 1986).

This predicament may partly be a reflection of severe methodological problems. It has been argued that a simple cross-sectional approach is bound to be inadequate as the impact of politics would take some time to become visible in policy outputs (Sharpe and Newton, 1984). On the other hand, a longitudinal approach means that our conclusion may be affected by sudden changes and by the fact that we restrict ourselves to countries with an abundance of data. Policies survive their originators and they are inherited by all, even the opponents of the policy in question (Rose, 1990). Given the fact of policy inertia and the difficulty to change past commitments, then how could policies matter longitudinally? Let us remember the Jackman insistence on that cross-sectional and longitudinal approaches are not always comparable. Cross-sectional analyses are particularly suitable for structural analyses of highly aggregate variables (Jackman, 1985).

From a theoretical point of view we argue that politics matter in relation to the fundamental choice of mechanism of allocation, between public resource allocation and market. These two forms for the making of collective choice can only be substituted to a certain extent. In relation to the so-called pure public goods there are no alternatives to choose from. This implies that politics should matter far less in relation to military expenditures than in relation to welfare spending where there is a real choice between state and market. It may be the case that it is difficult to pin down why politics matters for the detailed variation in various kinds of expenditures, but we argue that politics is a crucial determinant of the basic choice between state and market. Thus we expect to find that the total civilian public sector will be large and that overall welfare spending will be high in countries where the left is strong in various ways. However, politics enters into a context of policy-making which includes other factors which must be taken into account (Danziger, 1978).

Policy-determinant models

According to one seminal theme, *economic* factors are of crucial importance for public policy-making (Wilensky, 1975). A higher level of affluence is supposed to result in more public spending as the supply of, as well as the demand for, public policies increases with more abundant resources — *Wagner's law* (Wildavsky, 1985). This does not imply that the higher the economic growth the larger the public sector, only that nations that are more affluent will display a distinction between the public and the private that is different from that of poor nations. In terms of economic growth there is the counter-Wagner law claiming that rapid economic growth cannot be combined with rapid public sector expansion. Economic hypotheses about the variation in public spending either focus on supply factors or demand factors (Borcherding, 1977; 1984). Some emphasize some special economic variable like the openness of the economy (Cameron, 1978).

According to another seminal theme, slow, broad social change accounts for a reorientation of the distinction between the public and the private. As stated above, it is argued that *social structure* factors such as modernization or urbanization implies more of public spending for both indivisible and divisible goods and services. In a similar vein it is argued that broad demographic changes result in a demand for public policies. According to one hypothesis, the relative proportion of elderly has a definitive impact on various types of welfare spending (Wilensky, 1975).

A different hypothesis states the contrary, that rapid social change accounts for public sector expansion. External shocks like war or social upheaval have the result that public expenditures jump to a substantially higher level where they tend to remain— the *displacement hypothesis* (Peacock and Wiseman, 1961).

A third set of hypotheses focus on the impact of *politics* on the distinction between public and private. On the one hand, it has been argued that the political power of parties of the right is a decisive negative determinant of the size of the public sector (Castles, 1978; 1982). On the other hand, a different argument is that the strength of the position of parties of the left is conducive to public budget-making (Schmidt, 1982). A variety of indicators may be employed to measure the position of the left implying that there is a large number of hypotheses about the implications of politics, some referring to leftist governments, others to trade-union power or more generally to the power division between the left and the right in society, and still others to the relevance of various types of regimes (Weede, 1983; Cameron, 1984).

It seems relevant to include *institutionalization* as an independent variable. It denotes the time span of modern leadership in a polity. It is a different variable from modernization which refers to material well-being. It could be the case that institutionalization matters more than other political variables. According to the argument about institutional sclerosis, we may expect to find extensive policy-making in nations with a long and unbroken tradition of modern public institutions resulting in various kinds of policies that hamper the free operation of the market (Olson, 1982).

Since the publication of Wilensky's *The Welfare State and Equality* (1975) there has been an ongoing debate about the determinants of national public policies. Wilensky's emphasis on economic factors was derived from an analysis covering both rich and poor countries.

However, much of the later findings has been confined to the rich non-communist countries, pointing to the relevance of political factors (Schmidt, 1982). It is interesting to go back to the first more comprehensive approach and cover as many different nations as possible considering the availability of data. Is it then really true that affluence or modernization is such a powerful determinant of public policy-making? Is it really the case that political institutions or political parties matter so little when the sample of countries is made as broad as possible instead of narrowly restricted to Western Europe?

Determinants

The theoretical considerations presented above point in the direction of looking for indicators that measure a few latent variables. Considering the existing data sources and the ambition to cover a large set of countries, the following indicators are included in the analysis (Appendix 7.1):

Public Expenditures: measures of the total civilian public sector are included like total non-military outlays/GDP, just as indicators of subaggregates like defence expenditures, education and health expenditures. The reliability of the data may be questioned for some nations, which also applies to the indicators listed below. The data on public expenditures for the Communist countries appear to be most uncertain. We have calculated a ratio between total public budget and net material product which is not identical to GDP to arrive at a measure comparable to total civilian outlays of general government; the data for these countries have, with the exception for Romania, been taken from *Europa Yearbook*. They roughly refers to the mid-1970s.

Economy: level of economic affluence (GNP/cap.) in 1975, economic growth between 1960 and 1977, as well as the structure of employment in agriculture in 1977.

Openness of the economy: an index measuring the size of exports and imports in relation to the GNP.

Modernization: the level of modernization may be measured by two kinds of indicators; one refers to material aspects (energy consumption, radio or TV licences, telephones), while the other stands for health (life expectancy for males, proportion of physicians, infant mortality). Broad demographic changes may be described by indicators such as population density, the proportion of the population in major cities.

Politics and political structures: a set of democratically oriented nations may be identified by means of a human rights index for the late 1970s, and a democracy index for 1960 and 1965. In order to identify a set of communist regimes an index of the strength of the communist parties is employed. It also allows us to classify political systems as to the extent of radicalism. Moreover, we use two other indices of the strength of the left, an index of the strength of socialist parties as well as the dominance of the left in governments over the last decades.

Social structure: it refers to a set of indicators that taps the variation in social structure between nations, such as ethnic or religious fragmentation and proportion of Catholics and Moslems.

Institutionalization: an index measuring the introduction of modern leadership and modern political institutions.

Shock events: the occurrence of events such as war, social protest and domestic violence may be described by three separate indices.

The set of countries included in the analysis cannot be considered an entirely representative sample of the universe. However, an attempt has been made to cover three different regimes on a broad basis: advanced capitalist systems in the form of OECD countries, communist systems as they existed up to the 1989 upheaval in eastern Europe and developing countries — both so-called LDCs and NICs (Appendix 7.1).

Model estimation

In the literature models of determinants of public expenditures have been estimated mainly on OECD data (Swank, 1984). It is interesting to inquire into what the findings are when a much larger set of country data is resorted to. We estimate a number of regression models by a comparative analysis that includes at most seventy-eight countries: the twenty-four OECD countries, eight communist systems and forty-six Third World countries, selected on the basis of the availability of data. Let us present the findings under each separate dependent variable.

Total civilian outlays

The distinction between public and private is made in different ways in the world. Some nations trust public resource allocation whereas other nations emphasize the private sector and market allocation. What are the sources of these differences?

The regression analysis presented in Table 7.1 gives a number of estimates for three sets of nations, from the most inclusive one consisting of seventy-eight countries to the small set of OECD countries numbering twenty-four. The goodness of fit of the models is quite substantial, as the R-squared values indicate.

Table 7.1. Determinants of total civilian general government outlays

	(N = 78)		(N = 70)		(N = 24)	
Predictors	*Beta-W*	*t-stat*	*Beta-W*	*t-stat*	*Beta-W*	*t-stat*
GNP/cap 1975	.13	.80	.40	2.17	.04	.27
Modernization: health aspects	.35	2.32	.07	.36	.23	1.90
Economic growth: 1960-77	−.02	−.25	−.07	−.73	−.16	−1.23
Impex-index	.16	2.05	.24	2.77	.34	2.65
Proportion living in cities >100,000	−.14	−1.58	−.19	−1.90	−.27	−1.94
Social heterogeneity	.05	.58	−.09	−.86	.04	.28
War experience	.05	.65	.16	1.82	−.04	−.40
Left dominance in government	.36	3.91	.17	1.84	.35	2.95
Democracy index	−.21	−2.13	.11	.93	.13	1.02
Time for institutionalization	−.27	−2.13	−.19	−1.32	−.09	−.76
R^2	.66		.79		.92	
R^2A	.61		.63		.85	

Wealth and modernity is a potential source of policy-making. The state must have a certain amount of resources in order to employ public resource allocation for purposes other than those entailed in the minimal state. Public policy-making beyond the provision of pure collective goods is to be found in an economy with abundant resources. In poor countries the state will be smaller than the market.

The implication of wealth and modernity is clear when it is a matter of comparing all types of nations. The picture is more ambiguous when we look at the really rich nations. It seems as if there is a limit to the opportunities that affluence creates for public resource allocation. Once a nation has passed a certain threshold in terms of affluence public policy-making become less relevant. Most interestingly, a high rate of economic growth is negatively associated with total civilian outlays in the set of rich nations.

There can be no doubt about the importance of the political dimension for the overall structuring of the distinction between the public and the private. Whatever the set of nations studied, the position of the left within government or society has an impact on the division between state and market as long as we are not trying to account for the narrow variation in the welfare state in Western Europe. It is not only the case that public resource allocation is the only mechanism employed in those systems where the left has a hegemonic position. It also applies that the stronger the left is in non-communist regimes the larger the public sector. The hypothesis about the impact of institutionalization receives support. The longer a nation has been engaged in nation building, the more the state tends to be engaged in extensive policy-making.

The displacement effect hypothesis is hardly confirmed, but the impex hypothesis is clearly corroborated. Speaking generally, it is not the case that affluence is the major variable. While it is true that economic resources matter as predicted in the Wagner's law and the openness of the economy hypothesis, it is far from being the crucial variable as these hypotheses claim. Politics does matter.

Table 7.2. Determinants of general government educational expenditures

	(N = 78)		(N = 70)		(N = 24)	
Predictors	*Beta-W*	*t-stat*	*Beta-W*	*t-stat*	*Beta-W*	*t-stat*
GNP/cap 1975	.55	2.71	.59	2.73	.28	1.20
Modernization: health aspects	−.18	−.92	−.22	−1.02	−.37	−1.69
Economic growth: 1960-77	−.18	−1.76	−.03	−.25	.20	.84
Impex-index	.16	1.66	.07	.68	.23	1.00
Proportion living in cities >100,000	.00	.05	−.02	−.20	.14	.56
Social heterogeneity	.02	.21	.09	.71	.33	1.31
War experience	.20	2.05	.18	1.73	.06	.33
Left dominance in government	.34	2.90	.30	2.76	.52	2.38
Democracy index	.21	1.63	.24	1.68	.34	1.42
Time for institutionalization	.14	.86	.09	.53	−.01	−.06
R^2	.45		.50		.72	
R^2A	.37		.42		.51	

Education

Education is a kind of good that tends to be more in demand the more affluence there is. However, this does not mean that there has to be policy programmes providing education of various kinds. Affluence also means that citizens have a larger capacity to make their own choices suggesting that they may use the market to provide themselves with education opportunities. We may expect to find that wealth or modernity explains part of the variation in education expenditures but only a part. The findings in Table 7.2 confirm this interpretation.

Poor nations cannot afford to operate extensive programmes in the field of education. Rich nations on the other hand face a choice between public and private as they can afford to allocate resources to various kinds of education. Which mechanism of allocation is resorted to depends on other factors of which politics appears to be the most relevant one. The position of the left matters very much in relation to public spending for education. It is also the case that democratically structured nations favour public education systems.

Health

The provision of health tends to be larger in richer countries than in poorer ones, but this does not imply that affluence implies public spending for health. Health may be provided for privately in terms of market operations. The results stated in Table 7.3 confirm this hypothesis.

Wealth and modernity have a positive impact on health policy-making, up to a certain level. Once there is a certain level of public provision of health services, other factors will determine whether there will be public or private provision. Most important is politics, the left favouring public resource allocation.

Military effort

It may be believed that military spending is more favoured in authoritarian or communist systems than in democratic ones. Table 7.4 shows that this is not the case.

There is no relationship between democracy and a low level of military spending. What matters with regard to military effort is war experience. Countries that have this kind of experience emphasize military spending. Wealth and modernity have a limited impact, indicating that the richer a nation is the more resources there are

Table 7.3. Determinants of general government health expenditures

Predictors	(N = 78) Beta-W	t-stat	(N = 70) Beta-W	t-stat	(N = 24) Beta-W	t-stat
GNP/cap 1975	.32	1.84	.28	1.50	−.22	−.76
Modernization: health aspects	.14	.88	.15	.80	.35	1.28
Economic growth: 1960-77	−.13	−1.48	−.05	−.58	−.26	−.89
Impex-index	.01	.15	−.04	−.43	−.02	−.07
Proportion living in cities >100,000	.12	1.25	.12	1.22	.26	.84
Social heterogeneity	.07	.80	.13	1.21	.28	.90
War experience	−.02	−.21	−.03	−.35	−.07	−.31
Left dominance in government	.30	3.07	.27	2.82	.46	1.68
Democracy index	.13	1.25	.12	.98	.04	.13
Time for institutionalization	−.11	−.80	−.16	−1.09	.17	.61
R^2	.61		.63		.57	
R^2A	.55		.57		.23	

Table 7.4. Determinants of general government military expenditures

Predictors	(N = 78) Beta-W	t-stat	(N = 70) Beta-W	t-stat	(N = 24) Beta-W	t-stat
GNP/cap 1975	−.12	−.59	−.21	−.99	−.37	−1.50
Modernization: health aspects	.41	2.25	.58	2.66	.15	.66
Economic growth: 1960-77	.15	1.56	.14	1.29	.16	.65
Impex-index	.05	.55	.05	.53	−.43	−1.76
Proportion living in cities >100,000	.02	.18	.01	.11	−.34	−1.29
Social heterogeneity	.15	1.39	.21	1.75	.10	.38
War experience	.62	6.46	.60	5.87	.60	3.10
Left dominance in government	.22	1.97	.28	2.58	.28	1.20
Democracy index	−.05	−.38	−.19	−1.32	.01	.05
Time for institutionalization	.35	2.21	.34	1.98	−.36	−1.55
R^2	.49		.50		.69	
R^2A	.41		.42		.45	

available for such purposes, but still the most important or decisive determinant is the actual experience of war.

Conclusion

State or market in a country is a real choice opportunity when national public policy-making moves beyond the provision of pure public goods. And this choice opportunity becomes an actuality when nations have been modernized to such an extent that the state has large extractive capacities. Economic development and institutionalization of state structures opens up the *possibility* of extensive public policy-making. The few cases of poor nations with a large public sector refer to countries with heavy military commitments.

However, as nations and their economies modernize resources become available for civil public expenditures. But whether this possibility becomes a *reality* in terms of a large public sector depends not upon economic determinism but involves a real choice that implies a resolution based on political ideology. Once we move out of the focus on policy-making in Western Europe, then we have entirely different findings in the testing of models about policy determinants. We must recognize structural variability between independent and dependent variables in the debate on policy determinants. By taking a broader look including a much larger variety of countries we may establish that politics matters for policies.

As nations modernize their economy and social structure as well as institutionalize their public body they face the basic institutional choice between public resource allocation and market operations as the mechanism for allocating scarce resources to semi-public or private goods. And politics does matter very much for the way that choice is resolved. This applies in particular in relation to non-military expenditures which in advanced economies mainly refer to semi-public or private goods. Military expenditures appear to be a rather weak restriction on welfare spending. As the correlation between military spending and welfare expenditures is very low we must look for other determinants of non-military spending.

Public resource allocation is resorted to as nations grow richer and more modern, but there is a limit to the attractiveness of the state. In very rich countries the relevance of the market increases as citizens may wish to emphasize exit more than voice (Hirschman, 1970). In developing countries public resource allocation may be the more attractive alternative due to non-existence of a variety of markets or the need for political control, but there is a limit to the usefulness of this mechanism of collective choice. Technical considerations may give public resource allocation an advantage in relation to certain semi-public goods but in rich countries the attractiveness of public resource allocation is founded on political culture. There will be extensive policy-making where the left has a strong tradition of participation in government.

Politics does matter for the *fundamental choice* between public resource allocation and market operations. Although its impact on the detailed variation in expenditure levels or growth rates in the public sector in West European countries may be little as shown in Chapter 6, this simply reflects that politics does not matter for the *marginal* variation in welfare state spending. Public resource allocation is only necessary in relation to pure public goods. It may be an efficient mechanism of allocation in relation to semi-public goods. However, it is inferior to market operations when it is a question of allocation of private goods. Pure public goods will consume a smaller relative proportion of the resources as GDP grows when the economy is modernized. The tendency for public resource allocation to expand as a function of the modernization of the economy expresses a decision to trust one mechanism of allocation more than the other — and this decision is based more on *political considerations* than simply *economic determinism.*

Appendix 7.1. Indicators and sources

Indicator	Source
Employment in agriculture 1977	Taylor, 1981
GNP/capita 1975	Taylor, 1981
Modernization: Energy consumption/capita 1975	Taylor, 1981
Radios/1000 pop 1975	Taylor, 1981
TV sets/1000 pop 1975	Taylor, 1981
Telephones/1000 pop 1975	Taylor, 1981
Modernization: Life expectancy males 1975	Taylor, 1981
Doctors/million pop 1975	Taylor, 1981
Infant mortality rates 1975	Taylor, 1981
Economic growth 1960-77	World Bank World Tables
Economic growth 1970-78	World Bank World Tables
Impex-index: Imports and Exports/GNP 1975	Taylor, 1981
Proportion living in cities > 100 000	Taylor, 1981
Social heterogeneity: Ethnic and religious fragmentation	Taylor, 1981
Proportion Catholics	Taylor and Lewis, 1972
Proportion Moslems	Taylor and Lewis, 1972

Variable	Source
Protest index: Protest demonstrations, riots, political strikes per capita log	Taylor and Jodice, 1981
Violence index: Armed attacks, assassinations and deaths from domestic violence per capita and log	Taylor and Jodice, 1981
Strength of socialist parties	Day and Degenhardt, 1980 among others
Strength of communist parties	Staar, 1981 among others
Left dominance in government	Delury, 1983 Banks, 1978 among others
Democracy index: Human rights index c. 1978	Humana, 1983
Democracy index c. 1960	Bollen, 1980
Democracy index c. 1965	Bollen, 1980
Time for institutionalization	Taylor and Lewis, 1972
Total civilian general government outlays/GDP c. 1977: Total general government outlays minus defense expenditures	Taylor and Lewis, 1972; IMF, 1982
Defense expenditures/GDP	Taylor, 1981 Sivard, 1980
Educational expenditures/GDP	Taylor, 1981; Sivard, 1980
Health expenditures/GDP	Taylor, 1981; Sivard, 1980

Countries included:

002 USA	305 Austria	630 Iran
020 Canada	310 Hungary	640 Turkey
040 Cuba	315 Czechoslovakia	645 Iraq
042 Dominican Rep	325 Italy	651 Egypt
070 Mexico	345 Yugoslavia	663 Jordan
092 El Salvador	350 Greece	666 Israel
094 Costa Rica	355 Bulgaria	732 South Korea
095 Panama	360 Romania	740 Japan
100 Colombia	365 Soviet Union	750 India
101 Venezuela	375 Finland	770 Pakistan

130 Ecuador
135 Peru
140 Brazil
145 Bolivia
150 Paraguay
155 Chile
160 Argentina
165 Uruguay
200 UK
205 Ireland
210 Netherlands
211 Belgium
212 Luxembourg
220 France
225 Switzerland
230 Spain
235 Portugal
260 GFR
265 GDR
290 Poland
380 Sweden
385 Norway
390 Denmark
395 Iceland
433 Senegal
450 Liberia
452 Ghana
471 Cameroon
475 Nigeria
490 Zaïre
501 Kenya
510 Tanzania
530 Ethiopia
551 Zambia
553 Malawi
560 South Africa
580 Madagascar
600 Morocco
615 Algeria
616 Tunisia
780 Sri Lanka
800 Thailand
820 Malaysia
830 Singapore
840 Philippines
850 Indonesia
900 Australia
920 New Zealand

8 Institutions and economic growth in rich countries (OECD)

Introduction

In Chapters 5, 6 and 7 we assessed hypotheses about *inter alia* economic determinants of politics. One hypothesis claimed that economic affluence is a cause, or possibly *the* cause of democracy, whereas another hypothesis stated that socio-economic structure or development is a more powerful determinant of national policy variations than political factors. The main result in the test of these claims at economic determinism is that they are exaggerated, if not incorrect. The level of economic affluence does not determine how democratic a polity will be, nor can we say that politics does not matter for the variation in national policy programmes in different countries. Let us reverse the question: how about politics as a determinant of economic events like, for example, economic growth?

The theme of the *Rise and Decline of Nations* (Radon) by Mancur Olson (1982) belongs to this type of argument. Equating the rise and decline of nations with their growth rates in the overall economy, Olson ventures to state that the institutional fabric of society is a missing link in traditional theories explaining economic growth. Olson argues that a crucial factor in explaining the rise and decline of nations such as the United Kingdom, the Federal Republic of Germany, France, Sweden, Switzerland and Japan is a politically very relevant factor, the structure of pressure groups at various levels of government. These so-called distributional coalitions reduce economic growth by pushing for their special interests, thus bringing about national decline. The wealth of nations is not only a function of economic variables but the nature of the political authority structure is a very important factor. What is the relationship between political factors and economic growth? In this chapter we look at this problem with regard to the so-called rich market economies of the set of OECD countries.

Politics and economic growth

It is hardly astonishing that politics is mentioned as a potentially relevant explanatory factor when accounting for the variation in growth rates. Economic theory has concentrated on variables like labour, capital and technology (Ott, Ott and Yoo, 1975; Eltis, 1984; Chaudhuri, 1989; Scott, 1989), which it seems may be influenced by political decision-making. Thus the supply of labour may be augmented by policies that promote immigration, the availability of capital may depend on taxation rules, and technological advance may be stimulated by R & D policies. Two different types of models may be suggested in order to take the interaction between politics and economic growth in account. Politics may be singled out as a factor that besides the traditional economic variables condition growth rates, or politics may be modelled as a determinant of growth rates by means of its impact on the standard economic variables. Politics may explain what is left to explain after considering economic factors or politics may be conceived as a determinant of these very same economic variables.

The theme in the *Radon* singles out one kind of political factor, political institutions, and the argument is that the structure of these institutions matters very much for economic development. Thus the *Radon* argument is reminiscent of the current emphasis on institutionalism (March and Olsen, 1984; 1989). The more segmented the political structure in terms of the size and strength of distributional coalitions, the less the economic advance. What matters is not primarily political decision-making, because it is the overall structure of pressure groups in relation to state authority that determines growth rates. This would explain the country variation in growth rates, at least among the rich countries with a mixed economy.

The *Radon* argument is an attempt to employ the idea of a conflict or trade-off between efficiency and redistribution to explain the variation in growth rates at the national level. Following the argument in his *Logic of Collective Action* (1965), Olson advances a theory consisting of nine theoretical hypotheses focusing on the conflict between overall economic efficiency and growth on the one hand and the interests of distributional coalitions on the other. The nine theoretical propositions are all derived from the argument that economic growth is a public good which it is not rational to provide once a group of actors is large. Only small groups will provide collective interests of which public goods are simply one type, because in small groups it is possible to overcome the basic difficulties in public goods provision, the free rider problem and the preference revelation problem.

As spelled out in Chapter 3, economic growth rates vary considerably from one country to another and over time. Average growth rates or the mean rate of economic growth over a five- or ten-year period also differ very much between countries of various kinds — rich and poor, market regimes and Communist systems, West European, American and Third World countries — as well as between decades. How to account for the country and time variation in economic growth is a classical problem in economics (Solow, 1988; Scott, 1989).

A number of hypotheses have been put forward suggesting the factors that have an impact on growth rates in the long- and short-run perspective (Kalecki, 1954; Meade, 1961; Johnson, 1958; Hahn and Matthews, 1964; Södersten, 1964; Stiglitz and Uzawa, 1969; Hahn, 1971; Pasinetti, 1981):

(a) economic factors: labour, capital, technology, trade, level of affluence (Harrod, 1939; Kuznets, 1965, 1966, 1968; Hicks, 1965);
(b) social factors: agriculture, property rights (Lewis, 1955; Meier, 1984);
(c) cultural factors: religion, traditionalism (Myrdal, 1957; Thirlwall, 1986).

Where do we enter political factors among the determinants of economic growth? Let us start with testing the *Radon* theme that political institutionalization is of relevance for the explanation of the variation in economic growth among the OECD countries.

Short-run and long-run economic growth

Although the *Radon* has stimulated several attempts at testing the theory empirically it is difficult to make an overall assessment of the empirical evaluation. It has been argued that the theory has met with empirical corroboration, but also that there are severe counter-instances (Mueller, 1983; *International Studies Quarterly*, 1983). Moreover, it has also been claimed that the theory is very difficult to test, and what is even worse that it is framed in such a way that it cannot be refuted. By adding *ad hoc* hypotheses the argument could always be saved. It must be readily admitted that there is no straight-forward way of testing the nine hypotheses comprising the core of the argument.

First, it is far from clear how some of the concepts are to be measured or observed: what is a distributional coalition? How do we assess the influence and position of such an entity? What are the indicators on encompassing collective interests? Second, since economic growth is presumably affected by factors other than the structure of distributional coalitions, how can we devise a model that captures the interaction between the relevant variables allowing us to state the true partial impact of the political institutional structure on economic development?

The abstract nature of the *Radon* makes an empirical test of the theory a delicate business. Various tests may be devised, but is far from clear what their import is. What could we reasonably expect if the *Radon* argument is true? It is possible to measure the variation in growth rates among the OECD nations for the post-Second World War period. If these data are employed to test the Olson theory we would expect to find that there is a country variation in economic growth and that some measure of the status and position of distributional coalitions would explain at least some of this variation. If, on the other hand, political institutions matter very little, then we would be inclined to question the theory.

Testing the Olson hypothesis about a relationship between institutional sclerosis and economic growth has attracted a lot of attention. It has been argued that there are severe measurement problems involved in the Olson hypothesis (Saunders, 1986; Weede, 1986; Castles, 1991), particularly with regard to the indicator on institutional sclerosis. However, firstly we have to establish that there really exists a true country variation in growth rates.

Looking at the period between 1960 and 1983, the data about growth rates indicate that there is not only a country variation but also a variation over time. Given the emphasis of the *Radon* on the country differences to be explained by political institutionalism, we would expect to find that economic growth rates differ more between nations than within nations over time. A simple analysis of variance may be employed to test this implication of the *Radon*. As Table 8.1 shows, the test is negative: it is not the case that the yearly growth rates are more determined by country than by time, suggesting that the time variation is more pronounced than the intra-nation differences.

Table 8.1. Analysis of variance of GDP-growth rates 1961-1983 by country and time

	GDP Growth
Country (K = 24)	.12 (.00)
Year (K = 23)	.35 (.00)

Note: The eta-squared coefficient has been estimated on a data set for the OCED nations where the number of cases = 24 × 23 = 552. The larger the value of the coefficient - between 0 and 1 - the more variation is accounted for by the variable.

It is worth emphasizing that the within-nation differences over time are far larger than the between-nation differences with regard to the yearly variation in growth rates. This finding is a warning against any theory that focuses on country as a crucial determinant of economic development.

Since the structure of political institutions does not change radically from one year to another, the implication of the finding in Table 8.1 is clearly that the *Radon* argument cannot explain that part of the variation in economic growth or decline that is short-run. How about the long-run variation?

Even if the rate of economic growth hovers from one year to another, which cannot be accounted for by the structure of political institutions but perhaps by temporary political decision-making, it may still be the case that the average variation in growth rates displays a clear country identification. Table 8.2 shows various measures on the long-run variation in economic development.

Table 8.2. Average growth rates in the OECD nations: 1961-1970, 1971-1983, 1961-1983 (real GDP), 1960-1981 (real GDP capita) (in percent)

	Real GDP 1961-83	*Real GDP/capita 1960-81*	*Real GDP 1961-70*	*Real GDP 1971-83*
Australia	3.9	2.5	5.2	2.9
Austria	3.8	3.7	4.8	3.1
Belgium	3.6	3.4	5.0	2.5
Canada	4.2	3.1	5.2	3.4
Denmark	3.2	2.7	4.6	2.2
F R Germany	3.2	3.0	4.6	2.2
Finland	4.0	3.7	5.0	3.3
France	4.0	3.6	5.6	2.8
Greece	5.4	5.0	7.7	3.7
Iceland	4.1	3.3	4.5	3.7
Ireland	4.1	3.1	4.3	3.9
Italy	3.8	3.5	5.7	2.3
Japan	7.2	6.4	10.7	4.6
Luxembourg	2.7	2.3	3.5	2.0
Netherlands	3.4	2.7	5.2	2.1
New Zealand	2.8	1.6	3.7	2.0
Norway	4.2	3.6	4.4	4.1
Portugal	5.1	4.9	6.4	4.1
Spain	5.0	4.2	7.4	3.2
Sweden	3.0	2.6	4.7	1.7
Switzerland	2.7	2.1	4.8	1.1
Turkey	5.6	2.9	5.7	5.5
United Kingdom	2.2	1.8	2.8	1.8
United States	3.2	2.2	3.9	2.6

Note: Real GDP rates are based on OCED Economic Outlook, no 36 (1984) and 25 (1979); real GDP/captia growth rates are based on OCED Historical Statistics 1960-1981 (1983).

Bypassing the substantial yearly variations in growth rates it is possible to identify a stable variation over time. Considering the first time period (1961-70), the average growth rate varies between 10.7 per cent (Japan) and 2.8 per cent (United Kingdom). The country variation is not as extensive during the second time period as the difference between the maximum (Turkey = 5.5 per cent) and the minimum (Switzerland = 1.1 per cent) is down. It must be emphasized that the structure of the country variation is only partly the same during the two time periods as the correlation coefficient indicates ($r = 0.52$). This is again a warning against the attempt to identify a stable country variation during the post-war period. There is simply too much variation even between average growth rates over time. However, allowing for the substantial time variation we may single out four sets of nations that differ in the average growth rate between 1961-1983:

1. below 3.3 per cent: Denmark, West Germany, Luxembourg, New Zealand, Sweden, Switzerland, United Kingdom and United States;
2. 3.3-3.9 per cent: Australia, Austria, Belgium, Italy, Netherlands;
3. 4.0-4.9 per cent: Canada, Finland, France, Iceland, Ireland and Norway;
4. over 5.0 per cent: Greece, Japan, Portugal, Spain and Turkey.

How are we to account for this pattern of variation in average growth rates? Let us test a number of models that attempt to account for the long-run variation in economic growth. We will restrict our models by including politically relevant variables in order to search for evidence that indicates that politics matter. We ask if there is any evidence whatsoever for the theory that political factors have an impact on the average growth levels in advanced capitalist democracies.

Models

Let us specify a data set including a number of indicators tapping some latent variables to be measured across the OECD nations during the post-Second World War period, particularly since 1960. The data is based upon indicators on variables that figure in major theories about the sources of a country variation in economic growth (Kormendi and Meguire, 1985; Castles, 1990, 1991) and comprise:

1. *Rise and decline of nations*: various indicators measuring economic performance like average growth rates for various periods of time in overall GDP and GDP per capita, allowing for the fact that the quality of the data is not always the same (OECD, 1979, 1983, 1984).
2. *Wealth of nations*: the level of economic output as a starting point in e.g. 1957 measured by GNP per capita (Russett et al, 1964). The

catch-up hypothesis argues that the difference in average growth rates may be explained by the level of affluence at the starting-point, richer countries growing less rapid than less rich ones (Weede, 1986; Castles, 1991).

3. *Economic maturity*: it may be argued that high rates of economic growth should be found in economies with a rapidly expanding secondary sector, whereas the coming of a tertiary sector would mean a slow-down in economic growth. The explanation for this hypothesis is that the potential for productivity increases is far less in the tertiary sector. Thus we include a measure of the size of the tertiary sector (OECD, *Historical Statistics*).
4. *Institutionalization*: an index developed by Choi which taps the length of the period that a nation has had a political structure intact (Choi, 1983). The index has been extended to all OECD nations by additional estimates. It may be complemented by another measure of the age of a nation: a modernization index (Taylor and Hudson, 1972). However, it has been criticised as too simple for tapping institutional structure (Saunders, 1986; Castles, 1991).
5. *Structure of interest groups*: it is not easy to measure the structure of pressure groups nor to come up with some index that expresses valid generalizations about each and every pressure group. We will focus on the structure of the trade unions: a unionization index (Therborn, 1984; Kjellberg, 1983; Miele, 1983; Korpi, 1983) and a centralization index (Heady, 1970).
6. *Corporatist interest mediation*: if trade-union structure is not the only dimension in the nature of distributional coalitions, then perhaps the access of pressure groups to political power matters. Corporatist avenues to national decision-making may result in encompassing decision-making: two corporatization indices (Schmitter, 1981; Wilensky, 1976).
7. *Consociationalism*: broad social decision-making would be conducive to encompassing social solutions. Thus we include some indicators that measure the amount of political competition in the composition of government: a consociationalism index (Lijphart, 1979) and an index of oversized cabinets (Lijphart, 1984).
8. *Party government*: it is natural to take the colour of government into account when looking at the trade-off between economic growth and redistribution. Presumably, a socialist government favours redistribution whereas non-socialist governments emphasize economic growth. However, there is the counterargument that left-wing governments may find it easier to mobilize the population behind a policy favouring economic growth (Whiteley, 1982). We measure the composition of governments in the following way: an index of socialist and bourgeois dominance (Schmidt, 1983); government durability (Lijphart, 1984).

9. *Public policy*: pondering about the interaction between politics and economic growth one cannot bypass the impact of public policies on a long-run perspective. Since the dependent variable is the average growth rates we test some hypotheses about the effect of long-run public policies including the argument that a large public sector may promote economic growth (Korpi, 1985a. 1985b; Castles, 1990). Thus we include measures of the size of the public sector since 1960: total outlays, transfer payments and final government consumption, since the impact of these various items of public expenditure may differ with regard to economic growth (OECD: Historical Statistics).

Modelling the relationship between political variables and average economic growth some theoretical guidelines may be suggested. We single out economic performance as the dependent variable but employ three different indicators: real GDP growth, 1961-70, real GDP growth, 1971-83 and real GDP/capita growth, 1960-81. The substantial over-time variation means that the estimates may vary depending on which indicator is used. It is reasonable to expect that the level of economic performance has an impact upon the rate of economic growth. The lower the starting point, the higher the rate of change if there is a process of economic growth. Political variables may have an impact upon economic performance over and above that of the level of economic performance. We will test the contribution of each political variable in a regression equation comprising besides the wealth of nations the particular political variable in question. Such a stepwise procedure testing whether political factors mean anything over and above level of affluence will be used in relation to all political variables.

Model estimations and findings

It is not quite clear how the level of economic performance relates to the rate of change in economic performance. One may argue that countries at a low level tend to display a low level of economic growth as they are stuck in poor economic performance. The implication is that rich countries would tend to become even richer at a more rapid rate. Simon Kuznets argued along this line in his study of economic growth in a historical perspective (Kuznets, 1966, 1971). However, the opposite argument seems more plausible in relation to countries that have already reached a certain level of economic performance, as is true of the OECD countries. Here one would expect a negative relationship, i.e. that countries at a lower level of economic output tend to grow more rapidly than countries with a more mature economy — the catch-up hypothesis. In order to test these two alternative hypotheses a simple regression was run with economic level in 1957 predicting various measures of economic growth (Table 8.3).

Table 8.3. Economic level and growth rates

		Coefficient	*t-stat*	*Beta Wt*	R^2	R^2A
(1) GDP growth 1961-70	=	.0016 GNP/cap. 1957	−3.16	−.56	.31	.28
(2) GDP growth 1971-83	=	−.0010 GNP/cap. 1957	−2.95	−.53	.28	.25
(3) GNP/cap. growth 1960-81	=	−.0012 GNP/cap. 1957	−3.87	−.64	.40	.38

It appears that the second hypothesis is the correct one for the OECD nations as there is a considerable connection between economic performance and rates of change in the direction suggested by this second hypothesis. A substantial portion of the variation in growth rates in the 1960s and the 1970s may be accounted for by the level of economic performance. The high growth rates are to be found among nations at a low level of economic performance: Japan, Greece, Portugal, Spain and Turkey. However, this is hardly a complete explanation as even the best model explains less than half of the variation. Thus a basic economic variable like the level of economic output is clearly relevant to the explanation of growth rates, but what is the contribution of political factors? We now add each of the political variables listed above to the simple model relating economic growth to level of economic affluence.

Institutionalization

The basic hypothesis in the *Radon* states that the length of the time of institutionalization has a negative impact on growth rates. How is institutionalization to be measured? The concept of institutionalization is fairly similar to *modernization* as both refer to the emergence of a more or less constitutionally defined polity based on an industrial economy involving considerable portions of the citizens in political life. What matters in the concept of institutionalization according to the Olson interpretation is the length in time of unbroken institutionalization. Thus the occurrence of major societal disaster abolishing established institutions is of crucial importance in this variable.

An index of institutionalization or institutional sclerosis has been developed by Choi in a test of the *Radon* argument. It is fairly similar to a modernization measure identifying the years of consolidating a modernizing leadership. The correlation between the two measures is large, or Pearson's r = -0.75. Institutionalization may have an impact on economic growth either directly or in terms of its impact on level of economic performance. Since institutionalization refers to an extended period of time it may have an impact on both level and rate of change in economic performance. We will test a model comprising both institutional sclerosis and economic level.

Table 8.4. Institutionalization, economic level and growth rates

		Coefficient	*t-stat*	*Beta Wt*	R^2	R^2A
(1) GDP growth 1961-70	=	−.0001 GNP/cap. 1957	−.14	−.04	.45	.40
		−.0570 Institutional.	−2.33	−.64		
(2) GND growth 1971-83	=	−.0002 GNP/cap. 1957	.47	.12	.51	.46
		.0466 Institutional.	−3.09	−.81		
(3) GNP/cap. growth 1960-81	=	−.0004 GNP/cap. 1957	−.83	−.22	.50	.45
		−.0309 Institutional.	−1.94	−.51		

A model that includes institutionalization in addition to economic performance explains better than a simple economic equation. And the parameter estimated indicates that institutionalization is more important than economic level. Table 8.4 indicates a positive corroboration of the basic argument in the *Radon*: political institutions matter in relation to the average growth rates of nations. The goodness of fit of the model must be characterized as substantial. It may be argued that institutionalization merely measures another economic dimension, the economic maturity of the economy. Testing a model including an index of economic maturity — size of the third sector— does not change the findings, however (Table 8.5).

However, Francis Castles has the opposite finding in an analysis in a refined quantitative analysis (Castles, 1991). It seems to be the case that the way the severe methodological problems involved in the test of the Olson hypothesis is resolved has an impact on the findings (Saunders, 1986).

Table 8.5. Economic maturity, institutionalization, economic level and growth rates

		Coefficient	t-stat	Beta Wt	R^2	R^2A
(1) GDP growth 1961-70	=	−.0007 GNP/cap. 1957	−.93	−.26	.54	.47
		−.0762 Institutional.	−3.04	−.86		
		.0878 Service sector	1.93	.51		
(2) GND growth 1971-83	=	.0003 GNP/cap. 1957	.57	.16	.51	.44
		−.0440 Institutional.	−2.62	−.76		
		−.0107 Service sector	−.39	−.10		
(3) GNP/cap. growth 1960-81	=	−.0009 GNP/cap. 1957	−1.72	−.46	.59	.53
		−.0457 Institutional.	−2.84	−.76		
		.0635 Service sector	2.20	.56		

Unionization

Although the argument in the *Radon* concerns all kinds of distributional coalitions it is possible to test some implications concerning the impact of trade unions on economic growth. It is often believed that the mere existence of trade unions has a negative impact on economic growth. Olson adheres to this standard assumption but qualifies it by adding the reverse hypothesis that encompassing trade-unions promote economic growth. What is the relationship between trade unionization and economic growth in advanced capitalist societies? We will test a model that predicts economic growth by means of trade-union organization besides the general level of economic performance.

It appears that the contribution of trade-union organization to economic growth is slight when the level of economic performance is taken into account. Although there is an overall negative relationship between trade unionization and economic growth as well as an overall positive relationship between trade-union centralization and economic growth, these partial relations are not very strong. The argument about distributional coalitions implies that the relationship between trade-union density and economic growth constitute a U-shaped curve. Testing this implication for various time periods we may establish that there is little confirmation of this hypothesis except for the 1960s if the

Table 8.6. Unionization, institutionalization, economic level and growth rates

		Coefficient	*t-stat*	*Beta Wt*	R^2	R^2A
(1) GDP growth 1961-70	=	−.0002 GNP/cap. 1957	−.25	−.07	.46	.38
(N = 24)		−.0544 Institutional.	−2.11	−.61		
		−.0063 Union 1960's	−.41	−.07		
(2) GDP growth 1971-83	=	.0002 GNP/cap. 1957	.42	.11	.51	.44
(N = 24)		−.0458 Institutional.	−2.90	−.79		
		−.0020 Union 1970's	−.22	−.04		
(3) GNP/cap growth 1960-81	=	−.0005 GNP/cap. 1957	−.97	−.26	.52	.45
(N = 24)		−.0273 Institutional.	−1.67	−.45		
		−.0091 Unions 1970's	−.99	−.16		
(4) GNP growth 1961-70	=	.0001 GNP/cap. 1957	.16	.05	.52	.36
(N = 13)		−.0323 Institutional.	−2.22	−.69		
		.0016 Union centraliz.	.93	.22		
(5) GDP growth 1971-83	=	.0003 GNP/cap. 1957	.57	.22	.28	.04
(N = 13)		−.0305 Institutional.	−1.71	−.65		
		.0116 Union centraliz.	.06	.02		
(6) GDP/cap growth 1960-81	=	.0000 GNP/cap	.08	.02	.76	.68
(N = 13)		−.0313 Institutional.	−3.73	−.82		
		.0104 Union centraliz.	1.46	.24		

Note: Two indices are employed to tap trade union organization (membership) as well as centralization (influence). The two indices do not coincide and the selection of different points of time for the measurement of the variable results in alternative estimates of the impact of the variable depending on the number of cases involved.

analysis also includes Spain and Portugal with their high unionization within an authoritarian state system. It could be the case that trade-union organization has a more clear negative impact on economic growth, but that its partial impact will only be revealed in more complex models.

Other political factors

It has been argued that trade-union strength is only one political factor that is of crucial importance in a politico-economic perspective. Thus

Table 8.7. Institutional factors, institutionalization, economic level and growth rates

		Coefficient	*t-stat*	*Beta Wt*	R^2	R^2A
(1) GDP growth 1961-70	=	−.0004 GNP/cap. 1957	−.50	−.14	.52	.43
(N = 20)		−.0503 Institutional.	−1.19	−.52		
		−.6187 Socialist domin.	−2.02	−.38		
(2) GDP growth 1971-83	=	.0002 GNP/cap. 1957	.41	.13	.39	.27
(N = 20)		−.0397 Institutional.	−2.28	−.70		
		−.1075 Socialist domin.	−.53	−.11		
(3) GNP/cap growth 1960-81	=	−.0002 GNP/cap. 1957	−.42	−.11	.59	.51
(N = 20)		−.0431 Institutional.	−2.68	−.67		
		−.1478 Socialist domin.	−.79	−.14		
(4) GNP growth 1971-83	=	−.0002 GNP/cap. 1957	−.19	−.05	.54	.44
(N = 19)		−.0368 Institutional.	−2.30	−.60		
		−.0129 Oversized cab.	−2.14	−.38		

we find in the literature a number of hypotheses about the implications of corporatism, consociationalism and the type of party government (Castles, 1982; Wildavsky, 1985). The question we pose is whether these factors are equally valid for predicting the variation in growth rates. Therefore, we test a number of models predicting various measures of economic growth by means of economic level plus one political factor at a time. Table 8.7 reports only a few of these models, namely the models with the best goodness of fit.

The finding is that adding other political factors like corporatism, consociationalism or type of party government results in very minor changes in the basic explanatory power of the economic variable. It is clearly the case that economic level matters more for growth rates than these political variables. It may be pointed out that corporatist institutions may benefit economic growth whereas socialist dominance in party governments tends to have the opposite effect, as predicted in the standard assumption about socialist governments favouring redistribution. However, it is hardly possible to corroborate any strong hypothesis about the contribution of these political factors to economic growth.

Public Policy Variables

According to mainstream economic theory, an increase in public expenditure has two opposite consequences on economic growth. Whereas spending on collective and semi-collective goods would be conducive to economic growth adding to the infrastructure of society, an increase in transfer payments would have a negative impact favouring distribution before growth. Perhaps the variation between the OECD countries in terms of average growth rates could be accounted for by means of the variation in basic public sector dimensions: total outlays, final government consumption and social transfer payments. According to one hypothesis, public expenditures display an overall positive relationship with economic growth (Korpi, 1985; Castles, 1990). We test three models predicting economic growth by a combination of economic, institutional and policy variables (Table 8.8).

The finding is that political institutions matter more for economic growth rates than public policies. Adding various indicators on the size of the public sector does not change the finding that institutional sclerosis is the best single predictor of average economic growth. The relationships between various policy dimensions and economic growth are hardly strong, but the direction of the interaction is negative contrary to the hypothesis that on the whole public expenditures, in particular

Table 8.8. Public policy, institutionalization, economic level and growth rates

		Coefficient	t-stat	Beta Wt	R^2	R^2A
(1) GDP growth 1961-70	=	−.0000 GNP/cap. 1957	−.00	−.01	.48	.41
(N = 20)		−.0467 Institutional.	−1.79	−.53		
		−.1279 Gov. Fin. Cons.	−1.07	−.22		
(2) GDP growth 1971-83	=	.0002 GNP/cap. 1957	.46	.12	.51	.44
(N = 20)		−.0469 Institutional.	−2.86	−.81		
		.0025 Gov. Fin. Cons.	.05	.01		
(3) GNP/cap growth 1960-81	=	−.0004 GNP/cap. 1957	−.79	−.21	.50	.42
(N = 20)		−.0286 Institutional.	−1.65	−.47		
		−.0247 Gov. Fin. Cons.	−.39	−.08		
(4) GNP growth 1961-70	=	−.0002 GNP/cap. 1957	−.24	−.07	.46	.38
(N = 19)		−.0527 Institutional.	−1.98	−.59		
		−.0295 Social Sec. Trans.	−.47	−.08		
(5) GNP growth 1971-83	=	.0001 GNP/cap. 1957	.19	.05	.61	.55
(N = 19)		−.0359 Institutional.	−2.46	−.62		
		−.0660 Social Sec. Trans.	−2.24	−.34		
(6) GNP/cap growth 1960-81	=	−.0004 GNP/cap. 1957	−.79	−.22	.50	.42
(N = 19)		−.0312 Institutional.	−1.79	−.52		
		.0015 Social Sec. Trans.	.04	.01		
(7) GNP growth 1961-70	=	−.0003 GNP/cap. 1957	−.37	−.10	.54	.47

Table 8.8 continued

		Coefficient	t-stat	Beta Wt	R^2	R^2A
(N = 19)		−.0378 Institutional.	−1.52	−.43		
		−.0880 Total Outlays	−1.98	−.35		
(8) GNP growth 1971-83	=	.0001 GNP/cap. 1957	.21	.05	.54	.47
(N = 19)		−.0378 Institutional.	−2.28	−.66		
		−.0220 Total Outlays	−1.22	−.22		
(9) GNP/cap growth 1960-81	=	−.0004 GNP/cap. 1957	−.86	−.24	.50	.42
(N = 19)		−.0284 Institutional.	−1.56	−.47		
		−.0082 Total Outlays	−.32	−.06		

Note: The public policy variables refer to averages for the following periods: 1960-1967, 1974-1981 and 1960-1981 respectively; some data have been estimated for New Zealand.

transfer payments on final government consumption, tend to promote economic growth (Korpi, 1985a, 1985b). A large public sector, whatever its composition, does not appear to be conducive to economic growth. Again, Castles reports on the opposite finding employing different estimation techniques (Castles, 1990).

Conclusion

Economic growth rates are very important for the development of nations. It may not be the only relevant indicator on the rise or decline of nations but its crucial position in determining the fate of nations cannot be doubted. What determines economic growth? Looking beyond economic theory and the standard growth models we may search in less certain domains for the non-economic factors that condition economic development. The Olson hypothesis about the impact of social and political institutionalization is a step in this new direction of the research into the interaction between politics and economics.

Testing some of the implications of the argument in the *Radon* we find that the length of time of institutionalization matters very much for the understanding of the variation in national growth rates in the post-war period among OECD countries. We have not been able to corroborate any more specific hypothesis of the impact of political variables on economic growth. However, taking into account the interaction between the various factors tested in different models, it seems possible to arrive at a pattern. Figure 8.1 presents a path modeling of the crucial variables derived from the regression analysis.

Figure 8.1. Path analysis

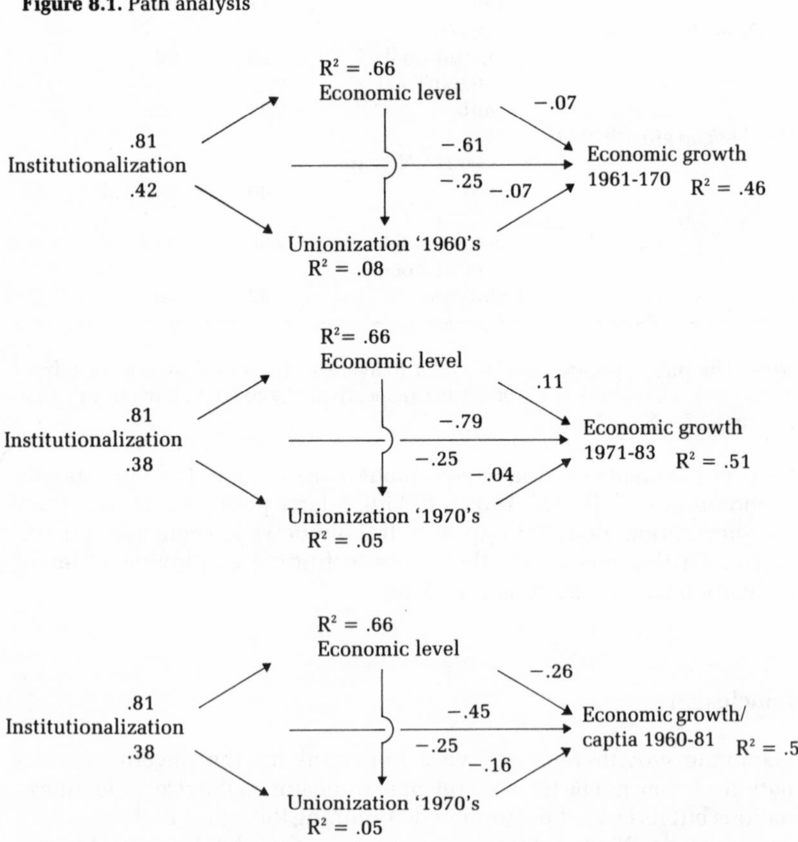

In a model that combines several political factors the finding is that a considerable portion of the country variation in economic development may be accounted for. It appears that if the extent of institutionalization is chosen as the basic variable, then an interpretable pattern shows up.

Institutionalization has a strong direct negative impact on economic growth. In addition it influences economic development indirectly by means of its impact on economic level and unionization.

Institutionalization seems to be conducive to a high level of economic performance which in turn has a negative impact on economic growth. Similarly, institutionalization goes together with unionization which also has a negative impact on economic growth. The relationships between institutionalization and unionization as well as between unionization and economic growth are weak, however. The interaction as portrayed in the path models is rather stable over time. The model explains somewhat better the first period of time which may depend upon a larger variation in the dependent variable. In particular, the connection between unionization and economic growth is almost non-existent in the last decade.

Institutionalization appears to have an impact on economic growth among the rich market economies besides its indirect effect via economic performance and unionization. It must be emphasized that there is a substantial time variation in economic growth rates which cannot be accounted for by an institutional model. Also there are contrary findings in the political economy literature (Weede, 1986; Castles, 1991). But looking at the average growth rates indicating the rise and decline of nations in a long-term perspective, the Olson analysis should be further tested and developed by taking a broader look at average economic growth among various types of politico-economic regimes. Let us move to an analysis of the relationship between political factors and average growth rates in a much broader set of countries.

Appendix 8.1. Indicators and sources

See Appendix 3.1, 5.1, 6.1, 7.1 and 9.1.

9 Politics and economic growth

Introduction

In the search for political determinants of economic growth it is argued that the traditional economic models of economic growth need to be supplemented or replaced by new ones that take into account the impact of political phenomena on the overall rate of change in the economy. As stated in Chapter 7 various political factors have been suggested as causes or conditions of the country variation in economic growth. According to one line of argument, the institutional fabric of the political system reduces the level of affluence as a function of the amount of institutional sclerosis (Olson, 1982), whereas another line of argument claims that the framing and conduct of an industrial market policy is of crucial importance for the possibility of a rapid process of economic growth (Zysman, 1983).

However, it remains an open question whether the addition of political variables really means anything to the understanding of the economic development of nations (Adelman and Morris, 1967, 1972). In this chapter we test various kinds of models of economic growth — economic, social and political — in order to create a firm ground for a discussion of the thesis that politics matter in relation to economic growth (Lange and Garrett, 1985).

Economic growth used to be approached as an endogenous variable determined by exogenous economic variables together with one or two instrument variables manipulable by means of economic policy. Olson's *Radon* meant a decisive break with this approach as Olson argued convincingly that a basic political variable is of fundamental importance for economic growth in rich countries: institutional sclerosis. Institutional sclerosis is related to a well-known concept in political science, namely modernization or the time of the introduction of modernized leadership. Modernization is the reverse of institutional sclerosis and the amount of institutional sclerosis affects the rate of economic growth in rich countries negatively. In Chapter 7 focusing only on the OECD countries we found empirical support for the institutionalization hypothesis, but how valid is this new political theory of economic growth?

Does the institutionalization hypothesis account for economic growth in Third World countries as well (Bairoch, 1975; Reynolds, 1985)? And what is the mechanism that relates modernization to economic growth? Once we begin to move towards a political economy of economic growth we need to integrate political variables with economic and social conditions that have an impact on economic growth. What is the place of political variables in an integrated model of economic growth? How about the empirical support for various political models of economic growth when a much larger set of countries is involved in the model estimation?

Economic growth and public choice

There are a number of growth models in economic theory that predict economic change on the basis of economic variables: the savings and investment function, labour supply, capital-output ratio, technological change and trade or exports (Hahn and Matthews, 1964; Hahn, 1971; Kuznets, 1965, 1966; Eltis, 1966; Solow, 1988; Chaudhuri, 1989). These models have been broadened in theories in developmental economics by the addition of social variables like industry, education or institutional variables (Hall, 1983). It is far from clear which variables are to be given major explanatory weights as there is no agreement in the fields of economic growth theory or development economics about which factors are crucial in processes of economic progress (Thirlwall, 1986). According to one theme, the standard growth models have limited applicability to the explanation of Third World development (Todaro, 1985; Syrquin, 1988).

Public choice theory bypasses the controversy between various economic models of growth by claiming that politics matter. Economic growth is part of a more general development phenomenon that is strategically influenced by political institutions and political behaviour. According to public choice theory, economic growth may be regarded as a public good characterized by a fundamental free rider problem. Since it benefits all indiscriminately but requires that each and every-one contributes, there is no individual incentive to supply the good. The stronger the distributional coalitions in a society the less the efforts to sustain a high level of economic growth, since it is in nobody's interest to supply the good for every group if the others are free riders. It pays more to increase the share of the income going to the group than to make a sacrifice for the increase in overall income. If on the other hand there is a strong consensus that economic growth is to be pursued because it is more to the advantage of each and everyone once all agree, then there will be a policy of state-sponsored growth that could be of decisive importance for the economic development of the country.

The question whether politics matter for the development of a nation may be approached in a broad way as the search for the economic, social and political sources of economic development. Taking an inductive approach, a number of variables may be related to indicators on economic development. Theoretical guidance is to be found in the basic economic models of economic growth as well as in the public choice approach to the political sources of economic development (Eltis, 1984; Buchanan *et al.*, 1980; Little, 1982; Gersovitz *et al.*, 1982).

Data and indicators

The test of models of economic growth is based on data for roughly sixty nations during the period of 1960-80. The selection of the countries is based on the idea that processes of economic development occur in both rich and poor countries but that the mechanisms that explain these processes may differ. The set of rich countries includes the OECD nations and the set of poor nations covers some forty Third World countries.

It could be argued that one should use overall GDP and not the GNP per capita measure when one studies economic development, because a strong increase in the population reduces the growth rates when economic development is measured by the per capita indicator. However, there is a considerable co-variation between the two measures (r = .81) (Figure 9.1). Among the independent variables we make a distinction between economic variables, social variables and political variables. The selection of the economic variables is based on the basic theories of economic development. Economic growth according to the production function model is the result of changes in capital formation, labour input and a residual consisting of productivity changes. Looking at economic growth from a wider perspective other factors will be considered: social variables measuring industry structure, population changes and educational opportunities.

It may be predicted that the rate of change in agricultural employment is related to economic growth, as an increase in industrial employment would be conducive to economic growth in the Third World. Whether a decrease in industrial employment characterizes the process of economic development in the rich countries is an open question. Population growth could be assumed to drive down economic growth,

Figure 9.1 GDP growth per capita and GNP per capita growth

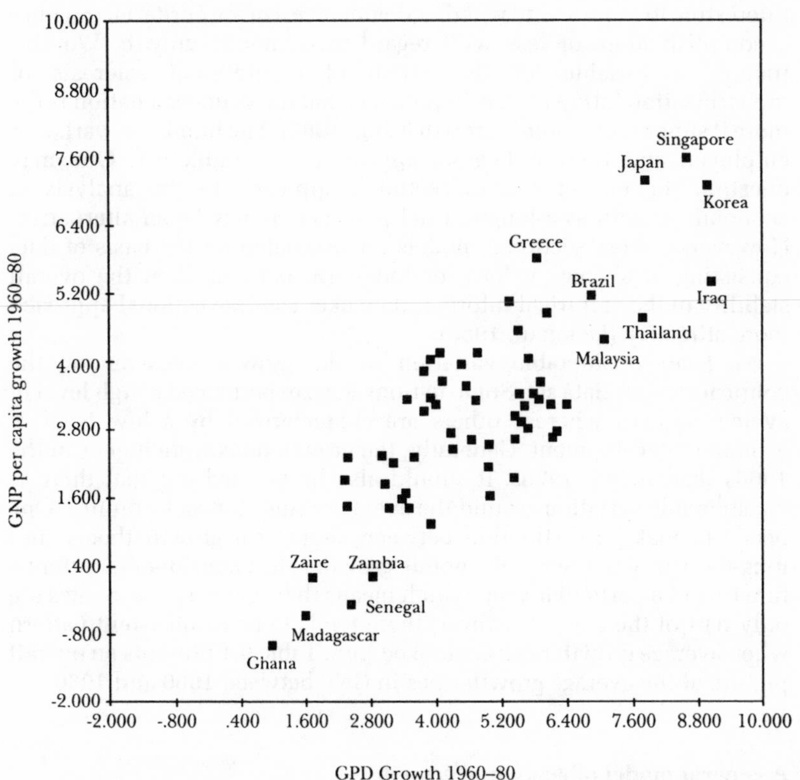

whereas education would have the opposite effect. There is disagreement whether the impact of inequality in the distribution of incomes is positive or negative.

Political variables may be assumed to have an impact on economic growth directly or indirectly in terms of their effects on economic variables. A government dominated by left-wing ministers may be assumed to be in favour of public policies that are more oriented towards the redistribution of incomes than towards the growth in affluence. It is interesting to inquire into whether democracies or authoritarian regimes accomplish more or less with regard to economic growth. We also include a variable for the extent of institutional sclerosis or modernization following the hypothesis that the younger a nation is the more it supports economic growth (Choi, 1983). The number of variables employed and their indicators appear in Appendix 9.1. One may question the use of a cross-sectional approach to the analysis of economic growth as a longitudinal perspective may be an alternative. However, if cross-sectional models are estimated on the basis of data consisting of average values for long-term periods, then the overall stability in the empirical information makes a cross-sectional approach more attractive (Jackman, 1985).

We face considerable variation in the growth rates among the countries in our data set. Some nations have experienced a high level of average growth whereas others are characterized by a low level of economic development. Generally, the growth rates were higher in the 1960s than in the 1970s. It should also be pointed out that there is considerable variation around the average values for each country. One needs to make a distinction between short-term growth theory and long-term growth theory. Economic growth is to a considerable extent a function of a particular year, which means that average growth rates are only part of the story. However, there tends to be a consistent pattern when average growth rates are looked into. Table 9.1 presents an overall picture of the average growth rates in GNP between 1960 and 1980.

A general model of economic growth

It is necessary to make a distinction between causes and concomitant properties when talking about economic growth. Processes of economic expansion have a number of implications for social systems, some of which are tied up with the process of economic change itself. It is difficult to separate these factors that go together with economic growth from factors that may be said to constitute causes of economic expansion. Rapid rates of economic growth tend to co-vary with major changes in the economic system, with a transformation of the social structure and they also display some implications for the political system. But the fact that economic growth tends to co-vary with a large

Table 9.1. Percentage increase in GNP per captia 1960-1980

Rapid increase:	*from 7.5% to 3.2%*	*Slow increase:*	*from 3.1% to −1.0%*
Singapore	7.5	Ireland	3.1
Japan	7.1	Colombia	3.0
South Korea	7.0	Malawi	2.9
Greece	5.8	Pakistan	2.8
Jordan	5.7	Philippines	2.8
Iraq	5.3	Kenya	2.7
Brazil	5.1	Australia	2.7
Portugal	5.0	Mexico	2.6
Tunisia	4.8	Venezuela	2.6
Thailand	4.7	Cameroon	2.6
Ecuador	4.5	Morocco	2.5
Spain	4.5	Sri Lanka	2.4
Malaysia	4.3	United States	2.3
Austria	4.1	Sweden	2.3
Nigeria	4.1	United Kingdom	2.2
Finland	4.0	Argentina	2.2
Indonesia	4.0	Bolivia	2.1
France	3.9	Tanzania	1.9
Belgium	3.8	Switzerland	1.9
Italy	3.6	New Zealand	1.8
Turkey	3.6	Chile	1.6
Norway	3.5	El Salvador	1.6
Dominican Rep	3.4	Liberia	1.5
Egypt	3.4	India	1.4
Canada	3.3	Uruguay	1.4
Panama	3.3	Ethiopia	1.4
Germany FR	3.3	Peru	1.1
Denmark	3.3	Zambia	0.2
Costa Rica	3.2	Zaire	0.2
Paraguay	3.2	Senegal	−0.3
Netherlands	3.2	Madagascar	−0.5
Algeria	3.2	Ghana	−1.0

number of other variables is of little relevance for the problem of causality. Only theoretical argument can guide the search for predictors of economic growth.

First, economic growth is assumed to be a function of the traditional economic variables: investments, labour supply, and trade — their levels and rates of change (Stigliz and Uzawa, 1969; Sen, 1970; Kregel,

1972; Hall, 1984). Second, social factors may have an impact on economic growth, either directly or in terms of their impact on the economic variables (Chenery and Srinivasan, 1988). Third, a set of political variables could be related to economic growth by means of their impact on the basic conditions for economic activity (Weede, 1986; Saunders, 1986; Castles, 1990, 1991). Thus we arrive at the following general model:

(1) EG = f(EV, SV, PV)

where EG is economic growth, EV stands for economic variables, SV for social variables and PV for political variables. We now proceed to test various models consisting of these variables.

Economic variables

Several economic models are plausible. What does a certain level of economic development mean for the growth rates over a decade or two (Horvat, 1974)? Is it the case that level of affluence in 1960 has any implications for the growth rates during the 1960s and 1970s? On the one hand, it could be argued that only the rich countries can afford a high level of investments which would guarantee high rates of economic development. On the other hand, there is the counter-argument that rich countries display a mature economy with low rates of economic growth whereas it is in the interest of the developing nations to mobilize resources for a high level of investments. Figure 9.2 shows the relationship between level of affluence in 1960 and average growth rates between 1980 and 1960.

It is not the case that level of affluence determines the growth potentially or the actual growth rates. We find considerable variation in growth rates among countries with a rather similar level of economic affluence and it is certainly not the case that rich countries tend to have higher growth rates than poor countries. One may predict from looking at Figure 9.2 that the classification of rich and poor countries in 1960 is bound to change after a few decades due to differential growth rates. Table 9.2 reports on the test of models relating growth rates to various indicators on levels of economic activity, proportion of investments to GDP, percentage of work-force and proportion of exports to GDP.

The emphasis in economic theory on a high level of investments as a condition for economic growth is amply supported in the model estimation. However, there is not much support for the other economic variables often adduced as crucial for economic expansion, level of labour force activity and level of exports. It seems as if a high level of exports is not a necessary condition for economic growth as some rich

Figure 9.2. Real GDP per capita in 1960 and GNP per capita growth 1960-80

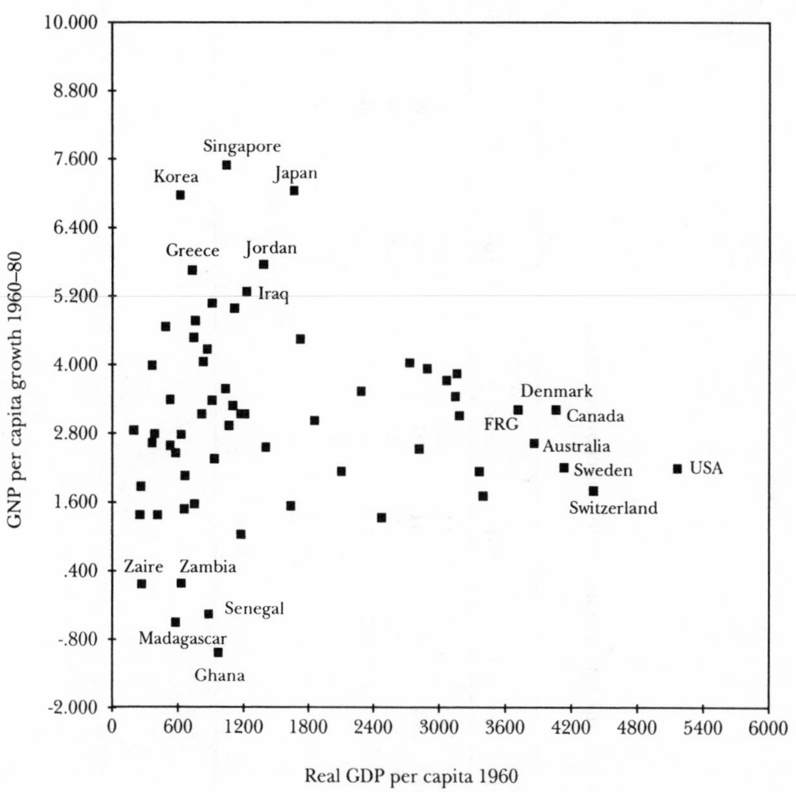

Table 9.2. Regression analysis: economic growth and levels of economic activity

		Total				*Third World*				*OECD*		
Predictors	*Coeff*	*Beta*	r	*t-stat*	*Coeff*	*Beta*	r	*t-stat*	*Coeff*	*Beta*	r	*t-stat*
GDInv	.16	.48	.52	4.03	.14	.38	.46	2.05	.18	.55	.46	2.75
Lab force	.02	.07	.14	.61	.01	.01	−.17	.05	−.02	−.04	−.09	−.19
Export	.01	.09	.23	.73	.02	.21	.36	1.26	−.04	−.42	−.31	−2.12
Constant	−1.92			−.90	−.80			−.15	1.31			.24
R2	.28				.25				.38			
R2A	.24				.19				.27			
N	61				40				21			

countries do not achieve high levels of economic growth although they have large exports. The fundamental place of a high level of investments is the same in rich as in Third World countries. On the other hand, we may look into the impact of the rate of change in a number of variables on economic growth. Here it is crucial to look at how increases in investments, labour-force changes and exports relate to economic growth. Table 9.3 has the findings of the test of such models.

Rapid increases in investments characterize countries with rapid economic growth, particularly in the Third World. The finding may be interpreted as indicating that economic growth processes are combined with heavy increases in the level of investments. Increases in the volume of exports also characterize processes of economic growth. Investment — level of and change in investments — is the key variable included in a pure economic model that according to the empirical evidence is of great importance (GCInv).

The crucial importance of capital growth for economic development in the Third World appears in the data. An increase in the number of people employed has a positive impact on economic growth in Third World countries. In rich countries economic growth leads to a reduction in the labour force. The importance of capital investments for economic growth, in particular in Third World countries, makes it crucial to look at the political condition for capital expenditure decisions.

Social variables

Social factors may be relevant to the country variation in economic growth as different social milieus or contexts may have different implications for basic parameters that determine economic growth, e.g. capital investments, labour input and technology. Thus a transfer of parts of the work force from agriculture to industry could raise productivity considerably and higher levels of educational attainment may result in economic growth because it increases the quality of labour. What is the macro importance of these factors in our set of data? Table 9.4 has the data.

Changes in agricultural employment have an impact on economic growth in the Third World nations. It is not the case that a reduction in industrial employment in rich countries leads to higher rates of economic growth. The level of education appears to be of limited importance contrary to the human capital hypothesis. There is little indication of any general relationship between population growth and economic growth. The overall correlation between GDP growth and population growth tends to be positive, whereas the correlation between growth in GNP per capita and population growth tends to be negative although these correlations are weak.

Table 9.3. Regression analysis: economic growth and economic change

Predictors	*Total*				*Third World*				*OECD*			
	Coeff	*Beta*	*r*	*t-stat*	*Coeff*	*Beta*	*r*	*t-stat*	*Coeff*	*Beta*	*r*	*t-stat*
GDInv	.26	.63	.66	6.37	.27	.68	.84	6.68	.34	.59	.65	3.64
Lab force	−.45	−.25	−.03	−2.69	.35	.12	.41	1.38	−.48	−.26	−.15	−1.69
Export	.14	.37	.65	4.17	.08	.22	.62	2.24	.20	.39	.66	2.47
Constant	1.50			4.30	−.35			−.62	1.10			1.68
R2	.67				.76				.68			
R2A	.65				.74				.62			
N	61				40				21			

Table 9.4. Regression analysis: economic growth and social structure

	Total				Third World				OECD			
Predictors	*Coeff*	*Beta*	*r*	*t-stat*	*Coeff*	*Beta*	*r*	*t-stat*	*Coeff*	*Beta*	*r*	*t-stat*
Secondary education	.01	.17	.37	.69	.02	.17	.39	.75	.02	.30	−.00	.94
Higher education	−.00	−.18	.22	−.97	−.00	−.05	.24	−.27	−.00	−.31	−.22	−1.07
Agricultural change	.03	.42	.44	2.07	.04	.42	.43	2.29	−.02	−.20	−.17	−.72
Constant	1.80			4.73	1.25			2.37	3.96			2.61
R2	.21				.26				.10			
R2A	.17				.20				.00			
N	61				40				21			

Political variables

It has been debated whether democracy affects economic growth positively or negatively (Weede, 1983; Weede, 1984). This is a version of the theme of the strong state. An authoritarian regime would promote economic growth due to its capacity to mobilize resources for investments. A similar line of argument has been suggested in a political hypothesis to the effect that left wing governments promote economic growth (Whiteley, 1982). Finally, there is the political hypothesis that a large public sector may have a net positive impact on economic growth although some types of public expenditures reduce rather than enhance economic growth (Korpi, 1985a, 1985b; Castles, 1990).

Political factors may affect economic growth by means of two mechanisms. On the one hand, specific policies conducted by governments for different periods of time may be conducive to a higher or lower rate of economic growth. On the other hand, the general political climate may be relevant for the economic factors that condition economic development. Tables 9.5 and 9.6 indicate that political factors are relevant for the explanation of the variation in average growth rates among nations. Let us begin with Tables 9.5A and 9.5B.

In the OECD set of countries it holds that the younger a nation the more rapid its rate of growth — institutional sclerosis as a negative determinant of economic growth according to one interpretation. There is little or no support for the other political hypotheses. The nature of the regime — democratic or authoritarian — does not matter and there is no indication of any link between socialist strength and high levels of economic growth. And the direction of the impact of public expenditures seems to differ among rich and poor countries, if indeed there is any impact at all.

It is interesting to look more closely at the impact of political factors on one crucial variable in economic growth, the investment function. Table 9.6A and 9.6B report findings that only support the institutionalization hypothesis. Neither the hypothesis about democracy reducing investments leading to economic growth, nor the hypothesis about left-wing governments enhancing investments promoting economic growth meet with empirical support.

The hypothesis that one political factor — institutional sclerosis — is related to economic growth is confirmed when the investment function is regressed on the political factors. The causal pattern is the same with regard to the variation in investments as with the variation in economic growth. Institutional sclerosis makes a difference for economic growth, especially among the rich OECD countries.

Mixed models

The model tests reported on so far show that some economic, social and

Table 9.5A. Regression analysis: economic growth and political structure

	Total				Third World				OECD			
Predictors	*Coeff*	*Beta*	r	*t-stat*	*Coeff*	*Beta*	r	*t-stat*	*Coeff*	*Beta*	r	*t-stat*
Institut. sclerosis	.01	.12	.11	.82	.01	.08	.07	.51	−.06	−.68	−.70	−3.68
Democracy	−.00	−.02	.04	−.16	−.01	−.08	−.06	−.47	−.00	−.04	−.33	−.19
Constant	2.79			4.63	2.82			3.37	7.08			7.28
R2	.01				.01				.49			
R2A	.00				.00				.43			
N	61				40				21			

Table 9.5B. Regression analysis: economic growth and political factors

Predictors	Total Coeff	Total Beta	Total r	Total t-stat	Third World Coeff	Third World Beta	Third World r	Third World t-stat	OECD Coeff	OECD Beta	OECD r	OECD t-stat
Socialist government	−.41	−.22	−.07	−1.38	−.35	−.14	−.12	−.85	−.03	−.02	−.39	−.08
Public expenditure	.03	.25	.12	1.58	.02	.11	.07	.65	−.06	−.49	−.50	−1.56
Constant	2.41			4.34	2.39			2.82	6.06			5.00
R2	.05				.02				.25			
R2A	.01				.00				.17			
N	61				40				21			

Table 9.6A. Regression analysis: investment growth and political factors

Predictors	Total Coeff	Total Beta	Total r	Total t-stat	Third World Coeff	Third World Beta	Third World r	Third World t-stat	OECD Coeff	OECD Beta	OECD r	OECD t-stat
Institut. sclerosis	−.03	−.20	−.29	−1.38	.00	.01	−.01	.04	−.09	−.65	−.69	−3.45
Democracy	−.03	−.18	−.28	−1.26	−.02	−.10	−.10	−.62	−.01	−.09	−.37	−.49
Constant	9.06			6.65	7.95			3.82	10.47			6.11
R2	.11				.01				.48			
R2A	.08				.00				.42			
N	61				40				21			

Table 9.6B. Regression analysis: investment growth and political factors

	Total				Third World				OECD			
Predictors	*Coeff*	*Beta*	*r*	*t-stat*	*Coeff*	*Beta*	*r*	*t-stat*	*Coeff*	*Beta*	*r*	*t-stat*
Socialist government	−1.22	−.28	−.35	−1.82	−1.55	−.25	−.23	−1.53	−.09	−.04	−.49	−.15
Public expenditure	−.04	−.13	−.29	−.83	−.05	.10	.03	.59	−.12	−.58	−.63	−2.11
Constant	8.26			6.54	6.71			3.24	9.51			4.98
R2	.13				.06				.39			
R2A	.10				.01				.33			
N	61				40				21			

Table 9.7A. Regression analysis: economic growth: mixed model

Predictors	Total Coeff	Total Beta	Total r	Total t-stat	Third World Coeff	Third World Beta	Third World r	Third World t-stat	OECD Coeff	OECD Beta	OECD r	OECD t-stat
GDInv level	.12	.36	.52	2.60	.11	.29	.46	1.71	.06	.20	.46	1.17
Prim & second education	.02	.29	.37	1.44	.03	.25	.39	1.36	.03	.41	−.00	2.13
Agricultural change	.02	.25	.44	1.18	.03	.25	.50	1.29	−.02	−.20	−.20	−1.08
Institut. sclerosis	−.03	−.40	.11	−2.45	−.02	−.21	.07	−1.35	−.06	−.75	−.70	−4.04
Constant	.16			.18	−.33			−.28	4.61			2.77
R2	.36				.35				.65			
R2A	.32				.27				.56			
N	61				40				21			

Table 9.7B. Regression analysis: economic growth: mixed model

Predictors	Total Coeff	Total Beta	Total r	Total t-stat	Third World Coeff	Third World Beta	Third World r	Third World t-stat	OECD Coeff	OECD Beta	OECD r	OECD t-stat
GDInv change	.29	.70	.66	9.61	.31	.77	.84	9.63	.15	.26	.65	1.21
Secondary education	.02	.27	.37	2.06	−.00	−.02	.39	−.17	.03	.40	−.00	2.06
Agricultural change	.03	.42	.44	3.41	.03	.34	.50	3.55	−.01	−.07	−.17	−.36
Institut. sclerosis	−.01	−.17	.11	−1.57	−.01	−.06	.07	−.66	−.05	−.67	−.70	−3.03
Constant	−.10			−.30	−.06			−.19	4.50			2.63
R2	.73				.81				.65			
R2A	.71				.78				.57			
N	61				40				21			

political variables are relevant to the explanation of economic growth. Could it be the case that some of these factors cancel each other out? Perhaps the relationship between institutional sclerosis and economic growth is spurious, to be explained in terms of other factors? Table 9.7A and 9.7B report on the the estimation of models that combine the factors that proved most relevant in earlier estimations of economic, social and political models.

There can be no doubt about the importance of the crucial economic variable — capital investments — or of changes in agriculture or education for economic development, but we note that the connection between institutional sclerosis and economic growth is not reducible to other factors. In the set of rich countries the variation in institutional sclerosis appears to be the best predictor of the variation in economic growth, whereas capital investments and social change matter more in Third World countries.

Conclusion

The argument that institutional sclerosis makes a difference for the average country growth rates in the economy meant an important contribution to the growing interest in the interaction between politics and economics. It carried the argument that political structure and economic system are interrelated further by adding a dynamic dimension: politics matter also for rate of change in the economy. There are a number of hypotheses that claim that political variables have an impact on average economic development. Testing these hypotheses with regard to both rich and poor countries results in a note of warning. Only one political factor — institutional sclerosis — appears to be of importance in the explanation of economic growth. And the effect is particularly strong in rich countries. The basic role of investments is strongly underlined in the findings reported on here (Sommers and Suits, 1971), whereas there is little evidence of public sector expansion promoting economic growth.

Economic growth is not determined by the level of affluence or the overall social structure. Economic growth is not predetermined by forces that cannot be influenced by political action. In the Third World economic growth is closely tied up with the overall investment behaviour which may be affected by government. In the rich countries economic growth is related to institutional sclerosis which is also affected by politics and policies. A deeper understanding of the impact of politics on economic growth would take us into an analysis of how and why nations differ in terms of crucial choices about the allocation of resources between the present and the future as well as about the status and power of distributional coalitions.

Appendix 9.1. Indicators and Sources

Indicator	Source
Economic growth: GNP/capita growth 1960-80	World Bank, 1982
Economic growth: GDP/capita growth 1960-80	World Bank, 1982
Economic level: Real GDP/capita 1960	Summers and Heston, 1984
GDInv.level: Gross Domestic Investment in per cent of GDP 1960, 1965, 1970, 1977, 1980	World Bank, 1982
GDInv.change: Growth in Gross Domestic Investment 1960-80	World Bank, 1982
Labour force level: male labour force participation rate 1960, 1980	World Bank, 1982
Labour force change: growth in labour force 1960-80	World Bank, 1982
Export level: export in per cent of GDP 1960, 1980	World Bank, 1982
Export change: growth in export 1960-80	World Bank, 1982
Secondary education: enrolment 1960, 1980	World Bank, 1982
Higher education: enrolment 1975	Taylor, 1981
Agricultural change: change in agricultural employment 1960-80	World Bank, 1984
Institutional sclerosis	Choi, 1983; Taylor and Hudson, 1972
Democracy c. 1965	Bollen, 1980
Socialist government: post-Second World War	Schmidt, 1983; Delury, 1983
Public sector expenditure in per cent of GDP c. 1977	IMF, 1982

10 Politico-economic regimes: an evaluation

Introduction

Perhaps the most controversial question in political economy is the evaluation of the performance of various types of economic systems or so-called politico-economic regimes. Which politico-economic system is the superior one? This is a problem to be decided ultimately by values, but the deliberation about pros and cons also involves matters of fact. Does capitalism do better than socialism in terms of economic growth? How about the degree of inequality in the distribution of resources in various countries? And which type of regime is more likely to run into double digit inflation or high national debts?

Not only are economic aspects relevant to the rise and decline of nations, but we also have to take into account how countries score on political criteria of evaluation such as, for example, democratic values. Moreover, what about welfare effort? There are a large number of relevant evaluation criteria: which are most appropriate? And any identification of politico-economic regimes or systems faces tremendous conceptual problems in relation to real-life systems where there is no such simple dichotomy as capitalism versus socialism. Is it at all possible to say something about the evaluation of regimes from a political economy perspective given this stage of theoretical and empirical knowledge?

Regimes

There are several relevant ways of classifying systems from a politico-economic perspective. In the mainstream economics literature the focus is on the concept of an economic system. And a few key kinds of economic systems are identified and evaluated. A definition of 'economic system' may look as follows:

> An *economic system* is a set of mechanisms and institutions for decision making and the implementation of decisions concerning production, income, and consumption within a given geographical area. (Lindbeck, 1977:214)

It follows from such an identification of the economic system in a country that it covers not only what traditionally counts as economic institutions like property and the market. Any description of an economic system would have to include a statement of the place of the state and the range of mechanisms for public resource allocation and income redistribution, i.e. political institutions. Thus, we may speak of *politico-economic regimes* in order to denote the various ways in which the market, the state, property institutions and public programmes for budget allocation and redistribution are mixed in different countries.

In their *Comparative Economic Systems* (1989) Gregory and Stuart employ a framework for the analysis of economic systems comprising four basic features which each has two modes: (1) organization of decision making: centralization and decentralization; (2) provision of information and coordination: market or plan; (3) property rights: private, cooperative and public; (4) the incentive system: moral or material. Gregory and Stuart use these categories to derive three main types of politico-economic regimes: capitalism, market socialism and planned socialism. Can we really speak of actually existing market socialist regimes? Is there some kind of pure model of capitalism which contain the essence of all non-socialist systems?

It is interesting to relate the standard categories in the literature on economic systems to the Gastil's framework, presented in *Freedom in the World* (1987) as it is a more refined one. Gastil categorizes politico-economic systems in the following way: (a) *capitalist*: a high degree of economic freedom and relatively little market intervention by the state; (b) *capitalist-statist*: substantial state intervention in markets and large public sectors, although the state remains committed to the institutions of private property; (c) *mixed capitalist*: an activist state with income redistribution, market intervention and regulation although the size of direct budget allocation of resources is not that large; (d) *mixed-socialist*: some economic freedom, private property and individual initiative within the framework of a socialist economy; (e) *socialist systems*: basically command economies with little economic freedom, private property and individual intiative.

Gastil classifies a large number of countries with the following politico-economic categories employing the legal status of voluntary exchange and ownership as the crucial charateristic, among others:

Capitalist: USA, Canada, Dominican Republic, El Salvador, Costa Rica, Colombia, Ecuador, Chile, Ireland, Belgium, Luxembourg, Switzerland, Spain, Germany FR, Iceland, Liberia, Cameroon, Kenya, Malawi, Jordan, South Korea, Japan, Thailand, Malaysia, Australia, New Zealand, Haiti, Barbados, Guatemala, Honduras, Cyprus, Niger, Ivory Coast, Sierra Leone, Gabon, Chad, Lebanon and Nepal.

Capitalist-State: Mexico, Panama, Venezuela, Peru, Brazil, Bolivia, Paraguay, Argentina, Italy, Ghana, Nigeria, Zaire, South Africa, Morocco, Iran, Turkey, India, Pakistan, Sri Lanka, Philippines, Indonesia, Jamaica, Trinidad, Mauritania, Central African Republic, Uganda, Saudi Arabia and Taiwan.

Mixed-Capitalist: Uruguay, United Kingdom, Netherlands, France, Portugal, Austria, Greece, Finland, Sweden, Norway, Denmark, Senegal, Tunisia, Israel, Singapore, Nicaragua, Guinea, Burundi, Sudan and Egypt.

Mixed-Socialist: Yugoslavia, Zambia, Madagascar, Guyana, Mali, Burkina Faso, Togo, Congo, Rwanda, Somalia, Libya, Syria, China and Burma.

Socialist: Germany DR, Hungary, Soviet Union, Bulgaria, Romania, Czechoslovakia, Tanzania, Ethiopia, Algeria, Iraq, Albania, Benin, Angola, Mozambique, Afghanistan, Mongolia, North Korea, Cambodia, Laos and Cuba.

There are a few major problems in relation to the Gastil framework and its classification. First, are the categories really conceptually distinct? Whereas it may be empirically feasible to distinguish the decentralized capitalist systems from the mixed-capitalist ones, the distinction between mixed-socialist and socialist is more troublesome to apply onto real world systems. Similarly, the separation between pure capitalist and capitalist-state is not all together easy to handle.

Second, any classification of countries into types of politico-economic regimes is bound to be time dependent. Gastil's classification refers to the late 1970s and early 1980s but politico-economic structures are not invariant over time. If the effort is to evaluate the performance of politico-economic regimes over time during the post-Second World War period, then the classification has to be reworked for some countries at certain points of time.

Third, when evaluating types of politico-economic regimes it is vital that enough countries be covered so that the conclusions apply to systems with different backgrounds. On the other, it is not necessary to include each and every country in the analysis, simply because the country background may be too deviant. Thus one could refrain from including countries that have had to face extended processes of internal or external instability such as, for example, war experience.

The description of the Federal Republic of Germany as only capitalist must be questioned given the strong tradition towards the welfare state in the 1949 constitution. Similarly, Portugal and Spain should be regrouped in the light of the strong state involvement in these societies, at least during the fascist period. The more detailed description of some African and Asian countries is open to discussion. In order to point out the difficulties in classifying countries in terms of politico-economic categories we will make a short geographical overview of the major countries on each continent employing *The Economist Atlas* (1989) and *Political Systems of The World* (1989). Which evaluation criteria should we concentrate on?

Performance

Gregory and Stuart evaluate the performance of their three types of economic systems by means of a set of outcomes: economic growth, efficiency, income distribution, stability, development objectives and national existence, where the overall finding is the precedence of the capitalist type on these evaluation criteria in relation to the others. However, why should we focus on these criteria? In order to evaluate how various types of politico-economic systems do in the real world one could employ both economic and political evaluation criteria.

Here we only attempt to suggest some preliminary steps towards the evaluation of politico-economic regimes. We will focus on five dimensions of politico-economic regimes which may be measured by means of specific evaluation criteria: two economic ones, two political ones and finally one social indicator. The average rate of economic growth over a number of years taps a dynamic aspect of politico-economic regimes whereas the average yearly rate of inflation captures a stability aspect. The evaluation criteria in a democracy index identifies several crucial performance aspects in relation to human values such as freedom and equality whereas a welfare effort index measures a different aspect on politico-economic performance. Finally, there is the inequality dimension to be measured by an indicator on the skewness in the distribution of income which is a standard outcome criterion.

To sum up, we will consider the following dimensions of a politico-economic regime in a country: economic growth, inflation, democratic rights and welfare effort by the state as well as the extent of inequality in the distribution of income. Thus, we have the following evaluation criteria: (i) *economic growth (EG)*: growth in real GDP per capita in international US dollars between 1980 to 1985; (ii) *inflation (I)*: average annual rates of inflation during 1980-1985; (iii) *democratic rights (D)*: the status of democracy about 1980 as measured by a complex index covering human rights, political competition and so on (Humana's index); (iv) *welfare effort by the state (W)*: a complex index calculated by Estes for roughly 1980; (v) *income inequality (Q)*: the share of the top quintile of the total national income measured on income data for about the 1970s.

These evaluation criteria — economic, political and social — have been measured on various data sources stated in Appendix 10.1. The rationale for the selection of these five evaluation criteria is simply that they are often used. Other criteria like unemployment, trade pattern and political stability could have been employed, but there is no natural limit where to stop. Let us take a close look at the country variation in politico-economic regimes and their performance around 1980 by moving from one continent to another focusing on economic growth, inflation, democratic performance, welfare effort and inequality. The data about the size of the population in various countries refer to about 1985.

America

The predominant orientation of the countries on the American continent towards some type of capitalist politico-economic regime is obvious, but there is much more to be said about the nuances. Firstly, there exist systems that fall outside of the set of capitalist regimes. It is true that the two examples of a socialist politico-economic regime — Cuba (10 million) and up to the 1990 election Nicaragua (3.3 million) — are small states when compared with the giant capitalist nations in this hemisphere. As there is hardly any case of a mixed-capitalist regime in America, the basic division among the countries on the American continent is between two types of capitalist regimes, decentralized capitalist and capitalist-state regimes. Besides Canada (25.4 million) the United States (239 million) belongs to the former category where also a number of small countries in the Caribbean islands and Central America should be placed: El Salvador (5.6 million), Dominican Republic (6.3 million), Barbados (0.3 million), Guatemala (8 million), Honduras (4.4 million) and Costa Rica (2.6 million).

The difficulty in drawing the demarcation line between capitalist and capitalist-state regimes is obvious with regard to Ecuador (9.4 million) and Chile (12 million), but we follow the Gastil classification here. The remaining countries should be classified as capitalist-state. Here, we have the giant countries in Latin America: Mexico (79 million), Brazil (136 million) and Argentina (31 million). Into the same type of politico-economic system enter a number of countries with fairly large populations: Venezuela (17.3 million), Peru (18.7 million), and Bolivia (6.4 million). To the same set belongs a few less populous countries like Paraguay (3.4 million), Panama (2.2 million), Trinidad (1.2 million) and Jamaica (2.2 million). It must be explicitly pointed out that the separation between decentralized capitalist and capitalism-state regimes is difficult to apply with precision. How to classify Uruguay (3 million) is an open question, as it is sometimes designated as a mixed-capitalist system. An overall picture of politico-economic performance on the American continent is given in Table 10:1.

Table 10.1. Politico-economic regimes in America

	EG 80-85	I 80-85	D 80	W 80	Q 75
Canada	1.27	6.3	94	16	41.0
USA	1.65	5.3	92	13	42.8
Mexico	−1.34	62.2	67	5	64.0
El Salvador	−2.51	11.6	30	6	54.4
Dominican Rep	−1.03	14.6	75	5	57.5
Guatemala	−2.94	7.4	30	2	58.8
Honduras	−2.54	5.4	75	1	67.8
Costa Rica	−2.10	36.4	90	6	50.6
Panama	.60	3.7	84	7	61.8
Colombia	.31	22.5	62	11	58.5
Venezuela	−3.30	9.2	89	4	54.0
Ecuador	−1.41	29.7	85	10	72.0
Peru	−2.32	98.6	81	9	61.0
Chile	−3.06	19.3	37	20	51.4
Bolivia	−4.80	569.1	50	8	61.0
Paraguay	.14	15.8	30	8	—
Brazil	−.37	147.7	70	16	66.6
Argentina	−3.29	342.8	44	12	50.3
Uruguay	−3.85	44.6	50	16	47.4

Note: EG 80-85 = average yearly economic growth between 1980-85; I 80-85 = average yearly inflation rate between 1980-85; D 80 = Humana's democracy index for about 1980; W 80 = Estes' welfare effort index for roughly 1980; Q 75 = inequality scores for the 1970s. The higher the score on D 80, W 80 and Q 75, the more of democracy, welfare effort and income inequality.

The performance data on politico-economic regimes in the Western hemisphere indicate severe problems of both an economic and political nature. Almost all countries in Latin America did badly on the evaluation criteria employed here in the late 1970s and early 1980s. The decentralized capitalist regimes score higher on most criteria compared with the state-capitalist regimes. Several large nations on the American continent have had to face not only income inequalities, hyperinflation

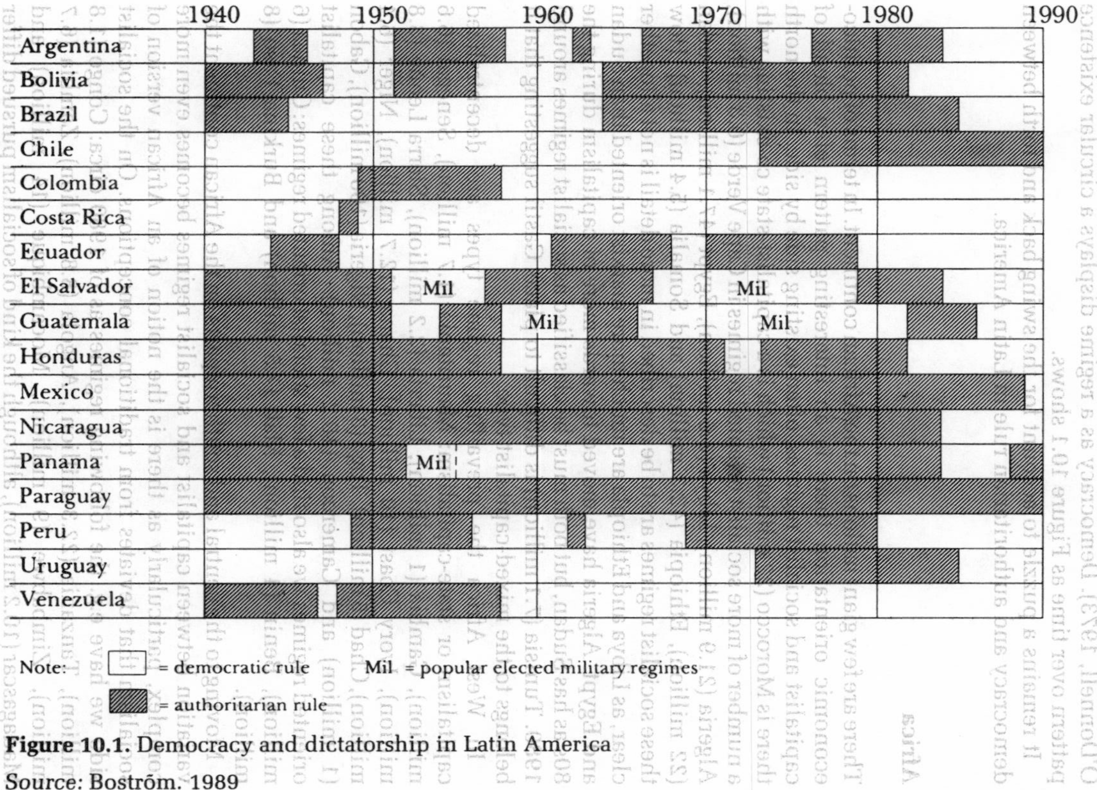

Figure 10.1. Democracy and dictatorship in Latin America

Source: Boström. 1989

and sluggish economic growth, but they have also scored low on democracy and welfare effort.

The status of democracy is confusing in Latin America. There is a conspicuous lack of a substantial and positive relationship between affluence and democratic political institutions in Latin America contrary to the well-known wealth model of democracy (Lipset, 1959; O'Donnell, 1973). Democracy as a regime displays a circular existence pattern over time as Figure 10.1 shows.

It remains a puzzle to account for the swing back and forth between democracy and authoritarian rule in Latin America.

Africa

There are few giant nations on the African continent. In terms of politico-economic orientation there is an interesting pattern of a blend of capitalist and socialist regimes, often existing side by side. In the north there is Morocco (22 million) which is a capitalist-state co-existing with a number of more socialist oriented regimes in Cape Verde (0.3 million), Algeria (21.9 million), Libya (3.6 million), Egypt (47.1 million), Sudan (22 million), Ethiopia (42.3 million) and Somalia (5.4 million). How these socialist regimes are to be described in more detail is not altogether clear, as Libya and Ethiopia are much more marxist oriented than Sudan and Egypt. Algeria have moved towards more of capitalism during the 80s as has Sudan, but both must be classified as socialist regimes around 1980. Tunisia (7.1 million) is difficult to place, Gastil suggesting that it belongs to the mixed-capitalist type.

In West Africa the prevailing regime types are decentralized capitalism or state-capitalism: Mauritania (1.7 million), Senegal (6.6 million), Gambia (1 million), Liberia (2.2 million), Sierra Leone (3.8 million), Ivory Coast (10 million), Ghana (12.7 million), Niger (6.4 million), Chad (5 million), Togo (3 million), Nigeria (100 million), Gabon (1 million) and Cameroon (10.2 million). Among these capitalist oriented regimes we also find a few socialist oriented regimes: Guinea (6 million), Benin (4 million), Mali (7.5 million) and Burkina Faso (8 million).

Moving to the central and southern parts on the African continent the variation between capitalist and socialist regimes becomes even more complex, particularly as there is the notion of an African version of socialism that deviates from traditional conceptions. On the socialist side we have e.g. the following regimes as of 1980 circa: Congo (1.8 million), Tanzania (22.3 million), Angola (8.8 million), Zambia (6.7 million), Zimbabwe (9 million), Mocambique (14 million) and Madagascar (10.2 million), although the kind of socialism pursued differ both with the country and the time period involved. The countries that had a politico-economic regime oriented towards some type of capitalism around 1980 are: Çentral African Republique (2.6 million), Zaire (31 million), Malawai (7.3 million), Kenya (20.4 million), Uganda (15.5 million), Burundi (4.7 million) and Rwanda (6 million). Table 10:2 presents some clues to the overall performance of several major African politico-economic systems around 1980.

Table 10.2. Politico-economic regimes in Africa

	EG 80-85	I 80-85	D 80	W 80	Q 75
Morocco	.31	7.8	57	9	65.4
Algeria	1.20	6.9	62	13	—
Tunisia	1.85	10.0	62	7	55.0
Libya	—	—	30	1	—
Egypt	3.23	11.0	64	5	47.5
Sudan	−2.86	31.7	55	4	49.8
Ethiopia	−.77	2.6	17	−1	—
Senegal	.22	9.7	89	6	60.9
Sierra Leone	−2.25	25.0	75	1	52.5
Ivory Coast	−2.85	10.0	75	5	57.2
Ghana	−2.85	57.0	50	1	—
Niger	−.45	8.5	50	2	—
Benin	−.28	9.7	—	4	51.7
Chad	−4.67	—	—	5	—
Nigeria	−4.92	11.4	69	1	—
Cameroon	4.19	11.8	50	4	—
Guinea	.11	8.3	50	6	—
Burkina Faso	.88	7.2	—	5	—
Liberia	−4.63	1.6	—	−1	—
Gabon	.73	—	—	—	67.5
Zaïre	−1.04	55.3	41	4	—
Kenya	−1.61	10.0	58	1	60.4
Uganda	5.84	—	50	1	—
Tanzania	.09	19.6	62	2	50.4
Burundi	.60	6.6	50	1	—
Rwanda	−1.67	7.6	50	2	—
Zambia	−3.07	14.7	58	2	61.1
Malawi	−1.20	11.4	50	1	50.6
Madagascar	−2.60	19.4	50	6	—

Note: see Table 10:1 for the abbreviations.

Generally, African politico-economic systems score low on the political performance evaluation criteria. On the economic ones, they vary considerably from one country to another. Some countries faced a very negative economic predicament in the early 1980s with an extremely bad rate of economic growth and sometimes hyperinflation. However, other countries did fairly well during the same time period when the world economy was sluggish in general.

Asia and Oceania

The populous nations on the Asian continent including Australia and New Zealand belong either to the set of socialist, capitalist or capitalist-state regimes. In Asia minor there is a number of capitalist or capitalist-state countries: Jordan (3.5 million), Lebanon (2.7 million), Saudia Arabia (11.5 million), United Arab Emirates (1.3 million), Oman (1.3 million), Qatar (0.3 million), North Yemen (6.3 million), Kuwait (1.8 million) and Iran (45.2 million). The classification of some of these countries onto types of regime is not unproblematic as their persistent war involvement has had an impact of the structure of their societies. Onto the socialist type may be entered the following countries: Syria (10.5 million), South Yemen (2.3 million), Iraq (15.7 million) and Afghanistan (18.2 million). How Israel (4.3 million) is to be described is an open question: mixed-capitalist, capitalist-state or mixed-socialist?

In East Asia we find the giant countries of the world, and they are either socialist, capitalist or capitalist-state. Thus, there is India (765.2 million) which perhaps should be identified as capitalist-state. Pakistan (95 million) belongs to the same type of politico-economic regime as did Sri Lanka (16.2 million) around 1980. Bangladesh (104 million) is capitalist-state whereas Burma (4.7 million) is a socialist regime. Examples of a capitalist politico-economic regime are to be found in Thailand (51 million), Malaysia (7.5 million), South Korea (40.7 million), Taiwan (19.6 million), Japan (121 million), Australia (15.8 million) and New Zealand (3.3 million).

How to separate a capitalist regime from a capitalist-state regime in this part of the world is not always easy. Thus, it has been argued that capitalist Singapore (2.6 million) belongs to the mixed-capitalist type, which is debtable to say the least. Populous Indonesia (162.2 million) may be designated capitalist-state as should the Philippines (54.7 million). Into the set of socialist politico-economic regimes enter mainland China (1 042 million), North Korea (20.4 million), Mongolia (2 million), Vietnam (62 million), Cambodia (7.3 million) and Laos (3.6 million).

In relation to the evaluation of the performance of politico-economic regimes in Asia one must take into account the enormous impact of long time periods of external or internal war. When presenting data on the performance of Asian politico-economic regimes we focus in particular on countries where about 1980 war involvement had not had a drastic effect on the country. Table 10.3 has the data.

Table 10.3. Politico-economic regimes in Asia and Oceania

	EG 80-85	I 80-85	D 80	W 80	Q 75
Israel	.34	196.3	73	7	39.9
Jordan	2.02	3.9	50	3	—
Syria	−.93	6.1	34	1	—
Iraq	−6.03	—	27	5	—
Iran	5.54	—	30	9	62.7
Saudi Arabia	—	—	29	—	—
Afghanistan	.36	—	30	—	—
Pakistan	2.76	8.1	42	3	—
India	3.69	7.8	70	6	49.2
Sri Lanka	4.73	14.7	75	5	44.5
Burma	2.55	2.6	50	3	—
Thailand	2.03	3.2	64	1	53.4
Malaysia	1.62	3.1	54	4	56.4
Singapore	11.51	3.1	61	4	—
South Korea	4.83	6.0	51	0	42.7
Taiwan	3.77	—	53	—	39.2
Japan	2.73	1.2	92	12	41.0
China	8.49	2.4	32	—	—
Indonesia	3.01	10.7	53	6	52.0
Philippines	−2.04	19.3	51	4	54.0
Australia	1.00	9.1	93	22	43.0
New Zealand	1.44	9.8	96	25	41.4
North Korea	—	—	22	—	—

Note: for the abbreviations see Table 10.1.

The overall picture when evaluating politico-economic regimes on the Asian continent including South East Asia is very much different from that of Latin America or Africa, even though the majority of countries are LDCs or NICs. Politico-economic performance has been on the whole much more impressive among the set of Asian countries. The average rate of economic growth tends to be higher and the level of inflation lower. Some countries display exceptionally high average growth rates in their economies. When it comes to the political criteria of evaluation things are not as bright as when the economic evaluation criteria were applied. It is true that there are quite a number of countries that score high on the democractic index, but there is also a large number of countries that are right-wing or left-wing authoritarian regimes. Besides the level of welfare state effort tends to be very low and the extent of income inequality substantial.

Europe

It remains to look at politico-economic performance in the old world, here covering both western and eastern Europe including the USSR and Turkey. On the European continent in this wide sense all the various politico-economic regime types may be found. It is not easy to draw a sharp dividing line between the various kinds of capitalist regimes, but a preliminary classification may be suggested for the early 1980s.

To the set of mixed-capitalist systems should be counted all countries with a strong welfare state combined with extensive market allocation. The set of mixed-capitalist regimes includes several small and a few large countries: Norway (4.1 million), Finland (4.9 million), Sweden (8.3 million), Denmark (5.1 million), Iceland (0.2 million), Netherlands (16.6 million), Belgium (9.9 million), United Kingdom (56.6 million), Ireland (3.6 million), Federal Republic of Germany (61 million), Austria (7.6 million), France (55.1 million) and Italy. Perhaps one may argue that Italy (57 million) could be placed among the capitalist-state regimes, but this applies only if the time period studied is the 1950s or 1960s. Equally debatable is the classification of Spain (38.7 million) and Portugal (10.2 million) which, however, is here placed among the set of capitalist-state regimes as we refer to the early 1980s. Into the category of capitalist regimes we enter Luxemburg (0.4 million), Switzerland (6.4 million), Greece (10 million) and Turkey (52 million), although Turkey could be placed among the capitalist-state regimes.

Up until 1989 the socialist regime type covered the entire Eastern Europe including the USSR. Thus, there is a number of populous socialist countries and one giant such system: Poland (37.3 million), German Democratic Republic (16.7 million), Czechoslovakia (15.5 million), Hungary (10.7 million), Romania (22.9 million), Bulgaria (9 million), Yugoslavia (23.1 million), Albania (3 million) and the Soviet Union (276 million). One may wish to distinguish between various types of socialist regimes, but it is far from evident how such distinctions are to be applied empirically in a systematic way.

Table 10.4 covers performance data for the European politico-economic regimes in the early 1980s. The tiny countries on the European continent have been excluded.

The mixed-capitalist regimes did not only do well on the political evaluation criteria which was expected, but they also showed fairly reasonable economic performance although certainly not doing exceptionally well. The communist regimes appear to begin to face severe economic problems in the early 1980s which have since aggravated. A few of the capitalist countries are plagued by hyperinflation, a phenomenon which is expressed — cueing — quite differently in the socialist systems. The level of income inequality tends to be rather low in Europe, although data are missing for some countries.

Table 10.4. Politico-economic regimes in Europe

	EG 80-85	I 80-85	D 80	W 80	Q 75
Norway	2.30	8.5	95	24	37.3
Finland	1.67	8.6	96	18	—
Sweden	1.96	8.6	94	23	37.0
Denmark	2.23	8.1	96	28	38.6
Netherlands	.10	3.5	94	25	40.0
Belgium	.88	5.9	92	25	39.8
Ireland	.93	10.8	86	25	39.4
UK	1.44	6.4	95	25	39.2
Switzerland	1.04	4.5	92	19	—
GFR	.40	3.2	91	29	45.2
Austria	1.42	4.9	92	28	—
France	.40	9.5	88	26	46.4
Italy	.61	14.2	88	26	46.5
Spain	.83	12.6	78	21	45.2
Portugal	−.02	22.7	86	13	49.1
Greece	.31	20.6	80	16	—
Turkey	1.54	37.1	43	5	58.6
Yugoslavia	1.16	45.1	55	19	41.5
Romania	1.38	—	32	17	—
Bulgaria	.71	—	37	20	—
Hungary	.78	—	54	22	33.4
CSSR	1.00	—	36	24	—
Poland	−.31	—	36	18	—
USSR	1.90	—	27	16	—
GDR	1.79	—	35	—	30.9

Note: abbreviations see Table 10:1.

We may conclude this elementary geographical overview by noting that there appears to exist a systematic variation across the four continents. Economic performance tends to be problematic on the American and African continents whereas countries in the Asian and European sets tend to do fairly well. High scores on the political performance criteria are to be found mainly on the European continent. However, such a geographical description is more misleading than clarifying as there are exceptions from the general pattern within each continent. What, then, accounts for the overall performance pattern for politico-economic regimes? Does some special type of political-economic regime matter for the economic and political performance? Let us move to an analysis of variance of the same information reported on above.

Evaluation

Having made a kind of geographical description of politico-economic performance in a number of countries on different continents, we now turn to an analysis in order to find out whether there is some pattern underneath the surface uncovered. Is it true that one kind of economic system or politico-economic regime — capitalism — performs better than its main competitor — socialism? How can we test this hypothesis? If it were true that capitalism did better than socialism, then performance data — economic growth and inflation, democracy and welfare effort and inequality — would tend to differ between regimes with regard to average performance scores. Is this the case? Since the dichotomy between capitalism and socialism is too crude we compare three types of capitalist regimes with the socialist type of politico-economic system. Let us try an analysis of variance of the differences between and within the four main categories of politico-economic regimes in order to test the hypothesis that all brands of capitalism perform better than socialism.

Below we report on the findings from an analysis of variance of the performance data on these four sets of regimes. Some statistics are rendered for each of the evaluation criteria: mean values, maxima and minima as well as CV scores and the eta-squared statistic. We are interested in how these different groups of politico-economic regimes perform in relation to each other as well as how much variation there is within the various groups of regimes. The basic question is this: is there more variation *between* the four sets of regimes than *within* these four subsets themselves? If the eta-squared statistic shows scores that are larger than 0.5, then we may conclude that the distinctions between the four politico-economic regimes are real. If, on the contrary, the eta-squared statistic is lower than 0.5, then there is more variation within these categories meaning that the regime property itself does not matter for the variation in performance.

Table 10.5 presents a tentative classification of politico-economic types. Starting from the Gastil framework we have done some changes when classifying countries into sets of politico-economic regimes. On the one hand, a few countries have been classified somewhat differently; Italy, for example, has been placed among the mixed-capitalist systems and not as a capitalist-state system. On the other hand, the two categories of mixed-socialist and socialist have been combined into one single category. The set of socialist regimes includes countries that have had a planned economy and a one-party state for a long period during the post-war period, although some of these countries abandoned the communist regime type in 1989 or 1990. We have reduced the number of countries (N=84) included in the analysis of variance of the performance scores, concentrating mainly on large countries. The classification has been checked with *The Economist Atlas* and *Political Systems of the World.*

Table 10.5. Classification of politico-economic regimes, 1980

Capitalist	*Capitalist-state*	*Mixed-capitalist*	*Socialist*
USA	Mexico	Ireland	GDR
Canada	Panama	UK	Yugoslavia
Dominican Rep	Venezuela	Netherlands	Hungary
El Salvador	Peru	France	Czechoslovakia
Costa Rica	Brazil	Italy	Bulgaria
Guatemala	Bolivia	Austria	Romania
Honduras	Paraguay		Soviet Union
Ecuador	Argentina	GFR	China
Colombia	Ghana	Sweden	Zambia
Chile	Nigeria	Denmark	Madacasgar
Switzerland	Zaïre	Finland	Burkina Faso
Greece	Morocco	Norway	Egypt
Niger	Iran	Belgium	Sudan
Kenya	Portugal		Libya
Malawi	India		Burma
Liberia	Pakistan		Tanzania
Cameroon	Sri Lanka		Algeria
Taiwan	Philippines		Iraq
Jordan	Indonesia		Benin
South Korea	Uganda		Afghanistan
Japan	Spain		North Korea
Thailand	Turkey		Poland
Singapore			
Malaysia			
Australia			
New Zealand			
Ivory Coast			
Sierra Leone			
Gabon			
Chad			

Note: This classification of politico-economic regimes follows Gastil's framework with some changes. The classification of countries like Spain and Portugal is debatable (Gastil, 1987).

Among the *capitalist* systems we find both OECD countries and Third World countries. This category is to be found on all the continents as it includes the United States and Canada, Ecuador and Chile, Greece and Switzerland, Niger, Ivory Coast and Kenya, Jordan, Thailand and Malaysia as well as Japan, and finally Australia and New Zealand. The *capitalist-state* type covers politico-economic regimes where the state plays a large role within the framework of an extensive private property system and market allocation. This category includes mainly Third World countries in Latin America: Argentina, Brazil, Mexico and Venezuela, or in Africa: Uganda, Morocco and Nigeria, as well as in Asia: Taiwan, the Philippines and Indonesia. How to apply this category onto OECD countries is debatable. Turkey is often designated as capitalist-state, but how about Spain and Portugal with regard to their fascist heritage?

There are several OECD countries in the set of *mixed-capitalist* systems. Actually, most of the West-European nations enter this category because of their welfare state orientation. Whether we also find some Third World countries in this category is to be doubted as welfare state spending is low among poor countries. The category of *socialist* countries covers a few Third World communist regimes besides the East European countries that adhered to a Leninist model of a politico-economic regime up until 1989-90. Thus all politico-economic regime types besides the mixed-capitalist category include both rich and poor countries. A necessary but not sufficient condition for welfare state spending on a grand scale — big government without socialism — is a rich economy, as argued in Chapter 7.

We will start with the economic dimension, including indices that measure the level of affluence and the average economic growth for various time periods during the post-World War Two period as well as an indicator on the extent of inflation between 1980-85. Then we will take up the political evaluation criteria.

Level of affluence

It is often argued that capitalist systems have a higher level of affluence than socialist ones. Is this true once we make the concepts of capitalism and socialism more refined? Tables 10.6 and 10.7 partly confirm the general impression that capitalism performs better than socialism in terms of economic prosperity, but we must take a closer look at various kinds of capitalist regimes comparing them with socialist regimes. Let us begin back in 1960 (Table 10.6).

Fifteen years after the end of the Second World War the capitalist and mixed-capitalist regimes had a higher level of affluence on an average than the socialist type of regimes. Since the mixed-capitalist type does

Table 10.6. Real GDP per capita in regime sets, 1960

	Mean	Max	Min	CV	Eta²
Capitalist (N=30)	1872	7380	237	1.11	
Capitalist-state (N=22)	1319	5308	314	.87	
Mixed-capitalist (N=12)	4427	5490	2545	.20	
Socialist (N=19)	1708	4516	208	.79	
Total (N=83)	2057	7380	208	0.89	0.30

Source: Summers and Heston, 1988.

not cover any Third World country the distance between the average score for the mixed-capitalist regime is far higher than the average affluence scores of the capitalist and the socialist regimes. Yet, the average real GDP per capita was higher in the capitalist set of countries than in the set of socialist countries. The difference was not that striking or $1 872 versus $1 708 on an average. The variation as measured by the CV scores was quite extensive among both capitalist and socialist regimes as opposed to the fairly homogeneous set of mixed-capitalist regimes which are mainly welfare states in Western Europe.

However, the state-capitalist regimes display a lower real GDP per capita than the socialist regimes when average scores are considered. Thus, we cannot say that generally capitalism is combined with a higher level of affluence than socialism. Moreover, the variation between and within the four sets of politico-economic regimes is such that a simple overall generalization that capitalism always does better than socialism in terms of country affluence is not warranted. The eta-squared score indicate that the variation within the groups is larger than the variation between the groups. This finding is supported by the very high CV scores measuring the within group variation. The socialist regimes and the capitalist-state regimes tend to have a lower level of affluence when mean values are focused on. We also note that the maximum values in these two sets are high as well as that there are low-scoring countries in all four sets of politico-economic regimes.

The prosperous period from the 1950s and the 1960s up to the mid-1970s with tremendous growth in output as well as in trade benefited all four types of politico-economic regimes about equally when we focus on average income per capita in various countries. The mean income for all the countries included here grew. A similar expansion took place in all the four sets taken separately, although the increase in the maximum values is much larger than the increase in the minimum values. Table 10.7 reports on how the different regimes performed when the world economy moved into a lower level of activity, if not some years of recession.

Table 10.7. Real GDP per capita in regime sets, 1985

	Mean	Max	Min	CV	Eta²
Capitalist (N=30)	3811	12532	254	1.01	
Capitalist-state (N=22)	2173	6437	210	.73	
Mixed-capitalist (N=12)	9359	12623	5205	.20	
Socialist (N=20)	3009	8740	355	.90	
Total (N=84)	3984	12623	210	0.91	0.40

Source: Summers and Heston, 1988.

During the 1970s and early 1980s the country mean average income measures rose again, although not as rapidly as during the 1950s and 1960s. The increase was, however, weak among the capitalist-state regimes which began to lag behind. Actually, the average level of affluence among the capitalist-state regimes was reduced in the early 1980s. The other major finding is the poor development in the socialist group of countries which no longer kept pace with the group of capitalist or mixed-capitalist regimes. It seems as if the mixed-capitalist group managed the economic crisis of the 1970s and early 1980s somewhat better than the set of capitalist regimes.

The general finding is that the gap between the capitalist and mixed-capitalist regimes on the one hand and the socialist and capitalist-state sets of regimes on the other hand has increased since the 1960s. Looking at country mean values the mixed-capitalist regimes in 1985 had a level of affluence three times that of the capitalist-state regimes as well as that of the socialist regimes, whereas the set of capitalist regimes displayed twice as high average income values as these two politico-economic regimes that lag behind. More specifically, it is found that politico-economic regimes that involve the state or the public sector to a large extent in the actual operations of the economy do worse than politico-economic regimes which trust markets more.

Interestingly, the higher eta-squared statistic for the 1985 data indicate that politico-economic regime does matter somewhat. The within group variation is only slightly larger than the between group variation. The mixed-capitalist do much better than the pure capitalistic regimes and the state-capitalist systems, simply because the welfare state is to be found among rich countries. The socialist regimes have not done well but also not that badly, as they tend to have a higher level of affluence than the capitalist-state regimes. However, they cannot compete with the capitalist ones or the mixed-capitalist regimes. Thus we may conclude that there is clear evidence for the claim that a socialist regime means less of economic affluence than a capitalist regime, but also that the hypothesis means an oversimplification.

Economic growth

The gap between the set of socialist politico-economic systems and two of the capitalist types of systems has increased in terms of GDP per capita. May we conclude that the rate of economic growth is higher among these two types of capitalist regimes than in the set of socialist regimes? Yes, but only for a longer time period like 1960-85. There is too much variation between the countries within all three sets with regard to different periods of time to permit any general conclusion that capitalism performs better than socialism with regard to yearly economic growth rates. Let us use more refined concepts for politico-economic systems and look at the average growth rates in the early 1980s? Table 10.8 has the data.

Tables 10.8. Economic growth among regime sets, 1980-85

	Mean	Max	Min	Eta²
Capitalist (N=30)	0.2	11.5	−4.7	
Capitalist-state (N=22)	0.1	5.8	−4.9	
Mixed-capitalist (N=12)	1.3	2.3	0.1	
Socialist (N=20)	0.5	8.5	−6.0	
Total (N=84)	0.4	11.5	−6.0	0.02

Source: Summers and Heston, 1988.

Any simple generalization about politico-economic systems fails to do justice to the real-world differences in average growth rates. During the five year period between 1980 and 1985 when the world economy was characterized by a low level of activity there are no principal differences in economic growth between the four sets of politico-economic regimes. All the variation is to be found within the four groups as the extremely low eta-squared measure shows. There are examples of very high average growth rates among capitalist, capitalist-state and socialist regimes just as there exist cases of very negative growth rates in the same categories of politico-economic regimes. We cannot say that generally speaking capitalism all the time and everywhere does better than socialism in terms of economic growth.

It is possible to broaden the evaluation of various politico-economic regimes by bringing in additional economic evaluation criteria. Here we will look quickly at inflation. The yearly rate of inflation has come to be regarded as a more and more important sign of stability in economic systems. The disruptive consequences of hyperinflation are feared all over the world. It seems as if governments in rich countries put more emphasis on the policy goal of a low average rate of inflation than on reducing unemployment. In any case, a high level of inflation is looked upon as a sign of fundamental economic instability. Are there any systematic differences tied to the various types of politico-economic regimes in terms of average level of inflation in the early 1980s? Table 10.9 presents an overview of the situation.

Table 10.9. Average rate of inflation 1980-85

	Mean	Max	Min	CV	Eta^2
Capitalist (N=27)	11.2	36.4	1.2	.80	
Capitalist-state (N=20)	75.7	569.1	3.7	1.84	
Mixed-capitalist (N=12)	7.7	14.2	3.2	.41	
Socialist (N=11)	15.5	45.1	2.4	.84	
Total (N=70)	29.7	569.1	1.2	2.68	0.02

Source: World Bank, 1987.

The overall finding when tracing a special pattern of inflation among the four categories or groups of politico-economic regimes is that the set of mixed-capitalist systems displays less spread between the maximum and minimum rates of inflation. The statistics reported on above single out capitalist-state systems as particularly vulnerable to hyperinflation.

Democratic rights

Since there is no standard measure of democracy we have to rely on some indices that attempt to rank countries on the basis of various legal and political considerations. Allowing for the difficulties involved in the construction of democracy indices as well as the problem of strictly comparing these indices, we may point to a few striking differences between the four politico-economic regimes. Not unexpectedly, the system variation with regard to democracy is more tied to the between-group variation than what was true of the economic evaluation criteria. The eta-squared score is much higher than noticed in the analysis of economic evaluation criteria (Table 10.10).

Tables 10.10. Democracy among regime sets, 1980

	Mean	Max	Min	CV	Eta^2
Capitalist (N=26)	67.8	96	30	.31	
Capitalist-state (N=22)	59.5	89	30	.30	
Mixed-capitalist (N=12)	92.3	96	86	.04	
Socialist (N=20)	42.7	64	22	.32	
Total (N=80)	62.9	96	22	0.36	0.48

Note: The Humana index ranges from 0 to 100 and is based mainly on the occurrence of human rights, including political rights (Humana, 1983).

In the mid-1980s democratic political rights occurred among the mixed-capitalist regime type. Here we have a number of countries that scored very high on the Humana democracy index. The mean value for the capitalist or capitalist-state is consistently lower, although these regime categories include countries that score high on the index: New Zealand, Australia, Japan among the capitalist regimes and India in the category of capitalist-state regimes. The democracy score among the three types of capitalistic regimes is higher than that of the socialist type of regime, but there exist some highly undemocratic regimes also in the set of capitalist and capitalist-state regimes.

The major finding is that this political evaluation criterion does discriminate between the various politico-economic regimes. The capitalist-state and the socialist regime types display much lower values than the mixed-capitalist. The capitalist regime kind also scores higher than the socialist regime type on this measure, but this type also includes countries with very low democracy scores, for example, Chad and Nigeria. Several socialist systems scored very low in 1980: Bulgaria, the Soviet Union, Czechoslovakia and East Germany. However, there remains one more relevant political evaluation criterion, the effort of the state at promoting social welfare by means of various public programmes.

Welfare effort

The Estes indicator on welfare effort in a country may be employed to map differences between politicio-economic regimes. It takes into account for how many years a country has employed social legislation. It is often believed that the capitalist systems do the least in terms of public programmes in order to enhance social welfare. Table 10.11 presents some data that pertain to this hypothesis about regime differences in welfare effort by the government.

Table 10.11. Welfare effort in regime sets, 1980

	Mean	Max	Min	Eta^2
Capitalist (N=28)	7.6	25	−1	
Capitalist-state (N=22)	7.0	21	1	
Mixed-capitalist (N=12)	25.2	29	18	
Socialist (N=18)	10.3	24	1	
Total (N=80)	10.7	29	−1	0.49

Note: The Estes index counts the number of years a country has had various types of social welfare legislation (Estes, 1984).

The welfare index measuring the effort at welfare state policies distinguishes between the four sets of politico-economic regimes. The eta-squared statistic is almost 0.50 as was also the case with the democracy index. This means that half of the country variation is to be found among the systematic differences between the types of politico-economic regimes. At the same time the picture is more complicated than what a simple dichotomy such as that between capitalism and socialism would involve. We note that the highest mean score is to be found among the mixed-capitalist regimes. Moreover, the average country welfare effort is hardly more extensive among the socialist regimes than among the capitalist or capitalist-state regimes. Welfare effort is not the same as welfare results. Let us look at an indicator on social outcomes, the distribution of the national income between households.

Income inequality

There is a large number of potentially relevant outcome measures that may be employed for the evaluation of politico-economic regimes. Perhaps the extent of income inequality is one of the most sensitive evaluation criteria, because it has figured so promimently in the ideologies tied to the distinction between capitalism and socialism. Is it true, may we ask, that various politico-economic regimes promote income equality differently? Table 10.12 provides some clues to the problem of how and if politico-economic systems are characterized by different structures of income distribution. The data available for socialist regimes is meagre.

Table 10.12. Income inequality, c. 1975

	Mean	Max	Min	CV	Eta^2
Capitalist (N=22)	52.7	72.0	39.2	0.18	
Capitalist-state (N=16)	56.2	66.6	44.5	0.13	
Mixed-capitalist (N=10)	40.9	46.5	37.0	0.09	
Socialist (N=8)	45.7	61.1	30.7	0.22	
Total (N=56)	50.6	72.0	30.7	0.16	0.33

Note: A top quintile index — income share of upper 20% of the population — has been used to measure the extent of income inequality. A higher score implies more of inequality in the distribution of income (Muller, 1985; 1988; Taylor & Jodice, 1983; Chan, 1989; Musgrave & Jarrett, 1979).

The eta-squared statistic being smaller than 0.5 indicates that the variation within the four fundamental categories is larger than the variation between these four sets of systems. However, there is one major finding: it is not the case that a socialist regime means more of income inequality per se. As a matter of fact, the mixed-capitalist regime type displays lower scores on all the statistics employed here. Thus the ideological commitment of socialist regimes to equality is one thing and matters of fact another thing. In the mixed capitalist systems a combination of economic affluence and political ambitions at redistributing income has resulted in much lower levels of income inequality than in other types of politico-economic regimes. Not very surprisingly, the standard statistics for the capitalist-state type of systems are worse than those of the capitalist-state regime type.

Conclusion

Much more remains to be done before there is a theory about the performance of politico-economic regimes. Here we have reported on a preliminary analysis based on economic, social and political evaluation dimensions. Six evaluation criteria using various indices were tested with regard to their discriminatory power in relation to four sets of regimes or systems. In order to move ahead in comparative research in the new field of political economy other evaluation criteria would have to be included and a more refined causal analysis be adopted in order to measure the partial impact of various factors. However, there are some novel findings in the empirical analysis conducted here.

First, we cannot reduce basic properties of politico-ecomomic systems like level of affluence, economic growth, democracy and welfare state effort to the standard crude dichotomy of capitalism versus socialism. A first step towards a refined assessment of the politico-economic performance of various countries is to employ categories like capitalist, mixed-capitalist, capitalist-state and socialist regimes on the basis of how the state recognizes the institutions of private property and of how much space there is for voluntary exchange in the allocation of resources. We simply cannot make sense of all the variation in the data about the performance of politico-economic systems by using the dichotomy between capitalism and socialism. The political evaluation criteria discriminate better than the economic ones between the basic kinds of politico-economic regimes. Although there is considerable within-regime type variation, we find some conspicuous between-regime differences

Second, the mixed-capitalist system tends to perform better on all evaluation criteria than the other regime types. The socialist regime type as well as the capitalist-state regime type tend to lag behind the other two types of capitalist regimes on the evaluation criteria employed here, in particular the average level of affluence measured by the GDP/capita indicator. Politico-economic systems where markets are given a prominent role tend to do better than politico-economic systems where the state is heavily involved in the economy.

Third, the failure of the socialist regime type to keep pace with the development rate among the two capitalist types of regimes is apparent already by 1970. Had reliable data about the late 1980s been available, the misfortunes of the planned economies would have been obvious. It remains to be seen what kind of politico-economic system will develop in Eastern Europe following the collapse of the Communist regimes in the fall of 1989.

Fourth, one brand of a capitalist regime — capitalist-state regimes — performs as badly as the socialist kind of regime. There are straightforward examples of failures even among the decentralized capitalist regimes. More research needs to be done on politico-economic regimes before we know why politico-economic systems differ in their overall performance profile. Evidently, the choice of a politico-economic regime matters but so do other factors.

Appendix 10.1. Indicators and sources

Real GDP/capita 1960	Summers and Heston, 1988
Real GDP/capita 1985	Summers and Heston, 1988
Economic growth 1980-85	Summers and Heston, 1988
Inflation rate 1980-85	World Bank 1987
Democracy rights c. 1980	Humana, 1983
Welfare effort c. 1970-80	Estes, 1984

Income inequality c. 1970-80	Muller, 1988, 1985 Taylor and Jodice, 1983 Chan, 1989 Musgrave and Jarrett, 1979

11 Conclusion

Introduction

Political economy is a rapidly expanding field of study on the borderline between political science and economics. A number of approaches or perspectives have contributed to the establishment of a set of theories modelling the short-run or long-run interaction or reciprocities between politics and economics (Brown, 1985). In this book we have drawn upon public choice theory, comparative politics, marxist perspectives on development, public policy and mainstream economic theory i.e. in particular growth theory (Stiglitz and Uzawa, 1970; Hahn, 1971; Sen, 1970). Bringing together political science with its strong emphasis on empirical research and the conduct of comparative inquiry with economic theory, so strongly oriented towards abstract modelling, must be a relevant social science endeavour during a time period when big government and huge public sector budgets loom large. Much more remains to be done and here we have only carved out a small piece of the expanding political economy cake which becomes more tasty as the number of interesting questions and models grow.

In the typical set of problems within modern political economy two main problems have been analysed at length in this small volume. Firstly, we have focused on the wealth theory of politics. It argues that economic factors constitute a crucial determinant of political phenomena like regime characteristics or public policy patterns. Secondly, we have looked at the political theory of economic growth which claims that political factors have a considerable impact on economic growth in the long run. More specifically, we examine the following questions:

1. Is economic affluence a key determinant of politics? More specifically, we deal with two arguments that come close to some

kind of economic determinism; one tries to account for the occurrence of different types of political regimes, especially democracy; and the other offers an economic explanation of the differences and similarities in national patterns of public policies.

2. Is politics a key determinant of economic phenomena? In particular, does the knowledge of political factors in a country help us account for the long-run dynamism of the economy, namely the average rate of economic growth?

A number of hypotheses referring to these two problem areas have been evaluated by means of a comparative framework for empirical analysis covering a large number of countries belonging to various politico-economic regime types. The exact number of countries has varied according to the specific problem dealt with, as has the time period chosen, although attempt has been made to cover both so-called rich and poor countries as well as several decades during the post-Second World War period.

Economics and politics

The claims of *economic determinism* cannot be confirmed. This applies to both the economic model of political regimes and the economic theory of policy patterns. The statistical associations are not strong enough to constitute the ground for a causal inference to the effect that economic factors determine regime characteristics or policy patterns.

The affluence theory

In the midst of a variety of modern political economy models one may identify a set that together constitute an *affluence theory of politics*, as it were. It predicts that there are strong connections between measures of economic affluence and various political variables pertaining to the regime or the public policy pattern of a country. However, we find that these empirical associations are not strong enough to support the claims of this affluence theory, as we call it. The strong versions of economic model explanations as, for example, the affluence model predicting democracy or public policies are not corroborated.

The regime model explaining democracy by means of economic affluence receives support in the data, but it leaves far too much of the variation unaccounted for. It is not possible to interpret the statistical association between high levels of affluence measured by means of the GDP per capita indicator and some standard index on democracy as an underlying necessary and sufficient condition. There are too many rich countries that are not democratic and there are poor countries that have managed to sustain democratic rule. Moreover, the empirical association between the level of affluence and democratic rule is not stable over different selections of country sets, indicating that we need some additional theory in order to explain why the countries in Latin America do not behave in accordance with the model.

Finally, it is not the case that increments in economic affluence tend to be associated with increments in the 'democraticness' of the regime of a country. The basic problem with the weath model of democracy is that it is impossible to make any causal inferences from the observed statistical correlation. The manifest relationship may be due to other factors that are conducive to both democracy and affluence or the correlation may be entirely accidental reflecting a historical association.

Wagner's Law

The hypothesis that economic factors are a crucial determinant of the growth of the public sector has a prominent place in the policy-determinant literature. It is called *Wagner's law* and it basically states that the richer a country becomes the larger the proportion of its national income will be transferred to the tax state and spent in terms of its public policy programmes. A variety of explanations have been adduced for this version of economic determinism with regard to policy-making: needs, income elasticity, infrastructure. However, a number of competing, non-economic hypotheses have been put forward to account for the variation in the national policy pattern as measured by means of public finance data. The policy literature has focused very much on Western Europe with their large welfare states.

Evaluating the different policy models — economic, sociological and political — we find that there is no single model type that can explain the policy or expenditure variation between the West European countries. When we focus upon only sixteen welfare states in Western Europe it is impossible to identify a one-factor model that may explain how levels of policy expenditure or growth rates in policy expenditure vary between countries and over time. The large number of models suggested that would account for the growth of the state indicates that the large public sector in Western Europe may be the result of over-determination. Against a common cultural background as well as a long period of depoliticization between the major ideologies it is no wonder that the fairly moderate public policy variation in Western Europe measured by means of public finance data cannot be explained by a few major factors. In any case, the economic models operate as poorly as the political counter-models in the famous 'Does politics matter' debate. Yet once we broaden the focus beyond the variation in the West European welfare state positive findings show up.

Looking at the various national policy patterns over the whole world by means of an inclusive selection of countries allows us to reaffirm the hypothesis that politics matters for policy-making. Economic affluence is only a necessary but not a sufficient condition for big policy spending. Decisive as to whether the government budget or the market will allocate a larger or smaller share of the resources is political ideology: the stronger the left in the state or in society, the more budget allocation or budget redistribution will be employed. Or if there is a widely shared belief in a political culture underlining equality of results, then budget allocation and redistribution will be trusted more than markets.

Politics and economics

If the exaggerated claims of economic determinism cannot be corroborated, then perhaps politics condition economics reversing the entire question of causal priority. Moving away from one-sided economic models opens up the possibility of interaction or reciprocities between political and economic variables. One well-known set of models state that politics affects economic growth. What are the findings when a variety of political models of economic growth are evaluated?

Growth theory and politics

Economic growth theory has traditionally focused on economic factors like technology, population and capital (Eltis, 1984; Solow, 1988; Chaudhuri, 1989), but political factors may have an impact on the country pattern of *average growth rates* either directly or indirectly through the impact on the crucial economic factors. Thus it has been argued that left-wing government would promote economic growth by favouring capital formation or strengthening effective demand by comprehensive transfer programmes. Another hypothesis underlines the importance of the year when a modernized leadership was introduced, predicting a higher average growth rate the younger the nation. Moreover, it has also been claimed that democratic regimes would enhance growth. At the same time, there are some counter hypotheses which state that a leftist government would reduce economic growth because of its redistributional inclination as well as that an authoritarian regime would be more able to stimulate economic growth.

The institutionalization hypothesis or the model of institutional sclerosis receives empirical support, particularly when the variation in economic growth among the OECD countries is analysed. The time when a modernized leadership was introduced seems to have a clear impact on the dynamism of the economy, at least with regard to the set of OECD nations. The other political models are not confirmed. There is no clear evidence for the hypothesis that democracy would be conducive to economic growth or that a strong position for the left would stimulate growth in the economy. Instead there is some indication that a large public sector reduces the rate of economic expansion in a country. In order to understand the differences in economic growth between Third World countries we must combine economic and sociological models.

Politico-economic regimes

It is often stated that capitalism performs better than socialism. How can we test this assertion? Better in terms of what criteria? What is a capitalist and a socialist regime? When one starts out to examine these important questions it becomes obvious that the simple framing of the problem — capitalism versus socialism — hides a host of difficult problems, both theoretical and empirical ones.

Some preliminary steps towards the evaluation of politico-economic regimes are taken here. We introduce explicit criteria, six all in all, for the evaluation of politico-economic systems to be measured by indices. The focus is on four types of overall economic systems:

- capitalist regimes
- capitalist-state regimes
- mixed-capitalist regimes
- socialist regimes.

These four regime types may be described by means of concepts that refer to the structure of ownership, the place of markets in the allocation of resources and the role of the state in redistributing income and wealth. Among the set of socialist regimes we enter the East European countries that adhered to a leninist politico-economic regime up until 1989. The set of capitalist regimes cover the countries that adhered to decentralized capitalism around 1980, whereas a capitalist-state regime stand for an economic system where private incentive mechanisms are combined with extensive state involvement in the economy, in particular state ownership of means of production. The mixed-capitalist regime corresponds to a welfare state in a country with an advanced capitalist economy.

There are three major findings in the evaluation of the performance of the countries in these regime sets. First, socialist and capitalist-state regimes tend to perform much worse than the decentralized capitalist and especially the mixed-capitalist regimes on all the evaluation criteria. Second, two of the types of capitalist regimes do perform better than the socialist regime type, but the capitalist-state regimes perform badly on the evaluation criteria. Third, the mixed-capitalist regime type performs better than the socialist regime kind on all the evaluation criteria and better than the decentralized capitalist type with the exception of economic growth.

Referring to the type of politico-economic regime a country has does not explain all the variation between various countries in terms of six basic economic and political aspects such as affluence, growth, inflation, democracy, welfare effort and inequality. The variation within the four sets of regimes is considerably larger than the variation between the four regime types when it is a matter of economic evaluation criteria.

Political economy models

We have only glanced at a few political economy models, viz those pertaining to problems clustering around development. The new field of political economy includes much more about the interaction between political and economic phenomena. Bypassing short run political economy models — the popularity function and the political business cycle — we have focused on some long-run political economy models concerning political regimes, public policy patterns and average country economic growth. Whereas the notion of economic development may be interpreted in a definitive way, the concept of political development is far more troublesome.

Although there is considerable country variation in both levels of affluence and growth rates, the standard theory accounting for these country differences may be questioned. It is indeed very questionable whether the so-called gap theory is correct or not. If one looks at the development since the Second World War in the various continents carrying out an analysis of variance for OECD countries, Communist systems, Latin American countries as well as Asian and African countries, the claims of the gap theory about an ever-increasing gulf between some rich or northern set of countries and some poor or southern set of countries cannot be corroborated. The emergence of the so-called NICs breaks up the picture that has been drawn by looking only at the so-called LDCs.

More research is needed in relation to the ambiguous notion of political development. The concept is truly a multi-dimensional one covering different political phenomena. Although theories of political system change are badly needed, it is not evident that all the problems may be solved when the notion of political development is employed as the basis for the change perspective. To enhance this type of political economy modelling more work is required to sort out various aspects of political development and to try to identify how economic factors interact with each of these dimensions separately. The institutionalization hypothesis accounting for the variation in average economic growth among the OECD countries is an example of such an improvement of political development analysis.

The road ahead

The new political economy implies a recognition of the relevance of *middle range theories* about reciprocities between politics and economics. By focusing on clearly defined problems for comparative research, for example,

- the conditions for democratic regimes
- the sources of extensive policy programmes
- the causes of average economic growth

the understanding of how politics and economics hang together may be enhanced. An empirical data base constructed on explicit criteria is necessary if political economy theory is not to remain *empty*, an abstract way of reasoning without empirical corroboration. At the same time the extensive information available at present about political and economic variables should be handled by means of explicit model building, or otherwise political economy will become *blind* as there is simply too much information about politics and economics around.

Finally, it is worth emphasizing the usefulness of a *comparative perspective* in political economy. Many models about the interaction between politics and economics can only be tested or developed by means of a comparative framework. There are many similarities and differences in political and economic phenomena in a number of politico-economic regimes. To identify these and unravel their interconnections will require explicit comparative modelling and testing. The new field of political economy benefits from the cross-fertilization of comparative politics with its empirical orientation and public choice theory and mainstream economic thought where abstract theory is strong.

Bibliography

Adelman, I. and Morris, C.T. (1967), *Society, Politics and Economic Development*, Baltimore, Johns Hopkins University Press. Revised edn. 1973.

Adelman, I. and Morris, C.T. (1972), 'The measurement of institutional characteristics of nations: methodological considerations', *Journal of Development Studies*, **8**, 3, 111-35.

Adelman, J. and Robinson, S. (1989), 'Income distribution and development', in Chenery, H. and Srinivasan, T.N. (eds) *Handbook of Development Economics*, vol. **II**.

Ahluwalia, M. (1976a), 'Income distribution and development: some stylized facts', *American Economic Review*, **66**, 2, 128-35.

Ahluwalia, M.S. (1976b) 'Inequality, poverty and development', *Journal of Development Economics*, **3**, 4, 307-42.

Ahluwalia, M.S., Carter, G. and Chenery, H.B. (1979), 'Growth and poverty in developing countries', *Journal of Development Economics*, **6**, 299-341.

Akerloff, G. (1970), 'The market for lemons : qualitative uncertainty and the market mechanism', *Quarterly Journal of Economics*, **84**, 488-500.

Albrow, M. (1970), *Bureaucracy*, London, Macmillan.

Almond, G.A. (1970), *Political Development: Essays in Heuristic Theory*, Boston, Little, Brown.

Almond, G.A. and Coleman, J. (eds) (1960), *The Politics of Developing Areas*, Princeton: Princeton University Press.

Almond, G.A. and Powell, G.B. (1966), *Comparative Politics: a Developmental Approach*, Boston, Little, Brown.

Almond, G.A., Flanagan, S.C. and Mundt, R.J. (eds)(1973), *Crisis,*

Choice, and Change: Historical Studies of Political Development, Boston, Little, Brown.

Alt, J. and Crystal, A.K. (1983), *Political Economics*, Berkeley, The University of California Press.

Anckar, D. and Ståhlberg, K. (1980), 'Assessing the impact of politics', *Scandinavian Political Studies*, vol. **3**, 191-208.

Apter, D.E. (1965), *The Politics of Modernization*, Chicago, University of Chicago Press.

Apter, D.E. (1971), *Choice and the Politics of Allocation*, New Haven, Yale University Press.

Apter, D.E. (1977), *Introduction to Political Analysis*, Cambridge, MA, Winthrop.

Apter, D.E and Andrain, C. (1968), 'Comparative government: developing new nations', in Irish, M.D. (ed.) *Political Science: Advance of the Discipline*, Englewood Cliffs, NJ, Prentice-Hall, 82-126.

Arrow, K.J. (1963), *Social Choice and Individual Values*, New York, Wiley.

Arrow, K.J. (1983), *General Equilibrium*, Oxford, Basil Blackwell.

Arrow, K.J. and Hurwicz, L. (1960), 'Decentralisation and Computation in Resource Allocation', in Pfouts, T. (ed.) *Essays in Economics and Econometrics in Honour of Harold Hotelling*, Chapel Hill, University of North Carolina Press.

Arrow, K.J. and Scitovsky, T. (eds)(1972), *Readings in Welfare Economics*, London, Allen and Unwin.

Ashford, D. E. (ed.)(1978), *Comparing Public Policies: new concepts and methods*, Beverly Hills, Sage.

Atkinson, A.B. and Stiglitz, J.E. (1980), *Lectures on Public Economics*, Maidenhead, McGraw-Hill.

Auerbach, A.J. and Feldstein, M. (eds) (1985), *Handbook of Public Economics*, vol.1, Amsterdam, North-Holland.

Auerbach, A.J. and Feldstein, M., (eds) (1987), *Handbook of Public Economics*, vol.2, Amsterdam, North-Holland.

Bain, G.S. and Price, R. (1980), *Profiles of Union Growth*, Oxford, Blackwell.

Bairoch, P. (1977), *The Economic Development of the Third World Since 1900*, Berkeley, University of California Press.

Balassa, B. (1989), *Comparative Advantage, Trade Policy and Economic Development*, London, Harvester Wheatsheaf.

Banks, A.S. (1971), *Cross-polity Time-series Data*, Cambridge, MA, MIT Press.

Banks, A.S. (1972), 'Correlates of democratic performance', *Comparative politics*, **4**, 217-30.

Banks, A.S. (1972b), 'Political characteristics of nation-states: a longitudinal summary', *Journal of politics*, **34**, 246-257.

Banks, A.S. (1974), 'Industrialization and development: a longitudinal analysis' in *Economic Development and Cultural Change*, **22**, 320-37.

Banks, A.S. (ed.)(1978), *Political Handbook of the World: 1978*, New York, McGraw Hill.

Banster, N. (1972), 'Development indicators: an introduction', *The Journal of Development Studies*, **8**, 1-20.

Bardhan, P. (1984), *The Political Economy of Development in India*, Oxford, Blackwell.

Bardhan, P. (1988), 'Alternative approaches to development economics', in Chenery, H. and Srinivasan, T.N. (eds), *Handbook of Development Economics*, vol. **I**.

Barone, E. (1935), 'The ministry of production in the collectivist state' in Hayek, von F.A. (ed.) *Collectivist Economic Planning*, London, Routledge and Kegan Paul.

Barry, B. (1970), *Sociologists, Economists and Democracy*, London, Collier-Macmillan,

Basu, D.K. and Sisson, R. (eds)(1986), *Social and Economic Development in India*, New Dehli, Sage.

Bator, F.M. (1958), 'The Anatomy of Market Failure', *Quarterly Journal of Economics*, vol. **72**, 351-79.

Baumol, W.J. (1965), *Welfare Economics and the Theory of the State*, Cambridge, Harvard University Press.

Bebler, A. and Seroka, J. (1989), *Contemporary Political Systems: classifications and typologies*, Boulder, Lynne Rienner.

Bell, D. (1973), *The Coming of Post-Industrial Society*, New York, Basic Books.

Ben-Dor, G. (1975), 'Institutionalization and political development: a conceptual and theoretical analysis', *Comparative Studies in Society and History*, **17**, 309-25.

Benjamin, R.W. (1972), *Patterns of political development*, New York, McKay.

Bergson, A. (1981), *Welfare, Planning and Employment*, Cambridge, MIT Press.

Bergson, A. and Levine, H.S. (1983)(eds) *The Soviet Economy: Toward the Year 2000*, London, Allen and Unwin.

Berry, B.J.L. (1966), 'By what categories may a state be characterized?, *Economic development and cultural change*, **15**, 91-3.

Beyme, K. von (1982), *Partiein in westleichen Demokratien*, Muchen, Piper.

Bhagwati, J.N. and Ruggie, J.G. (1984) (eds), *Power, Passions and Purpose: Prospects for North-South Negotiations*, Cambridge, MIT Press.

Bigsten, A. (1987), 'Growth and equity in some African and Asian countries', Stockholm, SIDA (unpublished manuscript).

Bill, J.A. and R.L. Hardgrave (1973), *Comparative Politics: The Quest for Theory*, Columbus, Merrill.

Binder, A.S. Solow, R.M., Breat, G.F., Steiner, P.O. and Netzer, D. (1974), *The Economics of Public Finance*, Washington, Brookings.

Binder, L. (1972), 'Political development in the Middle East', in Desai, A.R. (ed.) *Essays on Modernization of Underdeveloped Societies*, New York, Humanities Press.

Binder, L. (1986), 'The natural history of development theory', *Comparative Studies of Society and History*, **28**, 3-33.

Binder, L. Coleman, J.S., La Palombara, J., Pye, L.W., Verba, S. and Weiner, M. (1971), *Crises and Sequences in Political Development*, Princeton, NJ, Princeton University Press.

Bliss, C. (1989), 'Trade and development' in Chenery, H. and Srinivasan, T.N. (eds) *Handbook of Development Economics*, vol. **II**.

Blondel, J. (1969), *An Introduction to Comparative Government*, London, Weidenfeld and Nicolson.

Bohm, P. (1986), *Social Efficiency: A Concise Introduction to Welfare Economics*, London, Macmillan.

Bollen, K.A. and Grandjean, J. (1981), 'The dimension(s) of democracy: further issues in the measurement and effects of political democracy', *American Sociological Review*, **45**, 370-90.

Bollen, K.A. and Jackman, R.W. (1985), 'Political democracy and the size distribution of income', *American Sociological Review*, **50**, 438-57.

Bollen, K.A. (1979), 'Political democracy and the timing of development', *American Sociological Review*, **44**, 572-87.

Bollen, K.A. (1980), 'Issues in the Comparative Measurement of Political Democracy', *American Sociological Review*, **45**, 370-90.

Borcherding, T.E. (1977), *Budgets and Bureaucrats: The Sources of Government Growth*, Durham, Duke University Press.

Borcherding, T.E. (1984), 'A survey of empirical studies about causes of the growth of government', paper presented to the Nobel Symposium on the Growth of Government, Stockholm.

Boström, M. (1989), 'Political waves in Latin America, 1940-1988', in Ibero-Americana, *Nordic Journal of Latin American Studies,* **19**, 1, 3-19.

Brandt Report (1980), *North-South: A Programme for Survival*, London, Pan Books.

Brown, M.B. (1985), *Models in Political Economy: A Guide to the Arguments*, Boulder, Lynne Rienner.

Brunner, R.D and Brewer, G.D. (1971), *Organized complexity: Empirical Theories of Political Development*, New York, Free Press.

Brus, W. and Laski, K. (1990), *From Marx to the Market: Socialism in Search for an Economic System*, Oxford, Clarendon Press.

Buchanan, A. (1985), *Ethics, Efficiency and the Market*, Oxford, Clarendon Press.

Buchanan, J.M. (1967), *Public Finance in Democratic Process*, Chapel Hill, University of North Carolina Press.

Buchanan, J.M. (1986), *Liberty, Market and State: Political Economy in the 80s*, Brighton, Harvester Wheatsheaf.

Buchanan, J.M. Tollison, R.D. and Tollock, G. (eds)(1980), *Toward a Theory of the Rent-Seeking Society*, College Station, Texas A & M University Press.

Buchanan, J.M. and Flowers, M.R. (1980), *The Public Finances*, Homewood, Irwin-Dorsey.

Budge, I. and Farlie, D.J. (1981), 'Predicting regime change: a cross-national investigation with aggregate data 1950-1980', *Quality and Quantity*, **15**, 335-64.

Caiden, N. and Wildavsky, A. (1974), *Planning and Budgeting in Poor Countries*, New York, Wiley.

Cairncross, A. and Puri, M. (eds)(1976), *Employment, Income Distribution and Development Strategy*, London, Macmillan.

Cameron, D.R. (1974), 'Toward a theory of political mobilization', *Journal of politics*, **36**, 138-71.

Cameron, D.R. (1978), 'The expansion of the public economy: a comparative analysis', *American Political Science Review*, **72**, pp. 1243-61.

Cameron, D.R. (1984), 'Impact of political institutions on public sector expansion', paper presented to the Nobel Symposium on the Growth of Government, Stockholm.

Cantori, L.T. and Ziegler, A. (eds)(1988), *Comparative Politics in the Post-behavioural Era*, Boulder, Lynne Rienner.

Castles, F.G. (1978), *The Social Democratic Image of Society: A Study of the Achievements and Origins of Scandinavian Social Democracy in Comparative Perspective*, London, Routledge and Kegan Paul.

Castles, F.G. (ed.)(1982), *The Impact of Parties: Politics and Policies in Democratic Capitalist States*, London, Sage.

Castles, F.G. (1986), 'Whatever happened to the communist welfare state?, *Studies in Comparative Communism*, **19**, 213-26.

Castles, F.G., Lehner, F. and Schmidt, M.G. (1988), 'Comparative public policy analysis: problems, progress and prospects', Castles, F.G. (ed.), *Managing Mixed Economies*, Berlin, Walter de Gruyter: 197-223.

Castles, F.G. (1989), 'Big government in weak states', Canberra: Centre for Economic Policy Research (Discussion Paper no. 209).

Castles, F. and Dowrick, S. (1990), 'The impact of government spending on medium-term economic growth in the OECD 1960-85', *Journal of Theoretical Politics*, **2**, 173-204.

Castles, F. (1991), 'Democratic politics, war and catch-up: Olson's thesis and long-term economic growth in the English-speaking nations of advanced capitalism', *Journal of Theoretical Politics*, **3,4.**

Cave, M. and Hare, P. (1983), *Alternative Approaches to Economic Planning*, London, Macmillan.

Caves, R.E. and Jones, R.W. (1985), *World Trade and Payments*, Boston, Little, Brown and Co.

Chacholiades. M. (1985), *International Trade Theory and Policy*, London, McGraw-Hill.

Chan, S. (1989), 'Income distribution and war trauma: a cross-national analysis', *Western Political Quarterly, vol.* **42**, 263-81.

Chaudhuri, P. (1989), *The Economic Theory of Growth*, Brighton, Harvester Wheatsheaf

Chenery, H.C. (1983), 'Interaction between theory and observation in development', *World Development*, **11**, 10, 853-62 .

Chenery, H.B., Robinson, S. and Syrquin, M. (1986), *Industrialization and Growth*, Oxford, Oxford University Press.

Chenery, H.B. and Taylor, L. (1968), 'Development patterns: among countries and over time', *Review of economics and statistics*, **50**, 391-416.

Chenery, H. and Srinivasan, T.N. (eds)(1988), *Handbook of Development Economics*, vol. **I**, Amsterdam, North-Holland.

Chenbey, H. and Srinivasan, T.N. (eds) (1989), *Handbook of Development Economics*, vol. **II**, Amsterdam, North Holland.

Chilcote, R.H. and Johnson, D.L. (eds)(1983), *Theories of Development*, Beverly Hills, Sage.

Choi, K. (1983), 'A statistical test of Olson's model', Mueller, D. (ed.), *The Political Economy of Growth*, New Haven, Yale University Press, 57-78.

Choksi, A.M. and Papageorghiou, D. (eds) (1986), *Economic Liberalization in Developing Countries*, Oxford, Blackwell.

Clapham, C. (1985), *Third World Politics: An Introduction*, London, Croom Helm.

Claude, R.P. (1975), 'Comparative civil liberties: the state of the art', *Policy Studies Journal*, **4**, 175-180.

Cockcroft, J.D., Frank, A.G. and Johnson, D.L. (eds)(1972), *Dependence and Under-Development*, New York, Anchor Books.

Cohen, S.S. (1977), *Modern Capitalist Planning: The French Model*, Berkeley, University of California Press.

Coleman, J.S. (1968), 'Modernization: political aspects', in Sills, D.L. (ed.), *International Encyclopedia of the Social Sciences*, vol. **10**, New York, Free Press, 395-402.

Coleman, J.S. (ed.)(1965), *Education and Political Development*, Princeton, NJ, Princeton University Press.

Collier, D. (1978), 'Industrial modernization and political change: a Latin American perspective', *World Politics*, **30**, 593-614.

Collier, D. (ed.)(1979), *The New Authoritarianism in Latin America*, Princeton, NJ, Princeton University Press.

Coulter, P. (1971), 'Democratic political development: a systemic model based on regulative policy', *Development and change*, **3**, 25-61.

Cutright, P. (1963), 'National political development: measurement and analysis', *American Sociological Review*, **28**, 253-64.

Dahl, R.A. (1947), 'The science of public administration: three, problems, *Public Administration Review*, **7**, 1, 1-11.

Dahl, R.A. (1971), *Polyarchy*, New Haven, Yale University Press.

Dahl, R.A. (1985), *A Preface to an Economic Theory of Democracy*, London, Polity Press.

Dahl, R.A. and Lindblom, C.E. (1953), *Politics, Economics and Welfare*, New York, Harper and Row.

Dalton, G. (1974), *Economic Systems and Society*, London, Penguin.

Danziger, J.N. (1978), *Making Budgets: Public Resource Allocation*, Beverly Hills, Sage.

Davis, H. and Scase. R. (1985), *Western Capitalism and State Socialism*, Oxford, Blackwell.

Day, A.J. and Degenhardt, H.W. (1980), *Political Parties of the World: A Keesing's Reference Publication*, Harlow, Longman.

Debreu, G. (1959), *Theory of Value*, New York, Wiley.

de Schweinitz, K. (1964), *Industrialization and Democracy*, Glencoe, Free Press.

de Carvalho, J.A.M and Wood, C.H. (1980), 'Morality, Income distribution and rural-urban residence in Brazil, *Population and Development Review*, **4**, 3, 405-20.

Delury, G.E. (ed.)(1983), *World Encyclopedia of Political Systems*, Harlow, Longman.

Derbyshire, J.D. and Derbyshire, I. (1989), *Political Systems of the World*, Edinburgh, Chambers

Deutsch, K.W. (1961), 'Social mobilization and political development', *American Political Science Review*, **55**, 493-514.

Doel van den, J. (1979), *Democracy and Welfare Economics*, Cambridge, Cambridge University Press.

Diamant, A. (1966), 'The nature of political development' in Finkle, J. and Gable, W. (eds), *Political Development and Social Change*, New York, Wiley, 91-6.

Diamond, L, Linz, J. and Lipset, S.M. (eds)(1988), *Democracy in Developing Countries*, vol. **2**, Africa, Boulder, Lynne Rienner.

Diamond, L, Linz, J. and Lipset, S.M. (eds)(1989a), *Democracy in developing Countries*, vol. **3**, Asia, Boulder, Lynne Rienner.

Diamond, L, Linz, J. and Lipset, S.M. (eds)(1989b), *Democracy in Developing Countries*, vol. **4**, Latin America, Boulder, Lynne Rienner.

Dick, G.W. (1974), 'Authoritarian versus nonauthoritarian approaches to economic development', *Journal of Political Economy*, **82**, 817-27.

Dobb, M. (1940), *Political Economy and Capitalism*, London, Routledge and Kegan Paul.

Dowrick, S. and Nguyen, D.T. (1987), 'OECD economic growth in the post-war period: a test of the convergence hypothesis', Canberra, Centre for Economic Policy Research (Discussion Paper no. 181).

Drewnowski, J. (1961), 'The economic theory of socialism: a suggestion for reconsideration' in *Journal of Political Economy*, 341-354.

Dunleavy, P. and O'Leary, B. (1987), *Theories of the State*, London, Macmillan.

Dunsire, A. (1973), *Administration*, London, Martin Robertson.

Dye, T. (1966), *Politics, Economics and the Public*, Chicago, Rand Mc-Nally.

Dye, T.R. and V. Gray (eds)(1980), *The Determinants of Public Policy*, Lexington, Mass., Lexington Books.

Dye, T.R. and Zeigler, H. (1988), 'Socialism and equality in crossnational perspective', *Political Science and Politics*, **21**, 45-56.

Dyker, D.A. (1976), *The Soviet Economy*, London, Crosby Lockwood Staples.

Dyker, D.A. (1985), *The Future of the Soviet Planning System*, Cambridge, Cambridge University Press.

Easton, D. (1965), *A Systems Analysis of Political Life*, London, Wiley.

Eatwell, J., Milgate, M. and Newman, P. (eds)(1987), *The New Palgrave: A Dictionary of Economics*, London, Macmillan.

Eckstein, A. (1958), 'Individualism and the role of the state in economic growth', *Economic Development and Cultural Change*, **6**, 81-7.

Eckstein, A. (ed.)(1971), *Comparison of Economic Systems: Theoretical and Methodological approaches*, Berkeley, University of California Press.

Eckstein, H. (1966), *Division and Cohesion in Democracy: A Study of Norway*, Princeton, Princeton University Press.

Eckstein, H. (1971), *The Evaluation of Political Performance: Problems and Dimensions*, Beverly Hills, Sage.

Eckstein, H. (1982), 'The idea of political development: from dignity to efficiency', *World Politics*, **34**, 451-86.

Economist Atlas, (1989), London, Hutchinson

Eidem, R. and Viotti, S. (1978), *Economic Systems*, London, Martin Robertson.

Eisenstadt, S.N. (1962), 'Initial institutional patterns of political modernization', *Civilizations*, vol. **12**, 461-72.

Eisenstadt, S.N. (1964a), 'Political modernization: some comparative notes', *International Journal of Comparative Sociology*, **5**, 3-24.

Eisenstadt, S.N. (1964b), 'Breakdowns of modernization', *Economic Development and Cultural Change*, **12**, 345-67.

Eisenstadt, S.N. (1966), *Modernization*, Englewood Cliffs, NJ, Prentice-Hall.

Eisenstadt, S.N. (1973), *Tradition, Change and Modernity*, New York, Wiley.

Eltis, W.A. (1966), *Economic Growth: Analysis and Policy*, London, Hutchinson & Co.

Eltis, W.A. (1984), *The Classical Theory of Economic Growth*, London, Macmillan.

Ellman, M. (1979), *Socialist Planning*, Cambridge, Cambridge University Press.

Emerson, R. (1960), 'Nationalism and political development' *Journal of Politics*, **22**, 3-28.

Estes, R.J. (1984), *The Social Progress of Nations*, New York, Praeger.

Estrin, S. (1983), *Self-management: Economic Theory and Yugoslav Practice*, Cambridge, Cambridge University Press.

Evans, D. (1989), 'Alternative perspectives on trade and development', in Chenery, H. and Srinivasan, T.N. (eds), *Handbook of Development Economics*, vol. **III**.

Europa Yearbook 1978, London, Europa Publications.

Flanigan, W. and Fogelman, E. (1971), 'Patterns of political development and democratization: a quantitative analysis', in Gillespie, J.V. and Nesvold, B.A. (eds), *Macro-Quantitative Analysis: Conflict, Development and Democratization*, Beverly Hills, Sage, 441-73.

Flora, P. and Heidenheimer, A.J. (eds) (1981) *The Development of the Welfare States in Europe and America*, London, Transaction Books.

Foltz, W.J. (1981), 'Modernization and nation-building: the social mobilization model reconsidered' in Merritt, R.L. and Russett, B.M. (eds), *From National Development to Global Community*, London, Allen and Unwin, 25-45.

Frank, A.G. (1967), *Capitalism and Underdevelopment in Latin America: Historical Studies of Chile and Brazil*, New York, Monthly Review Press,

Frey, B. (1978), *Modern Political Economy*, London, Macmillan.

Galbraith, J.K. (1962), *The Affluent Society*, Boston, Houghton Mifflin.

Galbraith, J.K. (1969, 1974), *The New Industrial State*, Harmondsworth, Pelican.

Gastil, R.D. (ed.)(1987), *Political Rights and Civil Liberties 1986-1987*, New York, Greenwood Press.

Gersovitz, M.F. Diaz-Alejandro, C.F., Ranis, G. and Rosenzweig, M.R. (eds)(1982), *The Theory and Experience of Economic Development: Essays in Honor of Sir W. Arthur Lewis*, London, Allen and Unwin.

Goldsmith, A. (1987), 'Democracy, political stability and economic growth in developing countries: some evidence on Olson's theory distributional coalitions', *Comparative Political Studies*, vol. **18**, 517-31.

Goodwin, R.M. (1982), *Essays in Economic Dynamics*, London. Macmillan.

Gregory, P.R. and Stuart, R.C. (1989), *Comparative Economic Systems*, Boston, Houghton Mifflin.

Grew, R. (ed.)(1978), *Crises of Political Development in Europe and the United States*, Princeton, NJ, Princeton University Press.

Griffith-Jones, S. (ed.)(1988), *Managing World Debt*, London, Harvester Wheatsheaf.

Groth, A.J. (1971), *Comparative Politics: A Distributive Approach*, New York, Macmillan.

Gurr, T.R. and McClelland, M. (1971), *Political Performance: A Twelve-Nation Study*, Beverly Hills, Sage.

Gurr, T.R. (1974), 'Persistence and change in political systems, 1800-1971', *American Political Science Review*, **68**, 1482-1504.

Hahn, F.H. (1971), *Readings in the Theory of Economic Growth*, London, Macmillan.

Hahn, F.H. and Matthews, R.C.O. (1964), 'The theory of economic growth: a survey', *The Economic Journal*, **74**, 779-902.

Hall, P. (1983), *Growth and Development: An Economic Analysis*, Oxford, Martin Robertson.

Hamberg, D. (1971), *Models of Economic Growth*, New York, Harper and Row

Hanson, J.L. (1974), *A Dictionary of Economics and Commerce*, London, Macdonald and Evans.

Harff B. (1984), *Genocide and Human Rights: International, Legal and Political Issues*, Denver, University of Denver.

Harrod, R.R. (1939), 'An essay in dynamic theory' in *Economic Journal* **49**, 14-33.

Haug, M.R. (1967), 'Social and cultural pluralism as a concept in social system analysis', *American Journal of Sociology*, **73**, 294-304.

Hayek von, F.A. (ed.)(1935), *Collectivist Economic Planning*, London, Routledge and Kegan Paul.

Hayek von, F.A. (1940), 'Socialist Calculation: The Competitive Solution', *Economica*, **VII**, 125-49.

Hayek von, F.A. (1945), 'The Use of Knowledge in Society' in *American Economic Review*, vol. **XXXV**, 519-30.

Head, J.G. (1974), *Public Goods and Public Welfare*, Durham, Duke University Press.

Heady, B. (1970), 'Trade unions and national wage policies', *Journal of Politics*, **32**, pp. 407-39.

Heady, F. (1979), *Public Administration: A Comparative Perspective*, New York, Dekker.

Heal, G.M. (1973), *The Theory of Economic Planning*, Amsterdam, North-Holland.

Hedström, P. (1986), 'From political sociology to political economy', in Himmelstrand, U. (ed.), *Sociology: From Crisis to Science*, vol. **1**, London, Sage, 173-189.

Heidenheimer, A.J., Heclo, H. and Adams, C.J. (1983), *Comparative Public Policy: The Politics of Social Choice in Europe and America*, London, Macmillan.

Hewitt, C. (1977), 'The effect of political democracy and social democracy on equality in industrial societies: a cross-national comparison', *American Sociological Review*, **42**, 450-64.

Hibbs, D.A. (1987), *The American Political Economy: Macroeconomics and Electoral Politics*, Cambridge, Harvard University Press.

Hibbs, D.A. and Fassbender, H. (eds)(1981), *Contemporary Political Economy*, Amsterdam, North-Holland.

Hicks, J. R. (1965), *Capital and Growth*, Oxford, Clarendon Press.

Higgott, R.A. (1980), 'From modernization theory to public policy: continuity and change in the political science of development', *Studies in Comparative International Development*, **15**, 26-50.

Higgott, R.A. (1983), *Political Development Theory*, London, Croom Helm.

Hirschman, A. (1958), *Strategy of Economic Development*, New Haven, Yale University Press.

Hirschman, A.O. (1970), *Exit, Voice and Loyalty: Responses to Decline in Firms, Organizations and States*, Cambridge, Mass., Harvard University Press.

Hirschman, A.O. (1971), *A Bias For Hope: Essays on Development and Latin America*, New Haven, Yale University Press.

Hirschman, A.O. (1982), *Shifting Involvements: Private Interests and Public Action*, Princeton, NJ, Princeton University Press.

Hofferbert, R. (1974), *The Study of Public Policy*, Indianapolis, Bobbs-Merrill.

Hopkins, R.F. (1969), 'Aggregate data and the study of political development', *Journal of politics*, **31**, 71-94.

Horvat, B. (1974), 'The relation between rate of growth and level of development', *Journal of Development Studies*, **10**, 382-94.

Hozelitz, B.F. (1957), 'Economic growth and development: noneconomic factors in economic development', *American Economic Review*, **47**, 28-41.

Humana, C. (1983), *World Human Rights Guide*, London, Hutchinson.

Humana, C. (1986), *World Human Rights Guide*, 2nd ed., London, Economist Publications.

Huntington, S.P. (1965), 'Political development and political decay', *World Politics*, **17**, 386-430.

Huntington, S.P. (1968), *Political Order in Changing Societies*, New Haven, Yale University Press.

Huntington, S.P. (1971), 'The change to change: modernization, development and politics', *Comparative Politics*, **3**, 283-322.

Huntington, S.P. (1984), 'Will more countries become democratic?', *Political Science Quarterly*, **99**, 193-218.

Huntington, S.P. and Dominguez, J.I. (1975), 'Political development' in Greenstein, F.I. and Polsby, N.W. (eds) *Handbook of Political Science*, Vol. 3, *Macropolitical Theory*, Reading, MA, Addison-Wesley, 1-114.

IMF (1982), *Government Finance Statistics Yearbook*, Washington, DC; International Monetary Fund.

International Studies Quarterly (1983), Special Issue on Olson, M. (1982), *The Rise and Decline of Nations*.

Jackman, R.W (1973), 'On the relation of economic development to democratic performance', *American Journal of Political Science*, **17**, 611-21.

Jackman, R.W. (1974), 'Political democracy and social equality: a comparative analysis', *American Sociological Review*, **39**, 29-45.

Jackman, R.W. (1975), *Politics and social equality: a comparative analysis*, New York, Wiley.

Jackman, R.W. (1985), 'Cross-national statistical research and the study of comparative politics', *American Journal of Political Science*, **29**, 161-82.

Janda, K. (1980), *Political Parties: A Cross-National Survey*, New York, Free Press.

Johansen, L. (1977), *Public Economics*, Amsterdam; North-Holland.

Johansen, L. (1977, 1978), *Lectures on Macroeconomic Planning I-II*, Amsterdam; North-Holland.

Johansen, L. (1979), 'The bargaining society and the inefficiency of bargaining', *Kyklos*, **32**, 497-522.

Johnson, C. (1984) (ed.), *The Industrial Policy Debate*, San Francisco, Jossey-Bass.

Johnson, H. (1958), *International Trade and Economic Growth*, London, Allen and Unwin.

Johnson, H.G. (1975), *Technology and Economic Interdependence*, London, Macmillan.

Jones, R.W. and Kenen, P.B. (eds) (1984), *Handbook of International Economics*, Amsterdam, North-Holland.

Kahn, H. and Wiener, A. (1967), *The Year 2000*, London, Macmillan.

Kalecki, M. (1954), *Theory of Economic Dynamics*, London, Allen and Unwin.

Katzenstein, P. (1984), *Small States in World Markets*, Ithaca, Cornell University Press.

Kjellberg, A. (1983), *Facklig organisering i tolv länder*, Lund, Arkiv.

Kmenta, J. (1971), *Elements of Econometrics*, New York, Macmillan.

Kormendi, R.C. and Meguire, P.G. (1985), 'Macroeconomic determinants of growth: cross-country evidence', *Journal of Monetary Economics*, vol. **16**, no. 2, 141-63.

Kornai, J. (1980), *Economics of Shortage*, Amsterdam, North Holland.

Kornai, J. (1986), *Contradictions and Dilemmas. Studies on the Socialist Economy and Society*, Cambridge, MIT Press.

Kornai, J. (1990), *The Road to a Free Economy*, London, Norton Press.

Kornai, J. and Liptak, T. (1962), 'A mathematical investigation of some economic effects of profit sharing', *Econometrica*, **30**, 140-61.

Korpi, W. (1983), *The Democratic Class Struggle*, London, Routledge and Kegan Paul.

Korpi, W. (1985a), 'Economic growth and the welfare state: leaky bucket or irrigation system', *European Sociological Review*, vol **1**, 97-118.

Korpi, W. (1985b), 'Economic growth and the welfare state: a comparative study of 18 OECD countries', *Labour and Society*, vol. **10**, no. 2: 195-209.

Kregel, J.A. (1972), *The Theory of Economic Growth*, London, Macmillan.

Kreuger, A.O. (1978), *Liberalization Attempts and Consequences*, New York, National Bureau of Economic Research.

Kristensen, O.P. (1987), *Vaeksten i den offentlig sektor*, Copenhagen, Munksgaard.

Kuznets, S. (1955), 'Economic growth and income inequality', *American Economic Review*, vol. **45**, 18-25.

Kuznets, S. (1965), *Economic Growth and Structure*, New York, W.W. Norton

Kuznets, S. (1966), *Modern Economic Growth*, New Haven, Yale University Press.

Kuznets, S. (1968), *Toward a Theory of Economic Growth*, New York, Norton

Kuznets, S. (1971), *Economic Growth of Nations: Total Output and Production Structure*, Cambridge, Mass., Harvard University Press.

Laband, D.L. (1984), 'Is there a relationship between economic conditions and political structure?', *Public Choice*, vol. **42**, 27-37.

Lachman, L.M. (1986), *The Market as an Economic Process*, Oxford, Blackwell.

Lal, D. (1983), *The Poverty of 'Development Economics'*, London, Institute of Economic Affairs.

Lane, J.E. (ed.)(1985), *State and Market*, London: Sage.

Lane, J.E. (ed,)(1987), *Bureaucracy and Public Choice*, London, Sage.

Lange, O. (1936-37), 'On the economic theory of socialism', *Review of Economic Theory Studies*, vol. **IV**, 1-2.

Lange, O. (1942), 'The foundations of welfare economics' in Arrow, K.J. and Scitovsky, T. (1969) (eds), *Readings in Welfare Economics*, London, Allen and Unwin, 26-38.

Lange, O. (1964), 'On the economic theory of socialism' in Lange, O. and Taylor, F.M. (1964), *On the Economic Theory of Socialism*, Minneapolis: University of Minnesota Press.

Lange, P. and Garrett, G. (1985), 'The politics of growth: strategic interaction and economic performance in the advanced industrial democracies, 1974-1980', *Journal of Politics*, **47**, 729-827.

LaPalombara, J. and Weiner, M. (eds)(1967), *Political Parties and Political Development*, Princeton, NJ, Princeton University Press.

LaPalombara, J. (ed.)(1967), *Bureaucracy and Political Development*, Princeton, NJ, Princeton University Press.

Larkey, P., Stolp, L. and Winer, M. (1981), 'Theorizing about the growth of government: a research assessment', *Journal of Public Policy*, **2**, 157-220.

Layard, P.R.B. and Walters, A.A. (1978), *Microeconomic Theory*, New York, McGraw-Hill.

Lauterbach, A. (1989), *The Odyssey of Rationality*, Munich, Accedo Verlagsgesellschaft.

Leftwich, A. (1990), 'Politics and development studies' in Leftwich, A. (ed.), *New Developments in Political Science*, London, Edward Elgar.

Leeman, J.W. (ed.)(1963), *Capitalism, Market Socialism and Central Planning*, Boston, Houghton Mifflin.

Le Grand, J. and Estrin, S. (eds)(1989), *Market Socialism*, Oxford, Clarendon.

Lenski, G. (1963), *The Religious Factor: A Sociological Study of*

Religion's Impact on Politics, Economics and Family Life, Garden City, Doubleday.

Lenski, G. (1966), *Power and Privilege*, New York, McGraw-Hill.

Lerner, A.P. (1944), *The Economics of Control*, New York, Macmillan.

Lerner, D. (1958), *The Passing of Traditional Society: Modernizing the Middle East*, New York, Free Press.

Lerner, D. (1968), 'Modernization: social aspects', in Sills, D.L. (ed.) *International Encyclopedia of the Social Sciences*, Vol. **10**, New York, Free Press, 386-395.

Levy, M.J. (1952), *The Structure of Society*, Princeton, Princeton University Press.

Levy, M.J. (1966), *Modernization and the Structure of Societies*, Princeton, Princeton University Press.

Lewis, S.R. (1989), 'Primary exporting countries', in Chenery, H. and Srinivasan, T.N. (eds), *Handbook of Development Economics*, vol. **II**.

Lewis, W.A. (1955), The *Theory of Economic Growth*, London, Allen and Unwin.

Lewis, W.A. (1988), 'The roots of development theory', in Chenery, H. and Srinivasan, T.N. (eds), *Handbook of Development Economics*, vol. **I**.

Lijphart, A. (1968). 'Typologies of democratic systems', *Comparative Political Studies*, **1**, 3-44.

Lijphart, A. (1977), *Democracy in Plural Societies*, New Haven, Yale University Press.

Lijphart, A. (1979), 'Consociationalism and federation: conceptual and empirical links', *Canadian Journal of Political Science*, **21**, 499-515.

Lijphart, A. (1984), *Democracies: Patterns of Majoritarian and Consensus Government in Twenty-one Countries*, New Haven, Yale University Press.

Lindbeck, A. (1977), *The Political Economy of the New Left: An Outsider's View*, New York, Harper and Row.

Lindblom, C. (1977), *Politics and Markets*, New York, Basic Books.

Lindblom, C. (1988), *Democracy and Market System*, Oslo, Norwegian University Press.

Linz, J.J. and Stepan, A. (eds)(1978), *The Breakdown of Democratic Regimes*, Baltimore, The Johns Hopkins University Press.

Linz, J.J. (1975), 'Totalitarian and authoritarian regimes', Greenstein, F.I. and Polsby, N.W. (eds) *Handbook of Political Science*, Vol. **3** Macropolitical Theory, Reading, MA, Addison-Wesley, 175-411.

Lippincott, B.E. (ed.)(1938), *On the Economic Theory of Socialism*, Minneapolis, University of Minnesota Press.

Lipset, S.M. (1959), 'Some social requisites of democracy: eeconomic development and political legitimacy', *American Political Science Review*, vol. **53**, 69-105.

Lipset, S.M. (1963), *Political Man*, London, Heineman.

Little, I.M. (1982), *Economic Development: Theory, Policy, and International Relations*, New York, Basic Books.

Little, J. (1982), *Economic Development*, New York, Basic Books.

Little, I.M.D., Scitovsky, T. and Scott, M. (1970), *Industry and Trade in Some Developing Countries*, Oxford, Oxford University Press.

Loewenberg, G. and Patterson, S.C. (1979), *Comparing Legislatures*, Boston, Little and Brown.

Lydall, H. (1986), *Yugoslav Socialism*, Oxford, Clarendon Press.

Lybeck, J. (1986), *The Growth of Government in Developed Economies*, London, Gower.

Lybeck, J.A. and Henrekson, M. (eds)(1988), *Explaining the Growth of Government*, Amsterdam, North-Holland.

MacKie, T. and Rose, R. (1982), *The Internation Almanac of Electoral History*, New York, Free Press.

Macridis, R.C. (1955), *The Study of Comparative Government*, New York, Random House.

Madsen, H.J. (1978), *Poetics*, Aarhus, Dept of Political Science (mimeo).

Madsen, E.S. and Paldam, M. (1978), *Economic and Political Data for the Main OECD-countries 1948-1975*. Aarhus University, Institute of Economics.

Malinvaud, E. (1967), 'Decentralized procedures for planning' in Malinvaud, E. and Bacharach, M.O.L. (eds), *Activity Analysis in the Theory of Growth and Planning*, New York, Macmillan and Co.

Mandel, E. (1986), 'A critique of market socialism', *New Left Review*, no. 159.

March, J.G. and Olsen, J.P. (1984), 'The new institutionalism: organizational factors in political life', *American Political Science Review*, **78**, 734-49.

March, J.G. and Olson, J.P. (1989), *Rediscovering Institutions: The Organizational Basis of Politics*. New York, Free Press.

Mareshwari, S.R. (1968), *Indian Administration*, New Dehli, Orient Longman.

Mareshwari, S.R. (1984), *Rural Development in India*, New Dehli, Sage.

Margolis, J. and Guitton, H. (eds)(1969), *Public Economics: An Analysis of Public Production and Consumption and their Relations to the Private Sectors*, London: Macmillan.

Matheson D.K. *Ideology, Political Action and the Finnish Working Class*, Helsinki, Societas Scientarium Fennica.

Mathur, A. (1983), 'Regional development and income disparities in India: a sectorial analysis', *Economic Development and Cultural Change*, 475-505.

McAuley, A. (1979), *Economic Welfare in the Soviet Union*, London, Allen and Unwin.

McCormick, B.J. (1988), *The World Economy*, Oxford, Barnes and Noble.

Meade, J.E. (1961), *A Neo-Classical Theory of Economic Growth*, Oxford, Oxford University Press.

Meier, G.M. (ed.)(1984), *Leading Issues in Economic Development*, Oxford, Oxford University Press. New York,

Miele, S. (ed.)(1983), *Internationales Gewerkschaftshandbuch*, Opladen, Leeske und Budrich.

Mises, L.von (1936), *Socialism. An Economic and Sociological Analysis*, London, Cape.

Mishan, E.J. (1981), *Introduction to Normative Economics*. Oxford, Oxford University Press.

Montias, J.M. (1976), *The Structure of Economic Systems*, New Haven, Yale University Press.

Moore, B. (1966), *Social Origins of Dictatorship and Democracy*, Harmondsworth, Pelican.

Morishima, M. (1964), *Equilibrium, Stability and Growth*, Oxford, Clarendon Press.

Morris, M.D. (1979), *Measuring the Conditions of the World's Poor: The Physical Quality of Life Index*, London, Frank Cass.

Morris, C.T. and Adelman, I. (1980), 'The religious factor in economic development', *World Development*, **8**, 491-501.

Mueller, D.C. (ed)(1983), *The Political Economy of Growth*, New Haven, Yale University Press.

Mueller, D.C. (1986), *The Modern Corporation*, Brighton, Harvester Wheatsheaf.

Mueller, D.C. (1989), *Public Choice*, 2nd edn, Cambridge, Cambridge University Press.

Muller, E. (1985), 'Income inequality, regime repressiveness and political violence', *American Sociological Review*, vol. **50**, 47-61.

Muller, E. (1988), 'Democracy, economic development, and income inequality', *American Sociological Review*, vol. **53**, 50-68.

Musgrave, R.A. (1959), *Theory of Public Finance*, New York, McGraw-Hill.

Musgrave, R. and Jarrett, P. (1979), 'International Redistribution', *Kyklos*, **32**, 541-558.

Musgrave, R.A. and Musgrave, P. (1980), *Public Finance in Theory and Practice*, New York, Mc Graw-Hill.

Musgrave, R.A. and Peacock, A.T. (eds) (1967), *Classics in the Theory of Public Finance*, New York, St Martin's Press.

Myrdal, G. (1957), *Economic Theory and Underdeveloped Regions*, London, Duckworth.

Myrdal, G. (1961), ''Value-loaded' concepts', in Hegeland, H. (ed.) *Money, Growth, and Methodology and Other Essays in Honor of Johan Åkerman*, Lund, Gleerup.

Myrdal, G. (1968), *Asian Drama I-III*, New York, Pantheon Books.

Myrdal, G. (1970), *Objectivity in Social Research*, London, Duckworth.

Mytelka, L.K. (1979), *Regional Development in a Global Economy*, New Haven, Yale University Press.

Nash, M. (1959), 'Some social and cultural aspects of economic development', *Economic Development and Cultural Change*, vol. **7**, 137-50.

Nath, S.K. (1969), *A Reappraisal of Welfare Economics*, London, Routledge and Kegan Paul.

Nettl, J.P. (1967), *Political Mobilization: A Sociological Analysis of Methods and Concepts*, New York, Basic Books.

Neubauer, D.E. (1967), 'Some conditions of democracy', *American Political Science Review*, **61**, 1002-9.

Niskanen, W.E. (1971), *Bureaucracy and Representative Government*, Chicago, Aldine Publishing Company.

Nove, A. (1983), *The Economics of Feasible Socialism*, London, Allen and Unwin.

Nove, A. (1986), *The Soviet Economic System*, Boston, Allen and Unwin.

Nove, A. (1987), *An Economic History of the USSR*, 3rd edn, London, Unwin Heinemann.

Nurkse, R. (1961), *Equilibrium and Growth in the World Economy*, Cambridge, Harvard University Press.

Oates, W.E. (1972), *Fiscal Federalism*, New York, Harcourt Brace Jovanovich.

O'Brien, D.C. (1972), 'Modernization, order, and the erosion of a democratic ideal: American political science 1960-70', *Journal of Development Studies*, vol. **8**, no. 4, 351-78.

Ocampo, J.F. and Johnson, D.L. (1972), 'The concept of political development', in Cockcroft, J.D. *et al* (eds) *Dependence and Underdevelopment: Latin America's Political Economy*, Garden City, NY, Doubleday, 399-424.

O'Donnell, G. (1973), *Modernization and Bureaucratic-Authoritarianism: Studies in South American Politics*, Berkeley, Institute of International Studies.

O'Donnell, G. (1988), *Bureaucratic Authoritarianism: Argentina 1966-1973 in Comparative Perspective*, Berkeley, University of California Press.

O'Donnell, G. et al. (eds) (1986), *Transitions from Authoritarian Rule: Prospects for Democracy*, Baltimore: The Johns Hopkins University Press.

O'Donnell, G. and Schmitter, P.C. (1986), *Transitions from Authoritarian Rule: Tentative Conclusions about Uncertain Democracies*, Baltimore, The Johns Hopkins University Press.

OECD (1968), *National Accounts 1950-1968*, Paris, OECD.

OECD (1979), *Economic Outlook*, no. 29, Paris.

OECD (1979), *National Accounts 1960-1977, 1970-1980*, Paris, OECD.

OECD (1983), *Historical Statistics 1960-1981*, Paris, OECD.

OECD (1983), *National Accounts 1964-1981, 1985*, Paris, OECD.

OECD (1984), *Economic Outlook*, no. 36. Paris, OECD.

OECD (1987), *National Accounts 1973-1985*, Paris, OECD.

OECD (1988), *Labour Force Statistics*, Paris, OECD.

Olsen, M.E. (1968), 'Multivariate analysis of national political development', *American Sociological Review*, vol. **33**, 699-712.

Olsen, M.E. (1982), 'Linkages between socioeconomic modernization and national political development', *Journal of Political and Military Sociology*, vol. **10**, 41-69.

Olson, M. (1965), *The Logic of Collective Action*, Cambridge, Mass., Harvard University Press.

Olson, M. (1982), *The Rise and Decline of Nations: Economic Growth, Stagflation and Social Rigidities*, New Haven, Yale University Press.

Olson, M. (1983), 'The political economy of comparative growth rates' in Mueller, D. (ed.), *Political Economy of Growth*, New Haven and London, Yale University Press.

Organski, A.F.K. (1965), *Stages of Political Development*, New York, Knopf.

Ott, D.J., Ott, A.F. and Yoo, J. (1975), *Macroeconomic Theory*, New York, McGraw-Hill.

Pack, H. (1988), 'Industrialization and trade', in Chenery, H. and Srinivasan, T.N. (eds), *HaNDBOOK OF Development Economics*, vol. **I**.

Page, E.G. (1985), *Political Authority and Bureaucratic Power*, Brighton, Harvester Press.

Paine, J.L. (1989), *Why Nations Arm?*, Oxford, Blackwell.

Paldam, M. (1990a), 'How robust is the vote function. A comparative study of 197 elections in the OECD area 1948-85', in Lafay, J.D., Lewis-Beck, M. and Norporth, H. (eds) *Economics and elections in United States and Western Europe*. Ann Arbor, Michigan University Press.

Paldam, M. (1990b), 'Politics matters after all (1). A comparative test of Alesina's theory of partisan cycles', in Thygesen, N. and Velupillai, (eds) *Recent Developments in Business Cycle Theory - Methods and Empirical Applications*. London, Macmillan.

Paldam, M. (1990c), 'Politics matter after all (2). A comparative test of Hibb's theory of partisan cycles', in Guttman, J.M. and Hillman, A.L. (eds), *Markets and Politicians* (forthcoming 1991).

Palgrave, R.H.I. (ed.) (1899), *Dictionary of Political Economy*, London, Macmillan.

Park, T. (1973), 'Measuring the dynamic patterns of development: the case of Asia 1949-68', *Multivariate Behavioral Research*, vol. **8**.

Parsons, T, and Shils, E. (eds)(1951), *Towards a General Theory of Action*, New York, Harper and Row.

Parsons, T. (1951), *The Social System*, New York, Free Press.

Parsons, T. and Smelser, N. (1956), *Economy and Society*, London, Routledge and Kegan Paul.

Pasinetti, L. (1981), *Structural Change and Economic Growth*, Cambridge, Cambridge University Press.

Peacock, A. (1979), *The Economic Analysis of Government and Related Themes*, Oxford, Martin Robertson.

Peacock, A. and Wiseman, J. (1961), *The Growth of Public Expenditure in the United Kingdom*, Princeton, Princeton University Press.

Peacock, A. and Wiseman, J. (1979), 'Approaches to the analysis of government expenditure growth', *Public Finance Quarterly*, vol. **7**, 3-23.

Perlmutter, A. (1981), *Modern Authoritarianism: A Comparative Institutional Analysis*, New Haven, Yale University Press.

Peters, B.G. and Heisler, M.O. (1983), 'Thinking about public sector growth', in Taylor, C.L. (ed.), *Why Governments Grow: Measuring Public Sector Size*, Beverly Hills, Sage.

Phelps, E.S. (ed)(1962), *The Goal of Economic Growth*, New York, Norton.

Phillips, A. (1978), 'The concept of 'development'', *Review of African Political Economy*, **8**, 7-20.

Pindyck, R.S. and Rubinfeld, D.L. (1981), *Econometric Models and Economic Forecasts*, New York, McGraw-Hill.

Portes, A. (1976), 'On the sociology of national development: theories and issues', *American Journal of Sociology*, **82**, 55-85.

Pourgerami, A. (1988), 'The political economy of development: a cross-national causality test development-democracy-growth hypothesis', *Public Choice*, vol. **58**, 123-41.

Pourgerami, A. (1989), 'The political economy of development: an empirical examination of the wealth theory of democracy, (mimeo), Bakerfield, California State University, Dept. of Economics.

Pride, R.A. (1970), *Origins of Democracy: A Cross-National Study of Mobilization, Party Systems, and Democratic Stability*, Beverly Hills, Sage.

Pryor, F.L. (1968), *Public Expenditures in Communist and Capitalist Nations*, London, Allen and Unwin.

Przeworski, A. and Teune, H. (1970), *The Logic of Comparative Social Inquiry*, New York, Wiley.

Przeworski, A. (1975), 'Institutionlization of voting patterns, or is mobilization the source of decay?', *American Political Science Review*, vol. **69**, 49-67.

Przeworski, A. (1987), 'Methods of cross-national research, 1970-83: an overview', Dierkes, M. (ed.), *Comparative Policy Research: Learning from Experience*, Aldershot, Gower, 31-49.

Pye, L.W. (1958), 'Administrators, agitators, and brokers', *Public Opinion Quarterly*, vol. **22**.

Pye, L.W. (1966), *Aspects of Political Development*, Boston: Little, Brown.

Pye, L.W. (ed.)(1967), *Communications and Political Development*, Princeton, NJ, Princeton University Press.

Pye, L. (1987), 'Political development', in *The Blackwell Encyclopedia of Political Institutions*, Oxford, Blackwells.

Pye, L.W. and Verba, S. (eds)(1969), *Political Culture and Political Development*, Princeton, NJ, Princeton University Press.

Ranis, G. (1975), 'Equity and growth: new dimensions of development', *Journal of Conflict Resolution*, **19**, 558-68.

Rawls, J. (1971), *Theory of Justice*, Cambridge, Harvard University Press.

Reynolds, L.G. (1975), 'Agriculture in Development Theory: An Overview', in L.G. Reynolds (ed.) *Agriculture in Development Theory*, New Haven and London, Yale University Press.

Reynolds, Lloyd, G. (1985), *Economic Growth in the Third World, 1850-1980*, New Haven, Yale University Press.

Ricketts, M. (1987), *The Economics of Business Enterprise*, Brighton, Harvester Wheatsheaf.

Riggs, F.W. (1957), 'Agraria and industria: toward a typology of comparative administration', in Siffin, W.J. (ed.) *Toward a Comparative Study of Public Administration*, Bloomington, Indiana University Press, 23-116.

Riggs, F. (1964), *Administration in Developing Countries*, Boston, Houghton Mifflin.

Riggs, F.W. (1967), 'The theory of political development', in Charlesworth, J.C. (ed.) *Contemporary Political Analysis*, New York, Free Press.

Riggs, F.W. (1984), 'Development'. in Sartori, G. (ed.), *Social Science Concepts*, Beverly Hills, Sage, 125-203.

Robbins, L.C. (1934), *The Great Depression*, London, Macmillan.

Rokkan, S. *et al.* (1970), *Citizens, Elections, Parties: Approaches to the Comparative Study of the Process of Development*, Oslo, Universitetsforlaget.

Rose, R. (1973), 'Comparing Public Policy: An Overview', *European Journal of Political Research*, vol. **1**, 67-94.

Rose, R. (1984), *Big Government*, London, Sage.

Rose, R. (1985), 'Getting by in three economies: the resources of the official, unofficial and domestic economies', in Lane, J-E. (ed.) *State and Market*, London, Sage.

Rose, R. (1989), *Ordinary People in Public Policy*, London, Sage.

Rostow, W.W. (1960), *The Stages of Economic Growth. A Non-Communist Manifesto*, Cambridge, Cambridge University Press.

Rostow, W.W. (1971), *Politics and the Stages of Economic Growth*, Cambridge, Cambridge University Press.

Rotchild, K.W. (1989), 'Political economy or economics? Some terminological and normative considerations, *European Journal of Political Economy*, **5**, 1, 1-12.

Roth, G. (1975), 'Socio-historical model and developmental theory', *American Sociological Review*, vol. **40**, 148-57-.

Rubinson, R. and Quinlan, D. (1977), 'Democracy and social equality: a reanalysis', *American Sociological Review*, vol. **42**, 611-623.

Russett, B. Alker, H., Deutsch, K.W. and Lasswell, H.D. (1964), *World Handbook of Political and Social Indicators*, New Haven, Yale University Press.

Rustow, D.A. (1967), *A World of Nations: Problems of Political Modernization*, Washington, The Brookings Institution.

Rustow, D.A. (1970), 'Transitions to democracy: toward a dynamic model', *Comparative Politics*, vol. **2**, 337-63.

Rustow, D.A. and Ward, R.E. (1964), 'Introduction', in Ward, R.E. and Rustow, D.A. (eds) *Political Modernization in Japan and Turkey*, Princeton, NJ., Princeton University Press.

Samuelson, P.A. (1983), *Foundations of Economic Analysis*, Cambridge, Harvard University Press.

Sandbrook, R. (1976), 'The 'crisis' in political development theory', *Journal of Development Studies*, vol. **12**, 165-85.

Saunders, P. (1986), 'What can we learn from international comparison of public sector size and economic performance', *European Sociological Review*, vol. **2**, no. 1, 52-60.

Sartori, G. (1969), 'From the sociology of politics to political sociology', Lipset, S.M. (ed.) *Politics and the Social Sciences*, New York, Oxford University Press, 65-100.

Sartori, G. (1976), *Parties and Party Systems: A Framework for Analysis*, Cambridge, Cambridge University Press.

Sawyer, J.A. (1989), *Macroeconomic Theory*, London, Harvester Wheatsheaf.

Scalapino, R.A. (1964), 'Environmental and foreign contributions: Japan', in Ward, R.E. and Rustow, D.A. (eds) *Political Modernization in Japan and Turkey*, Princeton, NJ, Princeton University Press.

Schmidt, M.G. (1982), *Wohlfahrtsstaatliche Politik unter buergerlichen und sozialdemokratischen Regierungen: Ein internationaler Vergleich*, Frankfurt, Campus.

Schmidt, M.G. (ed.)(1983), *Westliche Industrie Gesellschaften: Wirtschaft, Gesellschaft, Politik*, München, Piper.

Schmidt, M.G. (1983), 'The welfare state and the economy in periods of economic crisis: a comparative study of twenty-three OECD nations' in *European Journal of Political Research*, vol. **II**, 1-26.

Schmitter, P.C. (1981), 'Interest intermediation and regime governability in contemporary western Europe and North America', in Berger, S. (ed.) *Organizing Interests in Western Europe*, Cambridge, Cambridge University Press, 285-327.

Schneider, F. (1989), 'Political economy or economics? A Comment', *European Journal of Political Economy*, **5**, 1.

Schumpeter, J. (1944), *Capitalism, Socialism and Democracy*, London, Allen and Unwin.

Scott, J.F. (1989), *A New View of Economic Growth*, Oxford, Clarendon Press.

Sen, A.K. (1970), *Penguin Modern Readings: Growth Economics*, Harmondsworth, Penguin.

Sen, A. (1988), 'The concept of development', in Chenery, H. and Srinivasan, T.N. (eds) *Handbook of Development Economics*, Amsterdam, North-Holland.

Share, D. (1987), 'Transitions to democracy and transition through transaction', *Comparative Political Studies*, vol. **19**, 525-48.

Sharkansky, I. (1969), *The Politics of Taxing and Spending*, Indianapolis, Bobs-Merril.

Sharpe, L.J. and K. Newton (1984), *Does Politics Matter?*, Oxford, Clarendon Press.

Sigelman, L. and Gadbois, G.H. (1983), 'Contemporary comparative politics: an inventory and assessment', *Comparative Political Studies*, vol. **16**, 275-305.

Sigelman, L. (1971), *Modernization and the Political System: A Critique and Preliminary Empirical Analysis*, Beverly Hills, Sage.

Singer, J.D. and Small, M. (1966), 'The composition and status ordering of the international system: 1815-1940', *World Politics*, vol. **18**, 236-82.

Singleton, F. and Carter, B. (1982), *The Economy of Yugoslavia*, London, Croom Helm.

Sivard, R.L. (1980), *World Military and Social Expenditures 1980*, Leesburg, VA, World Priorities.

Smith, A.K. (1969), 'Socio-economic development and political democracy: a causal analysis', *Midwest Journal of Political Science*, vol. **13**, 95-125.

Solow, R.M. (1988), *Growth Theory*, Oxford, Oxford University Press.

Sommers, P.M. and Suits D.B. (1971), 'A cross-section model of economic growth', *The Review of Economics and Statistics*, vol. **53**, 121-28.

Spulber, D.F. (1989), *Regulation and Markets*, Cambridge, MIT Press.

Spulber, N. (1969), *The Soviet Economy. Structure, Principles, Problems*, New York, Norton.

Staar, R.F. (1981), 'Checklist of communist parties and fronts, 1980', *Problems of Communism*, vol. **30**, 2, 88-92.

Staniland, M. (1985), *What is Political Economy?: A Study of Social Theory and Underdevelopment*, New Haven, Yale University Press.

Stigler, G. (1966), *The Theory of Price*, New York, Macmillan.

Stiglitz, J.E. (1988), *Economics of the Public Sector*, New York, Norton.

Stiglitz, J.E. and Uzawa, H. (1969), *Readings in the Modern Theory of Economic Growth*, Cambridge, M.I.T. Press.

Streeten, P. (1972), *The Frontiers of Development Studies*, London, Macmillan.

Summers, R. and Heston, A. (1984), 'Improved international comparisons of real product and its composition, 1950-80', *The Review of Income and Wealth*, vol. **30**, 207-262.

Summers, R. and Heston, A. (1988), 'A new set of international comparisons of real product and price levels estimates for 130 countries, 1950-1985', *Review of Income and Wealth*, vol. **34**, 1-25.

Sutton, F.X. (1963), 'Social theory and comparative politics', 67-81, in Eckstein, H. and Apter, D. (eds), *Comparative Politics: A Reader*, New York, Free Press.

Swank, D.H. (1984), 'The political economy of state domestic spending in eighteen advanced capitalist democracies, 1960-1980', paper presented to the 1984 APSA Meeting, Washington.

Syrquin, M. (1988), 'Patterns of structural change in Chenery', H. and Srinivasan, T.N. (eds), *Handbook of Development Economics*.

Szentes, T. (1983), *The Political Economy of Underdevelopment*, Budapest, Akadémiai Kiadó.

Södersten, B. (1965), *A Study of Economic Growth and International Trade*, Stockholm, Almqvist and Wicksell.

Tarschys, D. (1975), 'The growth of public expenditures: nine modes of explanation', *Scandinavian Political Studies*, vol. **10**, 9-31.

Taylor, (1966), *A New Dictionary of Economics*, London, Routledge and Kegan Paul.

Taylor, C.L. (1972), 'Indicators of political development', *The Journal of Development Studies*, vol. **8**, no. 3, 103-9.

Taylor, C.L. (1981), *Codebook to World Handbook of Political and Social Indicators*, vol. **I**, *Aggregate Data*, 3rd edn, West Berlin, IIVG.

Taylor, C.L. and Jodice, D. (1981), *Codebook to World Handbook of*

Political and Social Indicators. Vol. **II**, *Political Events Data*, 3rd edn, West Berlin, IIVG.

Taylor, C.L. and Hudson, M. (1972), *World Handbook of Political and Social Indicators*. 2nd edn, New Haven, Yale University Press.

Taylor, C.L. and Jodice, D. (1983), *World Handbook of Political and Social Indicators*, 3rd edn, New Haven, Yale University Press.

Taylor, J.G. (1979), *From Modernization to Modes of Production: a Critique of the Sociologies of Development and Underdevelopment*, Atlantic Highlands, NJ, Humanities Press.

Taylor, L. and Arida, P. (1988), 'Long-run income distribution and growth', in Chenery, H. and Srinivasan, T.N. (eds), *Handbook of Developmental Economics*.

Taylor, P.J. (1987), 'The poverty of international comparisons: some methodological lessons from world-system analysis', *Studies in Comparative International Development*, vol. **22**, 12-39.

Therborn, G. (1984), 'The prospects of labour and the transformation of advanced capitalism', *New Left Review*, no. 145, 5-38.

Thirlwall, A.P. (1986), *Growth and Development: With Special Reference to Developing Economies*, London, Macmillan.

Tilly, C. (1978), *From Mobilization to Revolution*, Reading, MA, Addison-Wesley.

Tilly, C. (ed.) (1975), *The Formation of Nation States in Western Europe*, Princeton, NJ, Princeton University Press.

Tinbergen, J. (1952), *On the Theory of Economic Policy*, Amsterdam: North-Holland.

Tinbergen, J. (1967), *Economic Policy: Principles and Design*, Amsterdam, North-Holland.

Todaro, M.P. (1985), *Economic Development in the Third World*, New York, Longman.

Toye, J. (1987), *Dilemmas of Development*, Oxford, Blackwell.

Tufte, E. (1978), *Political Control of the Economy*, Princeton, Princeton University Press.

Usher, D. (1981), *The Economic Prerequisite to Democracy*, Oxford, Blackwell.

Vanat, J. (1972), *The General Theory of Labor-Managed Economies*, Ithaca, Cornell University Press.

Vanhanen, T. (1984), *The Emergence of Democracy: A Comparative Study of 119 States*, 1850-1979, Helsinki, Societas Scientiarum Fennica.

Varian, H. (1984), *Microeconomic Analysis*, New York, Norton.

Verma, S.P. and Sharma, S.K. (1984), *Development Administration*, New Delhi, Indian Institute of Public Administration.

Von Vorys, K. (1973),'Toward a concept of development', in Masannat, G.S. (ed.) *The Dynamics of Modernization*, Pacific Palisades, Goodyear.

Wallerstein, I. (1974), *The Modern World-System: Capitalist Agriculture and the Origins of the European World-Economy in the Sixteenth Century*, New York, Academic Press.

Wallerstein, I. (1977), 'Rural economy in modern world society', *Studies in Comparative International Development*, vol. **12**, 29-40.

Wallerstein, I. (1979), *The Capitalist World-Economy*, Cambridge: Cambridge University Press.

Ward, R.E. and Rustow, D.A. (eds)(1964), *Political Modernization in Japan and Turkey*, Princeton, NJ, Princeton University Press.

Weber, M, (1949), *The Methodology of the Social Sciences*, Glencoe, Free Press.

Webber, C. and Wildavsky, A. (1986), *A History of Taxation and Expenditure in the Western World*, New York, Simon and Schuster.

Weede, E. (1980), 'Beyond misspecification in sociological analysis of income inequality,' *American Sociological Review*, **45**, 497-501.

Weede, E. (1983), 'The impact of democracy on economic growth: some evidence from cross-national analysis', *Kyklos*, vol. **36**, 21-39.

Weede, E. (1984a), 'Democracy and war involvement', *Journal of Conflict Resolution*, vol. **28**, 649-64.

Weede, E. (1984b), 'Political democracy, state strength and economic growth in LDCs: a cross-national analysis', *Review of International Studies*, vol. **10**, 297-312.

Weede, E. (1986), 'Catch-up, distributional coalitions and government as determinants of economic growth and decline in industralized democracies', *British Journal of Sociology*, vol. **37**, no. 2: 194-220.

Weiner, M. (1965), 'Political integration and political development', *Annals of the American Academy of Political and Social Science*, vol. **358**, 52-63.

Weiner, M. and Huntington, S.P. (eds)(1987), *Understanding Political Development*, Boston, Little, Brown.

Wesson, R. (ed.), *Democracy: a Worldwide Survey*, New York, Praeger.

Westlund, A. and Lane, J.E. (1983), 'The relevance of the concept of structural variability to the social sciences', *Quality and Quantity*, **17**, 189-201.

Whiteley, P. (ed.)(1980), *Models of Political Economy*, London, Sage.

Whiteley, P. (1982), 'The political economy of economic growth', *European Journal of Political Research*, vol. **11**, 197-213.

Whiteley, P. (1986), *Political Control of the Macroeconomy: The Political Economy of Public Policy Making*, London, Sage.

Wiarda, H.J. (1983), 'Toward a non ethnocentric theory of development: alternative conceptions from the Third World', *Journal of Developing Areas*, vol. **17**, 433-52.

Wildavsky, A. (1964, 1984), *The Politics of the Budgetary Process*, Boston: Little, Brown and Company.

Wildavsky, A. (1972), 'If planning is everything, then maybe it is nothing', *Policy Sciences*, vol. **4**.

Wildavsky, A. (1985), 'The logic of public sector growth' in Lane, J-E. (ed.) *State and Market*, London, Sage.

Wildavsky, A. (1976), *Budgeting: A Comparative Theory of the Budgetary Process*, Boston, Little , Brown and Company, 2nd edn., 1986, New Brunswick, Transaction.

Wildavsky, A. (1988), *The New Politics of the Budgetary Process*, Boston, Scott, Foresman and Company.

Wilensky, H. (1975), *The Welfare State and Equality*, Berkeley, The University of California Press.

Wilensky, H. (1976), *The 'New Corporatism', Centralization and the Welfare State*, Beverly Hills: Sage.

Williamson, O.E. (1975), *Markets and Hierarchies: Analysis and Antitrust Implications*, New York, Free Press.

Williamson, O.E. (1985), *The Economic Institutions of Capitalism*, New York, The Free Press.

Williamson, O.E. (1986), *Economic Organization: Firms, Market and Policy Control*, Brighton, Harvester Wheatsheaf.

World Bank (1980), *World Bank Atlas*, Washington, World Bank.

World Bank (1980), *World Tables 1980*, 2nd edn., Baltimore, The Johns Hopkins University Press.

World Bank (1980-1987), *World Development Report*, New York, Oxford University Press.

World Bank: (1984), *World Tables*, 3rd edn., Baltimore, Johns Hopkins University Press.

Wright, D.M. (1947), *The Economics of Disturbance*, New York, Macmillan.

Yarbrough, B.Y. and Yarbrough, R.M. (1988), *The World Economy*, Chicago, Dryden Press.

Yotopoulos, P.A. and Nugent, J.B. (1976), *Economics of Development, Empirical Investigations*, New York, Harper and Row.

Zaleski, E. (1980), *Stalinist Planning for Economic Growth*, London, Allen and Unwin.

Zysman, J. (1983), *Governments, Markets and Finance*, Ithaca, Cornell University Press.

Åslund, A. (1989), *Gorbachev's Struggle for Economic Reform. The Soviet reform process, 1985-88*, London, Pinter.

INDEX